U. S. Department of the Interior
BUREAU OF LAND MANAGEMENT

California
Desert
District

A Cultural Resources Overview
of the Colorado Desert Planning Units

by

Elizabeth von Till Warren, Robert H. Crabtree, Claude N. Warren.
Martha Knack and Richard Mc Carty

Cultural Resources Publications
anthropology - history

FORWARDS

In publishing this cultural resource overview of a greater portion of California's Colorado Desert, the Bureau of Land Management has fulfilled a strongly felt obligation to present the results of such studies to the public.

This overview was written as one of a series of supporting documents for the cultural resource element of the Bureau's California Desert Planning Program. A contract to undertake the work was initiated in 1978, with the final report approved in 1980. The authors were presented with no small task in compiling and synthesizing the considerable information available on such a vast area. This they have accomplished well, considering the limitations in both time and funding.

A companion volume in this series is Dennis Gallegos et al.'s, "Cultural Resources Inventory of the Central Mojave and Colorado Desert Regions, California", published by BLM in 1980. Together, they add immensely to our knowledge of past people and events in this low, very arid portion of the Desert West. Both will, we hope, assist in setting the stage for future research and judicious implementation of the now-approved California Desert Plan.

This work is relatively straight-forward, well-written, and carefully researched. While there already has been more recent archaeological work in this area, this volume will stand for quite some time as one of the basic reference documents for the history, ethnography, and archaeology for a major portion of the Colorado Desert.

Eric Ritter
General Editor

I wish to thank all of those who have supported the archaeology program in the California Desert in its efforts to print and disseminate cultural resource data to the general and professional public. Among those are, Gerald Hillier, Dick Freel, Bruce Ottenfeld, Bary Freet, Ronald Keller, and Bill Olsen. A special note of thanks goes to Clara Stapp who did the petroglyph drawings from photographs taken by Gerrit Fenega at Corn Springs.

The cover illustration is an element from Corn Springs taken from the business card of Heritage Research Associates of Holy City, California.

I hope that in these days of constrained budgets that the reprinting and dissemination of Cultural Resource Reports will be further accomplished and encouraged by management and staff alike.

Russell L. Kaldenberg
Cultural Resource Program Manager
Publications Coordinator
California Desert District

A CULTURAL RESOURCES OVERVIEW
OF THE COLORADO DESERT PLANNING UNITS

by

Elizabeth von Till Warren, Robert H. Crabtree, Claude N. Warren,
Martha Knack, and Richard McCarty

Eric W. Ritter
General Editor

Riverside, California
1981

TABLE OF CONTENTS

CHAPTERS

CHAPTER I. INTRODUCTION
Claude N. Warren

This overview pulls together existing data relating to the cultural resources of the Imperial, Santa Rosa, Orocopia, Twenty-Nine Palms, Bristol/Cadiz, Palen, Turtle Mountain, Whipple Mountain, Big Maria, and Picacho planning units of the Colorado Desert (Figure 1). The goals here are a description and evaluation of these resources that may serve as a basis for cultural resource recommendations and, in turn, for an educated and enlightened management of these resources.

The cultural resources have been presented in terms of the chronological sequences, quality of collections and special studies. These cultural resources are presented against a background of environmental conditions of the Colorado Desert. The primary direction of the study was to outline the cultural resources in terms of man's use of the desert from prehistoric times through the ethnographic present to European occupation of the area. Most of the data relevant to the relationship of man to past environment are still to be recovered through archaeological, ethnohistoric and historical fieldwork and analysis. Areas of greatest intensity of cultural activities have been identified for some periods. Land use in limited areas for short periods of time has been defined and the major direction in historical developments have been outlined. The paucity of data, however, makes it impossible to identify with any certainty the systemic relationships of the all too often isolated fragments that make up the cultural resources of the Colorado Desert. It is an area in which field research has gone on in "fits and starts" and no well-organized research program existed until the last decade. Consequently, this overview lacks the more formal presentation of settlement patterns, economic systems, and other aspects of prehistory to add greater meaning to the data.

The weakness in this overview, however, serves as an indication of the wealth and importance of the cultural resources that still lay unstudied in the Colorado Desert and underscores the great need for careful management and development of these resources.

The research and writing of this report has involved the cooperation of a large number of persons and institutions. Every individual and institution contacted, cooperated fully and we wish to thank the following:

The Contracting Officer, John Hunt, and the Contracting Officer's Authorized Representative, Eric Ritter; the administration and staff of the San Diego Museum of Man; San Bernardino County Museum; University of California Archaeological Research Facility at Berkeley; University of California Museum of Cultural History and Archaeological Survey, Los Angeles; University of California Archaeological Research Unit, Riverside; Imperial Valley College Museum; University of Nevada Archaeological Research Center, Las Vegas; Southwest Museum; Colorado River Indian Tribes Museum; National Park Service, Lake Mead Interpretive Center; Bureau of Land Management, Desert Planning Staff, Riverside; Archaeological Survey Association of Southern California; Joshua Tree National Monument, Visitors Center; Wells Fargo History Room, San Francisco; California State Library, Sacramento; Map Room,

Research Library, University of California Los Angeles; Los Angeles County Museum; Automobile Club of Southern California; Nevada Historical Society, Reno; Special Collection Department, Library, University of Nevada, Reno; Special Collection Department, Library, University of Nevada, Las Vegas; Bancroft Library; Mojave River Valley Museum; Riverside County Library. Arda Haenszel and Dennis Casebier. Office staff of the Institute for American Research: Andrea Karle, Jill Cowley, Lucille Calderon, Gary Coombs, and Myron.

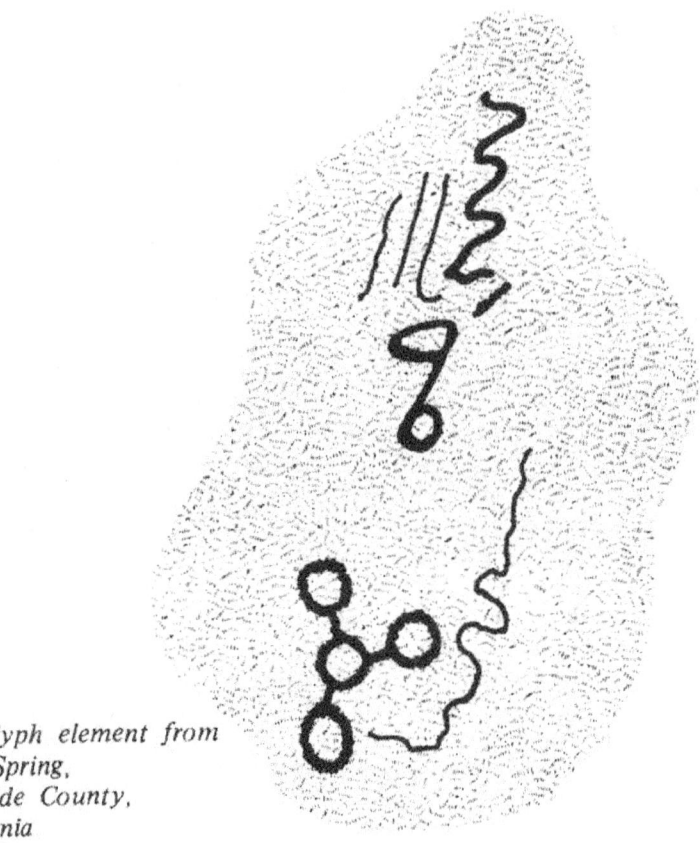

Petroglyph element from
Corn Spring,
Riverside County,
California

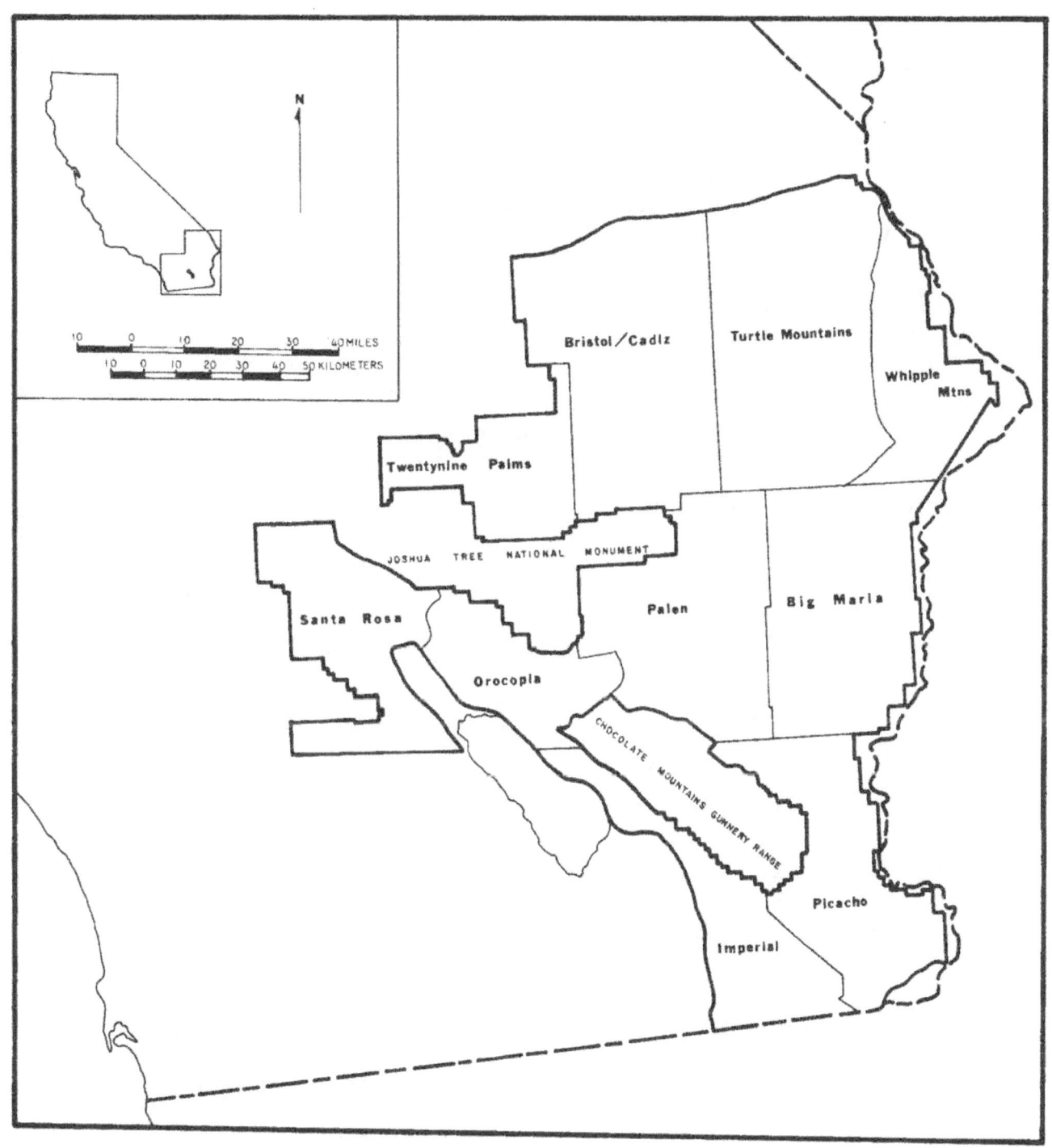

Figure 1. The Colorado Desert Planning Units

Chapter II. ENVIRONMENTAL BACKGROUND
Richard McCarty

A. Introduction

The Colorado Desert study area covers approximately 11,000 square miles (28,500 km. sq.) of which over two-thirds is managed by the Bureau of Land Management. The land is divided among the Imperial, Santa Rosa, Orocopia, Twentynine Palms, Bristol/Cadiz, Palen, Turtle Mountain, Whipple Mountain, Big Maria and Picacho planning units, which together will be referred to here as the Colorado Desert planning units (Figure 1).

The area is bounded on the north by Interstate 40. Its southern boundary is the United States/Mexican border, and its eastern boundary is the Colorado River and its delta lands. The western boundary is a winding line defined by the Twentynine Palms Marine Corps Base, Joshua Tree National Monument, the San Bernardino National Forest and the path of the Coachella and East Highland canals.

The Colorado Desert planning units are almost entirely in the low, hot desert below 2000 feet (610 m.). It is one of the harshest and most arid environments in North America (cf. Walter 1971) and present population figures reflect this. The interior of the Colorado Desert planning units is among the most sparsely settled in the United States.

Unfortunately, the formidable environmental conditions have also been a deterent to research in the area. The paucity of archaeological work, as discussed in this report, is equalled by the lack of necessary published information on the area by geologists, climatologists and biologists. The problem has become a nearly universal source of complaint among recent authors working in the area (cf. Burk 1977; Shlemon 1978; EECI 1978).

The terrain of the Colorado Desert planning units consists of a number of broad, shallow valleys that, in a general sense, trend to the southeast, draining into the Colorado River. These valleys contain five playas or closed basin sinks formed by the low-lying obstructions in the valley floor. The study area includes the transition from the Basin-Range Province's Mojavian to Sonoran system, and these playas make a graphic geomorphological transition between the closed basin systems found in the Mojave and the extensive drainage systems found in the Sonoran Desert. The position of the Colorado Desert planning units as a transitional zone between these two deserts is found in all of the environmental aspects of the study area.

The Salton Trough (the Imperial and Coachella valleys) with elevations below sea level, extends along the southwestern border of the Colorado Desert planning units. This valley system receives water from the Colorado River and is cut off from the Gulf of California by the Colorado River Delta which is filling the southern part of the Salton Trough. Along the western border of the study area, a sharp boundary is defined between the desert and the mesic chaparral woodlands of the San Jacinto and Santa Rosa mountains and the Peninsular Range.

Valleys in the interior of the Colorado Desert planning units surround and isolate a number of small, severely weathered mountain ranges. These ranges run generally north-south in the northern areas and northwest-southeast in the southern portions. Peaks range to 4000 feet (1220 m.) in the north and 2000 feet (610 m.) in the south. Valley elevations extend from 800 feet (245 m.) to 200 feet (-61 m.) below sea level.

The rather uniform low elevation of the area is coupled with a convectional/frontal climatic regime that brings summer precipitation and mild winter temperatures. As a result, the vegetation found over much of the area is related to Sonoran Desert varieties of Arizona and Sonora, Mexico.

There are very few environmental aspects that the Colorado Desert planning units hold inclusively and exclusively. Its low elevation, its geology, its climate and its vegetation are all shared, at least partially, with other, surrounding deserts. Therefore, in dealing with the specific aspects of landform, climate and botany, it is important to view the study area as a transition zone between the Mojave Desert in the north and the Sonoran Desert to the south and east.

The transitional nature of the Colorado Desert region is largely the source of the differences in the interpretations of the desert's boundaries. Figure 2 shows four lines that are popular limits to the Colorado Desert and serve as a demonstration of the differences in interpretation among writers. It is worth noting that the major discrepancies occur between fields of study; within each discipline there are only minor differences.

Geologists and geomorphologists (Figure 2, line A) have the narrowest interpretation of the Colorado Desert and one that almost excludes it from the Colorado Desert planning units. The term "Colorado Desert" was first applied to this region in 1853 by the geologist, William P. Blake. His definition of the desert clearly referred to the area of southern California and Mexico that "owes its origin to the (Colorado) River by the deposition of alluvions and the displacement of sea-water" (MacDougal et al. 1914:6). Blake was referring to the banks of the Colorado River and its delta soils. He strongly discouraged any broader interpretation of the desert. For geologists, there is little reason to make any distinction between the Mojave Desert and the desert valleys and ranges of the Colorado Desert planning units. They commonly refer to the area as the southeastern arm of the Mojave Desert (Shlemon 1978).

Botanists (Figure 2, lines B and C) commonly define the Colorado Desert's boundaries by the occurrence of Woodland Wash community members, especially Cercidium and Olneya. They also use the distribution of the distinctive plant types such as ocotillo, Fouquieria splendons, as boundary markers. The minor differences among botanists relate to the explanation of why these plant boundaries occur where they do. Jaeger (1957), argues that increased precipitation, lower wash elevations and increased water supply near the Colorado River are the deciding factors, and makes his line run essentially north-south. Burk (1977) argues that the winter (sub 0 degrees C) temperature is the limiting factor and relies on Turnage and Hinckley's survey reports (1938) to define an east-west boundary at approximately the 34 degree parallel.

Most botanists agree that there is a difference between the vegetation of the arid desert ranges and the vegetation found in the Salton Trough. Marks (1950) refers to the environments of the Salton Sea as the Lower Colorado Desert.

Climatologists comprise the third group defining the boundaries of the Colorado Desert, however, their interpretations usually defy linear boundaries. The one line that is traceable is Bailey's (1966) distinction between high and low deserts (Figure 2, line D), separating valleys above and below 2000 feet (610 m.). This includes much of the area usually defined as the eastern Mojave.

The history of human populations and human activities in the Colorado Desert (or more appropriately the transitional Colorado Desert planning units) is tied closely to the processes of landform, climate, flora and fauna. If we could understand these environmental aspects and their interwoven relationship to each other, we would be much closer to explaining and predicting man's past activities in this arid desert.

B. Landform

There are 38 defined mountain ranges in or adjoining the Colorado Desert planning units. Thirty-four of these are described as isolated, weathered and lowlying. These are referred to as "desert ranges". The other four, the San Jacinto, Santa Rosa, Little San Bernardino and Hexie mountains, adjoin the planning area and form parts of its western boundary. Since they are part of the Peninsular Range and are much higher, with woodland communities and geomorphology radically different from the desert ranges, they are termed "boundary mountains."

The boundary mountains have an average height of 8325 feet (2538 m.). By contrast, the desert ranges have an average peak elevation of 3450 feet (1052 m.). The northern desert ranges are nearly 1000 feet (300 m.) higher than this average; while southern peaks, with the exception of the Chuchwallas, are generally 1000 feet lower.

This pattern of increasing height as one moves northward through the Colorado Desert planning units is associated with a similar pattern of consolidation of mountain ranges and a general increase in the size of the ranges. North of the Colorado Desert planning units this pattern persists throughout the California Desert as summits become higher and mountain regions take up a greater proportion of the area.

The desert ranges within the Colorado Desert planning units are often barren exposures of rock outcrop, talus slopes and steep, dissected canyons. The angle of slope for most of the mountain region is between 15 and 60 degrees, but often approaches 90 degrees on outcrop faces. Two very different examples of shear slopes in the desert ranges are visable from the highways in the region's interior. The smooth granite faces of the Turtle Mountains contrast sharply with the talus covered pinnacles of the Palo Verde Mountains to the south.

The structural geology of the desert ranges, like much of the Sonoran sections of the Basin-Range Province, is a complicated array of rock types that have been exposed by extensive folding and thrust and block faulting that took place during the Mesozoic and early Cenozoic (Tertiary). As a result, adjacent ranges and even parts of the same range are often composed of very different rock types. All of the desert ranges show signs of disturbance by an unpatterned series of fault lines. The exposed geology in the ranges include granite, schist, gneiss and lesser amounts of limestone and sandstone. They date from the Mesozoic or pre-Mesozoic age, the majority being Cambrian and pre-Cambrian metamorphics (Bishop et al. 1963a). These early rocks have been intruded by rhyolites and basalts, dating to the Tertiary and later (Parker 1963; Murray et al. 1976). These intrusives and volcanics have formed extensive outcrops along the northern border of the study area (Amboy, Goffs and Turtle Mountains) and throughout the southeastern portion of the area (Crystal Peak area and the Black Hills).

A line of geographically recent volcanic activity (55000-16000 BP., according to Muffler and White 1969) runs along the base of the Salton Trough from the Gulf of California to the Salton Sea. The rhyolite buttes of the Red Hills area at the south end of the Salton Sea are one of the landmarks of this activity.

There is a large and growing amount of published work on the Salton Trough and its soils, faultlines and volcanics. But the rest of the Colorado Desert planning units has been virtually ignored by researchers. The lack of geologic mapping has hampered both our interpretations of the mountain regions and the valley systems that are filled with the alluvium of the weathered ranges. Most of the information on the desert soils has come from specific area studies such as the Sun Desert report (Shlemon 1978) and the EECI report on the soils of the Turtle Mountains (EECI 1978).

From these specific studies emerges a picture of valley systems with a relatively uniform morphology (pediment, pediment plain, base level plain) and a complicated geology of schists, granites, rhyolites and basalts that make up the alkaline and often calcareous gravels and soils.

There are ten large scale valleys in the Colorado Desert planning units which take up nearly seventy-five percent of the total region. From profiles down the length of the valleys of the desert ranges (Figure 3), they can be categorized into two types. The first consists of short steep valleys, definably shaped by a continuous wash channel. These include the Vidal, Chemehuevi and Arroyo Seco or Milpitas wash valleys (Figure 3a). The second type is the long shallow valley systems that are actually a series of contiguous valleys (Figure 3b,3c,3d). Under more pluvial conditions, these valleys have the potential to overflow their blockades and become a continuous drainage. Three valley systems fit this category: the Bristol/Cadiz basin, fed by the Fenner and Bristol valleys; the Ward/Rice valley system, with the Danby Dry Lake and a slight basin in the Rice Valley; and the Pinto/Chuckwalla valleys, with Palen and Ford dry lakes. With enough water to flood the impass, the Bristol/Cadiz system could just as easily overflow into either of the other two drainages.

The cross-section profile of the valley almost anywhere along the valley course presents a very broad "V" or "U" shaped pattern. The cross-section is remarkably uniform throughout the California deserts and has been one of the most studied and most controversial aspects of desert morphology (Cooke and Warren 1973:172-173; Cooke 1970a). Figure 4 gives an idealized profile, labeling the important features of the valley, especially in the piedmont/mountain boundary and the slopes of the pediment (15 to 5 degrees) and the lower valley (less than 5 degrees). In going from the mountain to the base level plain, there are some important and easily distinguishable gradients. The first of these is that the soils generally become smaller in size, ranging from mostly cobbles at the pediment down to sands and loams at the valley center. The other important gradient is in age. In areas where the runoff is largely confined to channels, such as in the southern portion of the Colorado Desert planning units along the Milpitas Wash, soils in the upper pediments date in the neighborhood of 2 million years. Two increasingly younger soil types are passed through before reaching the lower piedmont plain soils, dating from 15000 years to active wash deposits (Shlemon 1978).

One easily definable index that provides some insight into the relationship of the desert ranges to the valley systems surrounding them (Table A) is the point of inflex (the boundary between mountain and valley pediment). It can be plotted from topographic maps. Point of inflex elevations in the southern portion of the Colorado Desert planning units are often quite high. One extreme example is on the northeastern side of the Chocolate Mountains where the inflex point is 2500 feet (762 m.), just below its highest peak of 2900 feet (885 m.). In the northern sections, the highest point of inflex occurs generally 1000 feet (305 m.) higher than in the south. When this high pediment height is combined with the lowest pediment height and the peak elevation, a consistent 1000 foot interval pattern shows up in the northern mountains. The southern mountains have no definable pattern of this type.

The height of the low pediment or point of inflex has a general downward depression moving from the northern to southern mountain ranges. Another pattern is that this index has a large number of readings at or close to the 1000 foot (305 m.) interval contour. Many of these readings are closely associated with the two major drainage systems, suggesting some relationship to these drainages. At least for the Bristol/Cadiz basin, this may be related to the shoreline at the overflow point of the basin into either the Ward/Rice Valley system or the Palen/Chuckwalla Valley system. The reason behind this morphological pattern has not yet been fully understood.

The Bristol/Cadiz and Ward/Rice drainages were chosen by Blackwelder (1953) as the course of the overflow of the Pleistocene Mojave and Death Valley lake systems. This often cited speculation has some serious flaws that make it very unlikely (cf. Gallegos et al. 1979). Longwell (1954) reports that a blockage of the Colorado River below the Whipple Mountains was the cause of the Chemehuevi Lake deposits found through the northeastern corner of the Colorado Desert planning units. Clearly, much more detailed geologic work is needed on the soils and tectonics before any of these speculations can be addressed.

A rather unimposing sand dune formation is to be found at the base (base level plain) of the larger desert range valley systems (Figure 5). These dunes generally measure 15 feet (4.5 m.) in height and are usually of sand sheet or transverse dune types (Dean 1977). The dunes are stabilized by vegetation, but wind activity has slowly moved the formations to the east, down the valleys. In places, such as Rice Valley, the formations occur very high on the sides of the ranges, creating sand bajadas.

Sand dune formations are also a common sight in the Salton Trough, although these dunes are generally more impressive than those of the desert ranges. The dunes in the upper end of the Coachella Valley have been studied extensively as models for weathering, composition and dune movement (Sharp 1964; Cooke and Warren 1973). The barchan dunes at the base of the Santa Rosa Mountains and the Algodones Dunes are major tourist attractions.

Water supply in the interior of the Colorado Desert planning units is limited to a very few springs and seeps in the mountains and higher washes. These springs are associated with fault activity, usually in granites, and occur where these geologic discontinuities surface. Another type of spring or seep area is at the end of large gravel fans formed at the base of bajadas. High evaporation rates limit the length of time that natural bedrock tanks could be used as a water source. Runoff water throughout the desert occurs as sheetwash or as shortlived flows, quite often in the form of flash floods. Ground water in the deep sandy soils of the valleys usually requires extensive deep drilling and is well beyond the reach of vegetation.

The eastern and southwestern borders of the Colorado Desert planning units abound with water and riparian resources. The constant flow of the Colorado River and its recent very rich soils, such as in the Palo Verde Valley, at one time provided extensive grassland, mesquite groves and other resource areas. Today these alluvial soils produce large quantities of farm produce.

At one time, the drainage of the Colorado River into the Imperial Valley supported Lake Cahuilla, a very large fresh water lake in the Salton Trough. At its equilibrium maximum (high shore line), it covered an area of approximately 2000 square miles (5000 square km.) (Weide 1976:13). It has fluctuated dramatically during its history due to changes in environment and amount of flow from the Colorado River. The lake has dropped from its maximum during the Pleistocene (in excess of 50,000 years BP, according to Hubbs, Bien and Suess 1965), to its dessication in approximately A.D. 1680. A shift in the course of the river in A.D. 1907 began a period of refilling of the lake but this was promptly stopped by the Southern Pacific Railroad. A thorough report of Lake Cahuilla is in MacDougal et al.(1914) and Weide (1976).

While Quaternary alluvium covers most of the eastern and northern sections of the area, tectonic activity is the major force responsible for the character of the terrain in the south and west portions of the Colorado Desert planning units. Tectonic forces are responsible for the uplift of the Cis-montane regions and for the large graben or rift valley known as the Salton Trough. Formation of the valley, in over-simplistic terms, is the result of spreading of the earth's crust (Phinney 1968) which has dropped and broken up the surface and allowed a rise in the basalt magma below the crust.

The two-directional thinning of the crust is associated with extensive lateral shifting along fault axes. The most notable faults are the San Andreas, Elsinore, Imperial and San Jacinto lines; all running parallel to the Salton Trough, the Chocolate Mountains and the Peninsular Range. Odd formations, such as the Orocopia green shists, are the result of the metamorphics involved in the thinning of the earth's crust and the lateral and thrust faulting along the sides of this graben. Geologists believe that the San Andreas is the newest of these faults and moves at the rate of approximate 2.2 cm (0.86 inches) per year (Wyss and Brune 1968:4692).

C. Climate

The climate of the Colorado Desert planning units is classified as sub-humid or sub-tropical with evaporation greatly outstripping precipitation. Summer temperatures of July through September average above 86 degrees F (30 degrees C) with daytime maximum temperatures often nearing 110 degrees F (43 degrees C) and ground temperatures exceeding 140 degrees F (59 degrees C). Winter temperatures for December through February average 50-70 degrees F (10-20 degrees C) which makes for a mild, cold season. Temperatures in the southern portion of the study area normally do not drop below 32 degrees F (0 degrees C) during the year.

Precipitation in the Colorado Desert planning units is near 3 inches (7.6 cm) per year with substantial yearly variability between locations in the amount of rain. The range of variability is from 0 to 10 inches (0-25 cm.). Jaeger (1957: 13) reports that the longest recorded drought in North America occurred in the northwestern corner of the project area with only 1/100 of an inch (0.025 cm.) recorded in slightly over three years.

The weather patterns responsible for bringing precipitation to the California deserts are a combined result of two global-scale weather systems and a blockage of weather by the boundary mountains, the Peninsular, Transverse and Sierra Nevada ranges. The blockage creates a rainshadow that either stops weather as it comes from the Pacific Ocean, or lifts it high aloft, above the desert ranges. The influences of this rainshadow are strongly felt on the western side of the desert but diminish considerably by the time storms reach the eastern side of the Mojave and Sonoran deserts.

The dominant weather system during the winter months is the frontal pattern of the Pacific High. This brings generally clear skies, but occasionally drops some precipitation from winter storms. In the Colorado Desert planning units, the summer months are characterized as a fluctuation between the high pressure system and a tropical, waterladden convectional system that comes off the Gulf of California. This convectional system is sometimes able to penetrate the frontal system, bringing very localized, late afternoon and early evening thundershowers.

The expected pattern from these combined features is an increase in the amount of rainfall from west to east across the desert as the influences of the rainshadow diminish. Also we would expect an increase in the amount of summer rainfall, creating a bimodal yearly pattern, as we move from north to south through the Colorado Desert region.

The reports from the various weather stations in the study area only partially support this pattern (Figure 5). The effects of the rainshadow and its decline toward the east is strongly supported. Precipitation recorded at six stations on the western side of the study area average 5.81 cm. (2.29 inches) and the three stations along the eastern border are more than double this amount (13.6 cm, 5.35 inches). However, the increased summer precipitation to the south and the bi-modal pattern are not noticeable from weather station information. Both Daggett (34%) and Twentynine Palms (47%) are among the highest percentages for summer precipitation, and they are supposedly outside the influence of the convectional storm system. Other readings show no pattern. Part of the reason for this erratic summer precipitation pattern results from the random pattern of summer thunder showers that drop most of the recorded summer precipitation in a matter of days or even hours (Cooke and Warren 1973:21). Another reason is that because of the low elevation of the peaks in the area, much of the convectional storms pass over the Colorado Desert planning units area and bring precipitation father north. Huning (1978:124) marks the area around Halloran Springs and Mountain Pass as benefitting most from the tropical weather pattern.

The disadvantage of low elevation in stopping storm systems illustrates another critical variable operating in the desert which is especially pertinent to the Colorado Desert planning units. This is the thermopluvial gradient that fluctuates in direct response to elevation: with an increase in elevation, there will be a decrease in temperature and an increase in moisture/precipitation. In other areas of the California Desert, this is reflected in gradient zones of vegetation. In the Colorado Desert planning units, however, we have only the lower end of the scale so that there are almost no elevational distinctions of vegetation. Rather, vegetation is represented by its ability to maintain itself at the bottom of this gradient.

D. Vegetation

The vegetation of the Colorado Desert planning units is tied closely to the climate, soils and topography of the area. Salinity, water availability and thermal factors are among the most important criteria which directly affect the configuration of the desert flora and the composition of the desert floral communities. There are other, more subtle influences (such as the direction of exposure and elevation) that also play a significant role.

A few plant types in the Colorado Desert planning units are limited specifically to the area (Salvia vaseyi, wand sage; Parosela californica; Ambrosia ilicifolia, holly-leaved burrobush). However, the majority form a transitional gradient, either as a Mojave/Colorado desert continuum (Atriplex hymenelytra, desert holly; Coleogyne ramosissima, blackbrush; Lycium cooperi, peach thorn; Ephedra californica, joint fir); as a Yuman/Colorado continuum (Olneya tesota, ironwood; Hyptis emoryi, desert lavender; Fouquieria splendens, ocotillo); or as a continuation through all three deserts (Ambrosia dumosa, burrobush; Prosopis glandulosa var. torreyana, mesquite; Eriogonum inflatum, desert trumpet). The interregional fit of the Colorado Desert with its northern neighbor the Mojave Desert and with the other Sonoran deserts in Arizona and Mexico is an important relationship. The position of the Colorado Desert planning units in relation to these deserts shows why the study area is likely to emphasize the transitional nature of the region.

The dominant plant type in the Colorado Desert planning units is Larrea tridentata (creosote bush). It is also the dominant plant of the Mojave Desert and is a very common plant in the Arizona-Sonoran deserts. Within the study area, it forms a uniformly monotonous coverage as it spreads itself in varying densities and heights over the valleys, bajadas and even the mountain areas of the region. Its favorite location is in the deep, well drained soils of the pediment plain, where it often occurs alone or with a single associate, Ambrosia dumosa (burrobush). It also has a large number of lesser associates (Petalonyx thurberi, Thurber sandpaper plant; Eriogonum trichopes, little trumpet; Acacia greggii, cat's-claw) that change with variations in soils and topography.

The creosote scrub community surrounds a number of smaller, specialized communities. One of these is the cactus scrub community, formed in fine soils and usually on south facing slopes of the desert valleys (Burk 1977: 876; Marks 1950). The most common members include Echinocactus acanthodes (barrel cactus), Echinocereus engelmannii (calico cactus), Mammillaria tetrancistra (corkseed cactus), Opuntia bigelovii (Bigelow cactus). Often associated with this community are non-cactus types, such as Fouquieria splendens (ocotillo) and Encelia farinosa (brittle bush). A few individuals of Carnegiea gigantea (sahuaro cactus) are reported from the eastern end of the Little Chuckwalla Mountains, the Whipple Mountains, the Mule Mountains and the Chocolate Mountains near Laguna Dam.

The sand dune community is another community surrounded by creosote. It is usually situated along the bottoms of the large, segmented valley systems and often reaches to the bajadas. In the areas bordering the Imperial Valley, this dune community has a slightly different character. The common types include Parosela fremontii (Fremont dalea), Hilaria rigida (big galletagrass), Oenothera deltoides (dune primrose), Palafoxia linearis (spanish needle), Ephedra californica (joint fir) and at elevations below 500 feet (152 m.) Coldenia palmeri (Palmer coldenia) (Dean 1977).

On the bajadas, these species are often joined by the Cis-montane Croton californicus (desert croton), Parosela schottii (indigo bush) and Coldenia plicata (plicate coldenia). On the Algodones dunes, many of these species or close relatives occur with some localized plants, such as Euphorbia pediculifera (sand mat).

The desert range valleys and the Salton Trough contain a number of closed basins that form playas or areas of high salt concentration. Where these occur, the creosote scrub community gives way to a succession of increasingly more salt tolerant species. The xerophytic creosote zone is replaced by a more halophytic one, often including Atriplex canescens var. linearis (narrow-leaved wingscale) and areas of mesquite bosque or sand hummocks, Prosopis glandulosa var. torreyana. This zone is replaced by halophytes of increasing salt tolerance: Atriplex canescens (wingscale), Haplopappus acradenius ssp. eremophilus (alkali golden bush), Suaeda torreyana ramosissima (iodine weed), Allenrolfea occidentalis (pickleweed) (Marks 1950).

In a few areas in the interior of the Colorado Desert planning units, at springs, seeps, wells and areas along the Colorado River, there is sufficient ground water supply to support the specialized communities of Pluchea sericea (arrowweed) and the introduced Tamarix chinensis. Usually associated with these two are Aster spinosus (Mexican devil-weed), Salix exigua (slender willow) and Baccharis sergiloides (desert baccharis). This community depends on a high ground water table and can occur in almost any desert soil type, from clays to sands and at very high alkali levels (Marks 1950). Locating water sources in the desert ranges is made simple by the striking pure stands of arrowweed and large Tamarix trees.

One of the most prominent communities, and one that is important in defining the limits of the Sonoran Desert, is the woodland wash community. The defining members are the thorn arboreals: Olneya tesota (ironwood) and Cercidium floridum (border palo verde). Another somewhat hardier Sonoran arboreal, Parosela spinosa (smoke tree), ranges just past the northern borders of the study area. Still another arboreal, Chilopsis linearis (desert willow) ranges throughout the high desert of the Mojave and joins the Colorado Desert woodland wash communities in their higher and more protected stands. It apparently has a lower tolerance to heat than the other arboreals in the study area (Strain and Chase 1966). Other members of the community include Lycium Andersonii (Anderson thornbush), Prosopis glandulosa var. torreyana (mesquite), and Baccharis sarothroides (broom baccharis). A number of other perennials and annuals are associated with the riparian zone, as well as some parasitic plants, such as Phoradendron californicum (desert mistletoe) which is common in Prosopis and Olneya. One uncommon type of Sonoran arboreal, found only in the Whipple Mountains in the Colorado Desert, is Cerdicium microphyllum (little-leaved horse bean) (Jaeger 1941: 93; Hastings et al. 1972).

The Salton Trough and the Imperial and Coachella valleys pose a somewhat different set of environmental conditions than are found in the desert ranges. As a result, these areas have some different vegetational communities. The most noticeable is the palm oasis community, found along the base of the San Jacinto and Santa Rosa mountains and in the Indio Hills. Washingtonia filifera (California fan palm) occurs in the steep canyons and along the hillsides of regions that can supply permanent water and are well drained. These palms usually have an understory vegetation that is also water dependant and salt tolerant: Pluchea sericea (arrow-weed), Haplopappus acradenius (alkali goldenbush) Sporobolus airoides (dropseed), Juncus acutus var. sphaerocarpus (wire grass).

Still another community represented in the Colorado Desert planning units is found at the higher elevations along the northern section of the study area. In the western most extension of the northwest arm (Twentynine Palms Planning Unit) one encounters the Joshua Tree Woodland community. It occurs on the valley slopes and along the edges of the Pinto Mountains where elevations exceed 3000 feet (915 m.). Besides Joshua Tree (Yucca brevifolia), plant members include Grayia spinosa (spiny hop-sage), Atriplex hymenelytra (desert holly), Salvia mohavensis (Mohave sage) and Ephedra spp. (joint fir). This Mojave, high desert community grades into the Juniper/Pinyon Woodland community at higher elevations (above 4500 feet, 1370 m.). The Juniper/Pinyon community is also found at the top of the northern end of the Old Woman Mountains in the northeastern section of the study area.

E. Climatic and Environmental Reconstructions

A necessary task in explaining the lifeways of prehistoric and historic populations is the reconstruction of environments facing these peoples. Within archeology, two different approaches to this problem have been used. One is to focus on the large scale movement and development of people throughout western North American, based on the fluctuations of environments (i.e. Baumhoff and Heizer 1965). The other approach is framed in the model of human ecology, answering questions about adaptive responses to changes in specific environments (i.e. Davis 1978; Warren and DeCosta 1964).

Because of the necessary reliance on environmental factors, archaeologists in the California Desert have worked closely with the related fields of geology and botany and are obliged to integrate data from these diverse and fast growing fields into their own interpretations.

Unfortunately, in the Colorado Desert planning units there is only a few scattered sources of information available on past climates. Paleobotanical information comes from the northeast corner of the region (Van Devender and King 1971; Van Devender 1976; Van Devender and Spaulding 1979; Waters 1979). The Sundesert Project has been the main contributor to various fields of information on past climate in the southeast portion of the study area. In the area of Lake Cahuilla there have been intriguing studies of the relationship of the lake's shorelines and environmental factors (Weide 1976; Babcock 1974).

Geologists and geographers have provided a broad field of climatic and environmental information over the last one hundred years. Studies of Basin-Range shorelines in the mid 1800's have been complimented by more recent analysis of cores from these ancient lakes, presenting an increasingly sophisticated scheme of Pleistocene, Post-Pleistocene and Holocene environments throughout the Basin-Range Province.

The work was initiated by Russell (1885) with his pioneering analysis of shorelines in the northern Great Basin. Refined interpretations have since been presented by Morrison (1965) and Smith (1968), showing dramatic fluctuation in climate throughout the late Pleistocene (40,000-10,000 BP) but an overall climate that was much cooler and moister than today. The pluvial maximums of this period filled many of the basins of the arid west with a system of lakes and streams. Floral communities during this period differed radically in both composition and elevational limits.

Holocene (10,000 BP to present) environments have been generally hotter and dryer than the previous period but have also shown signs of significant fluctuation. Antevs (1948; 1955) developed a scheme that, with some slight modification, represents our general understanding of Holocene climate. His model consists of three parts: The Anathernal (10,000-7000 BP) having warm and moist conditions, the Altithermal (7000-4500 BP) characterized as hot and dry, and the Medithermal (4500 to present) again having warm and moist conditions. Changes in climate responsible for these periods were, according to Antevs' hypothesis, based on shifts in the position and the magnitude of the Pacific High Pressure cell in relation to the wetter Aleutian Low Pressure cell. Fluctuations of these global-scale weather systems have been responsible for both Pleistocene and Holocene patterns, with a compression of these weather systems toward the equator during the moister and cooler periods. Aschmann (1958), however, has presented an alternative view.

In the past 20 years, information on climate from the field of biology (bioclimatology) has added a new dimension to the geologic data. Bioclimatology has made possible the comparison of plant community locations through time. This field has also permitted an analysis of changes in the structure of the plant community (e.g. adding and dropping of community members and changes in the ratio of members).

Bioclimatology is here divided into two sub-fields, pollen analysis and the study of plant macro-fossils. The study of plant macro-fossils is itself divided between coprolite analysis and pack rat midden analysis. Coprolite analysis gained a reputation very early with the discovery and study of ground sloth dung from Gypsum Cave in southern Nevada (Laudermilk and Munz 1934, 1938; Long and Martin 1974). Recently analysis of pack rat (Neotoma spp.) middens has supplied large amounts of data from throughout the Mojave and Sonoran deserts.

Wells and Berger (1967) recognized the importance of pack rat middens because of the animal's unique pattern of collecting and preserving surrounding flora. This pattern involves a somewhat random sampling within a very restricted area (150 feet, 45m.). Their middens are built stratigraphically by long term and often sequential habitation. Excreta in the midden solidifies and preserves twigs, seeds, bark and other portable material found within the packrat's collecting range. The favorite habitation for packrats is in limestone formations and often on very steep slopes. Whether this special habitat accurately represents the conditions of the rest of the desert area is a major concern of people working with midden analysis. The problem is only partially overcome by the very large amount of information and the environmental situations in which middens are found. An advantage of data from middens is that it is easily and usually quite accurately dated by C-14.

At least two sets of bioclimate authors dealing with comparisons between the Mojave and the Sonoran deserts during the late Pleistocene, have touched upon parts of the Colorado Desert planning units in order to show the area's transitional nature. Wells and Berger (1967) reported on two middens found in the Turtle Mountains. The most abundant of the two (T-2) is at an elevation of 730 meters (2394 feet) and dates to 13,900 $\pm$ 200 BP. Material from this site includes three plant types that are no longer in the area: Juniperus osteosperma (Utah juniper), Pinus monophylla (single-leaved pinyon) and Ribes velutinum (goose berry). All of these plants now occur 1000 to 1500 feet (305-457 m.) higher.

Neotoma middens from the Whipple Mountains have been analysed by Van Devender and others (Van Devender 1977b; Van Devender and Spaulding 1979) and these have been used to compare the results from macro plant fossils and from pollen in the same samples .(King and Van Devender 1976). The middens occurred at a number of locations at elevational ranges of 1050 feet (320 m.), dating to approximately 11,500 BP; 1197 feet (365 m.), dating to approximately 12,500 BP; and 1706 feet (520 m.), dating to 9000 to 13,000 BP. Juniper was represented in all of the samples and pinyon in all but the earliest. Other species included: Cercocarpus intricatus (little-leaved mahogany), which is a plant described by Munz (1974) as preferring limestone cliffs; Opuntia acanthocarpa (deer-horn cactus); Ephedra nevadensis (Mormon tea); Salvia mohavensis (Mohave sage); and Yucca brevifolia (Joshua tree). Yucca brevifolia is quite common in the sites. Cactus species and other plant types indicate that the sites were heavily influenced by the Mohave Desert during the late Pleistocene. Perennials found in the middens indicate a mixture of Mojave and Sonoran influences, and the annuals recovered are now associated with xeric Conifer Woodland communities and the Mojave Desert (Rowlands 1978:128-132, tables 14,15,17).

This information shows that during the late Pleistocene there was at least a 2000 foot (610 m.) depression of the woodland plant communities in the northern portions of the Colorado Desert planning units and a considerable intermixing of plant types. The relationship that this may have had on the central and southern portions of the Colorado Desert planning units is unclear. Van Devender has postulated that a sub-tropical refugia existed in the northern Mexican deserts (Van Devender 1977:192). The refugia was established by a tropical low pressure system, and this weather pattern possibly could have extended westward through the southern portions of the Colorado Desert planning units and into the Salton Trough. Munz (1974: 5) has noted that a number of plant types found in the lower mountainous regions and valleys are relic species that have moved up from Mexico during periods of moist climate and are now cut off from their relatives to the southeast by the Colorado Desert. He lists Arctostaphylos glauca eremicola (desert manzanita) and Fremontodendron californicam (California slippery elm) and others.

For the present, our interpretations of earlier environments of the study area can be limited to the immediate areas of sound information. Comparison of Pleistocene animal middens with present day communities demonstrates that plant communities do not move en masse with fluctuations in climate. Rather the communities are composed of a variety of individual plant members that are brought together by their common suitibility to a particular set of environmental factors related to climate and soils (cf. Rowlands 1978:131).

Wells and Berger (1967) have argued against climatic reconstructions on a large scale, because of our limited and fragmented knowledge of these complex factors. Recently Van Devender and Spaulding (1979) have proven that with the amount of new information available some general schemes relating to vegetation dynamics and past climates are possible. Yet for the Colorado Desert planning units, where the area has served as a transitional zone during the Pleistocene and Holocene climatic regimes, and where the area has been subjected to refugias and rainshadows, a clear understanding of past climate and associated plant dynamics is still in the future.

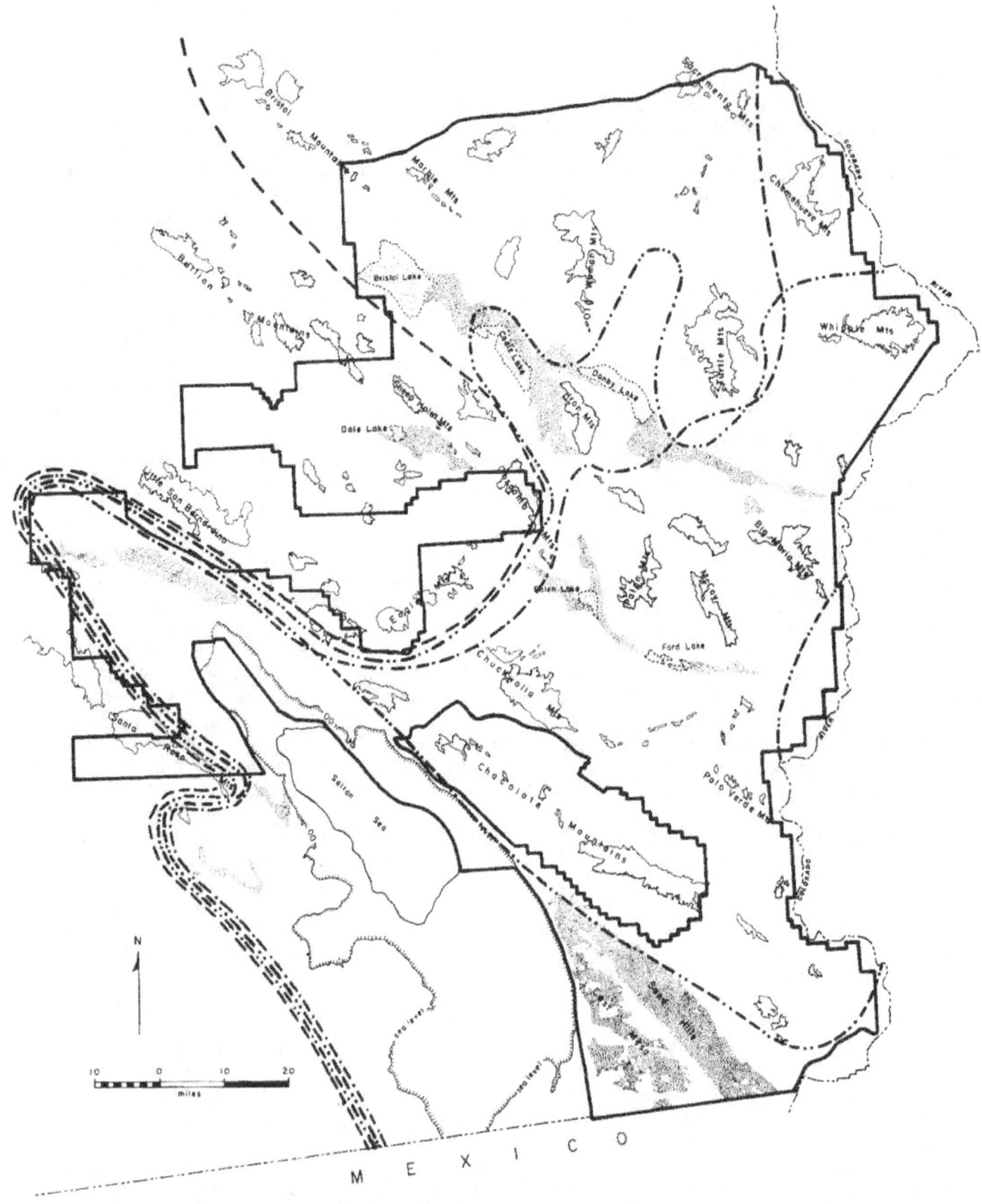

Figure 2. Proposed Boundaries of the Colorado Desert

A ——————— (Blake 1854, Jahns 1956)
B ——————— (Burk 1977)
C ——————— (Jeager 1957)
D ——————— (Bailey 1966)

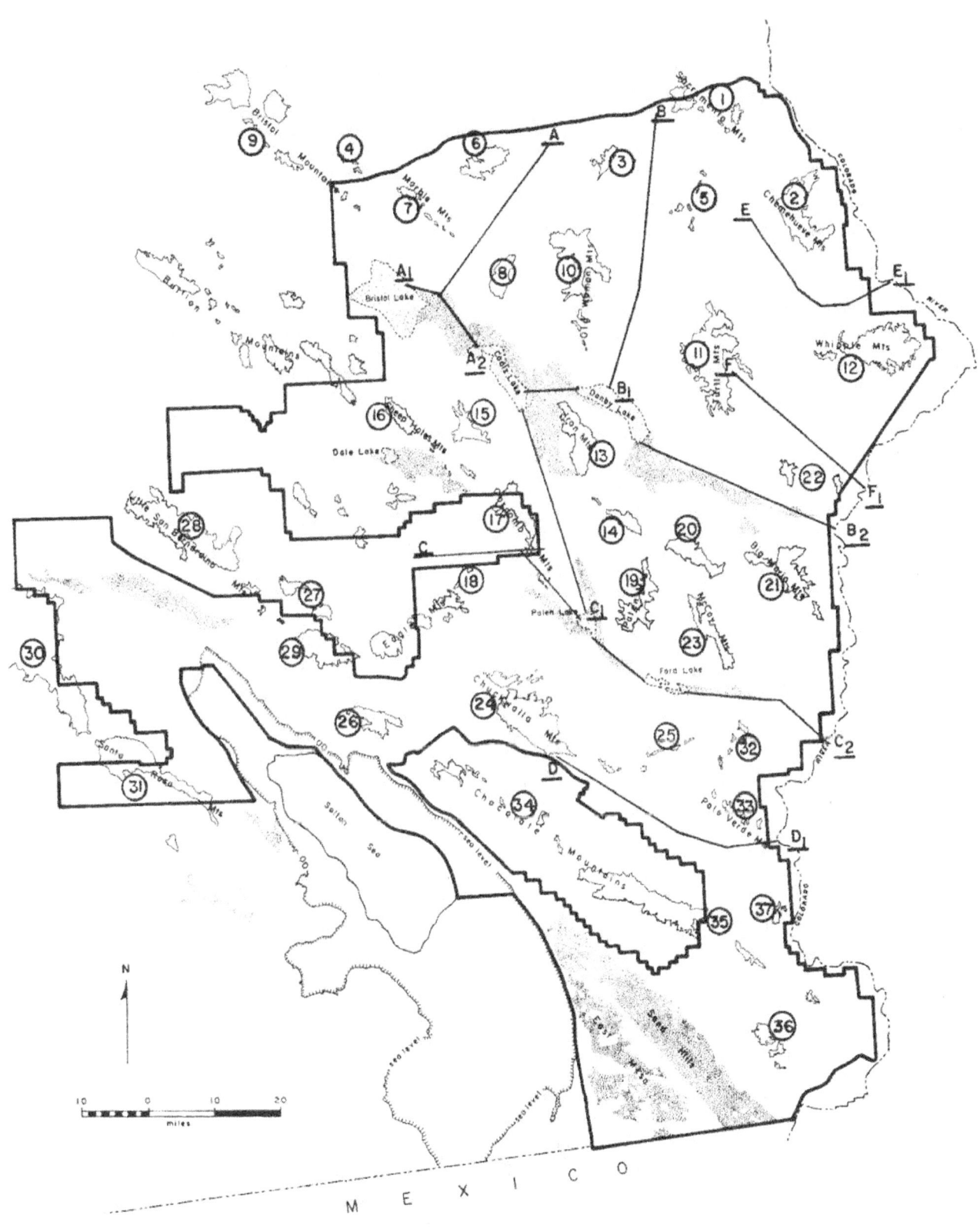

Figure 3.   Major Mountain Ranges and Profile Locations

TABLE A. MOUNTAIN RANGE DATA

No.	Range	Area	Orientation	Height	Pediment	Springs	Terrain
1.	Sacramento	44	NW-SE	3308	11-22	0	MB
2.	Chemehuevi	78	---	2988	10-24	3	M
3.	Paiute	35	N-SW	4165	28-32	4	MB
4.	Old Dad	27	NW-SE	4000	30-35	0	B
5.	Stepladder	20	N-S	2683	17-20	0	B
6.	Clipper	32	NE-SW	4604	20-30	3	M
7.	Marble	22	NW-SE	3842	10-30	0	MB
8.	Ship	14	N-SW	3239	10-14	0	M
9.	Bristol	(51)	NW-SE	3609	10-23	0	B
10.	Old Woman	105	N-S	5326	10-32	12	MB
11.	Turtle	130	N-S	4231	13-23	8	MB
12.	Whipple	165	E-W	4131	8-22	2	M
13.	Iron	36	NW-S	3296	10-14	0	M
14.	Granite	20	NW-SE	4353	18-21	0	M
15.	E. Sheephole	45	NW-SE	3702	10-28	0	MB
16.	Sheephole	23	NW-SE	4685	19-22	0	MB
17.	Coxcomb	89	N-SE	4416	10-22	0	M
18.	Eagle	204	NE-SW	5350	12-32	3	M
19.	Palen	78	N-SW	3600	10-16	0	M
20.	Little Maria	34	NW-SE	3043	10-16	1	M
21.	Big Maria	110	N-S	3500	6-14	0	M
22.	Riverside	18	N-S	2252	4-12	0	MB
23.	McCoy	48	NW-SE	2835	6-12	0	M
24.	Chuchwalla	168	NW-E	4504	8-28	6	MB
25.	Little Chuchwalla	21	E-W	1600	8-12	0	MB
26.	Orocopia	98	---	3815	2-22	5	M
27.	Hexie	--	W-SE	4747	20-40	1	M
28.	Little S. Ben	--	NW-SE	5462	10-40	1	M
29.	Cottonwood	28	E-W	4375	18-32	2	M
30.	San Jacinto	--	NW-SE	10804	3-11	1	M
31.	Santa Rosa	--	NW-SE	8714	0-10	1	M
32.	Mule	14	NE-SW	1801	4-8	0	B
33.	Palo Verde	48	NW-SE	1795	4-6	1	B
34.	Chocolate	230	NW-SE	2967	0-25	5	M
35.	E. Chocolate	22	NW-SE	1538	4-10	1	B
36.	Cargo Mucho	18	NW-SE	2129	5-10	0	M
37.	Mid Way	12	---	1400	8-10	1	B

KEY: AREA is provided in square miles.
HEIGHT is for the highest peak, in feet.
PEDIMENT figures are elevations, in hundreds of feet, for low and high
pediment locations (see Figure 4).
TERRAIN: M=Mountainous, B=Broken.
SPRINGS refers to the number of springs found in the range.

SOURCE: USGS 1:250,000 and 18' topographic maps.

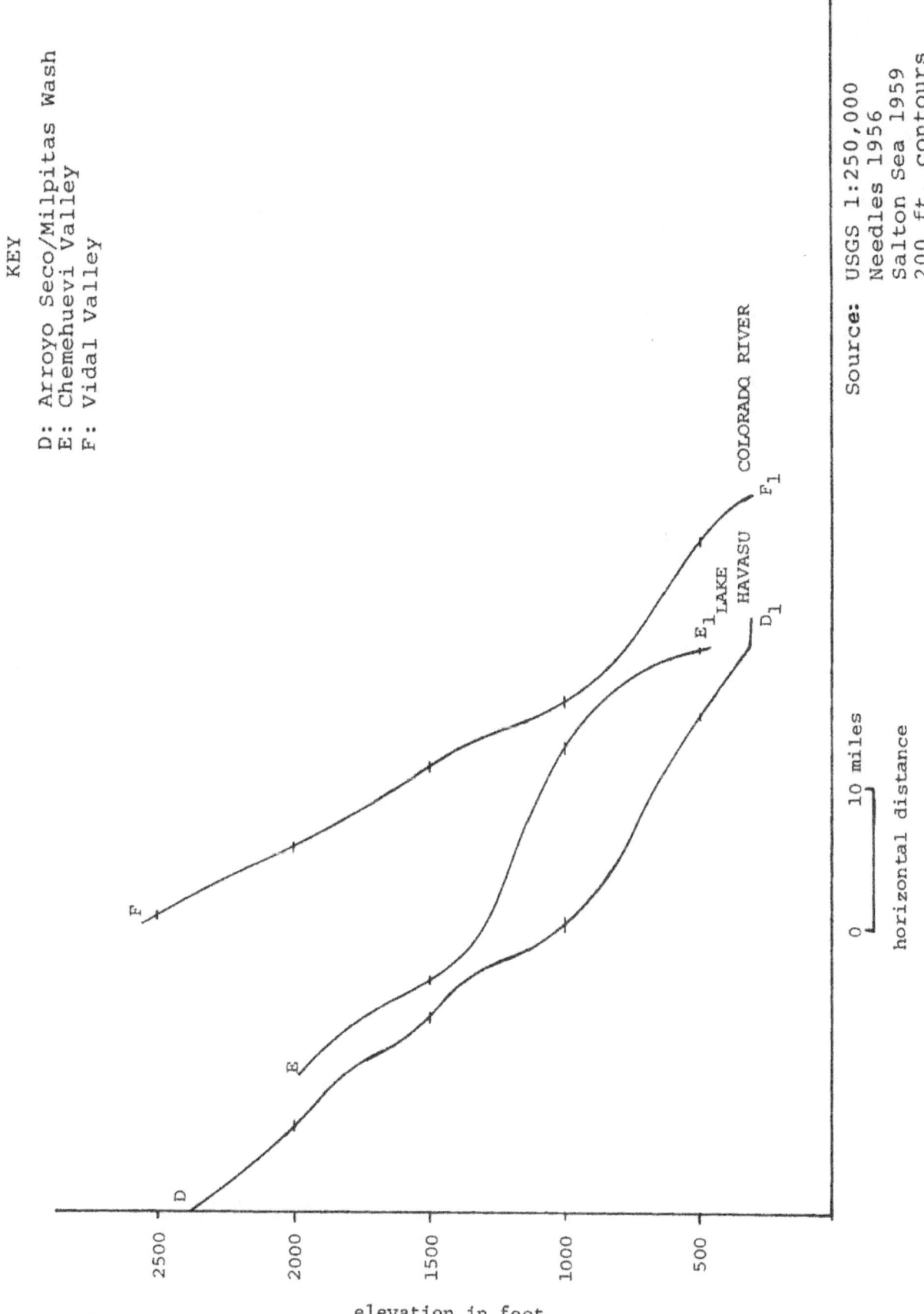

KEY

D: Arroyo Seco/Milpitas Wash
E: Chemehuevi Valley
F: Vidal Valley

Source: USGS 1:250,000
Needles 1956
Salton Sea 1959
200 ft. contours

Figure 3a.

Profiles of Arroyo Seco/Milpitas Wash, Chemehuevi and Vidal Valleys

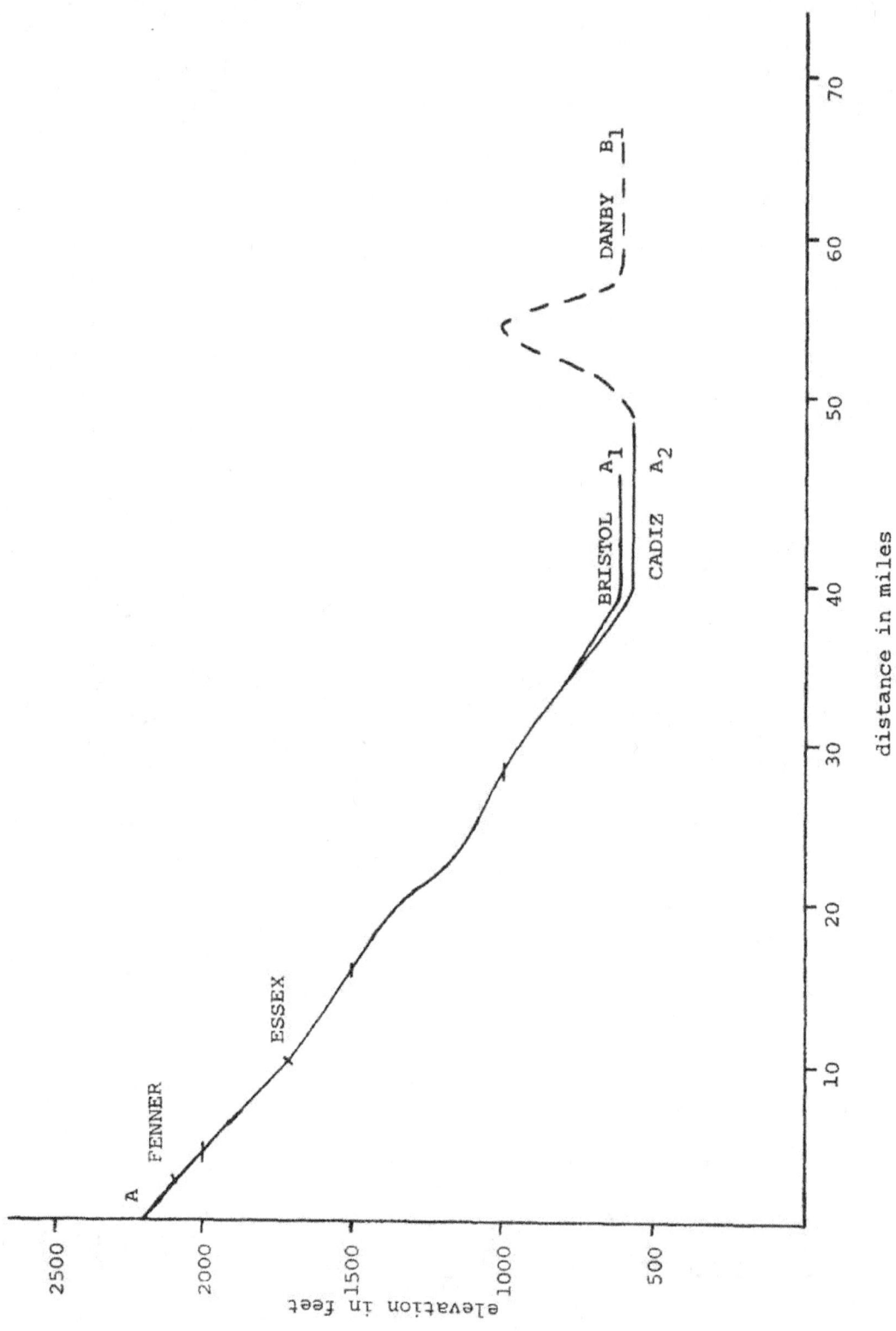

Figure 3b. Profile of Fenner Valley

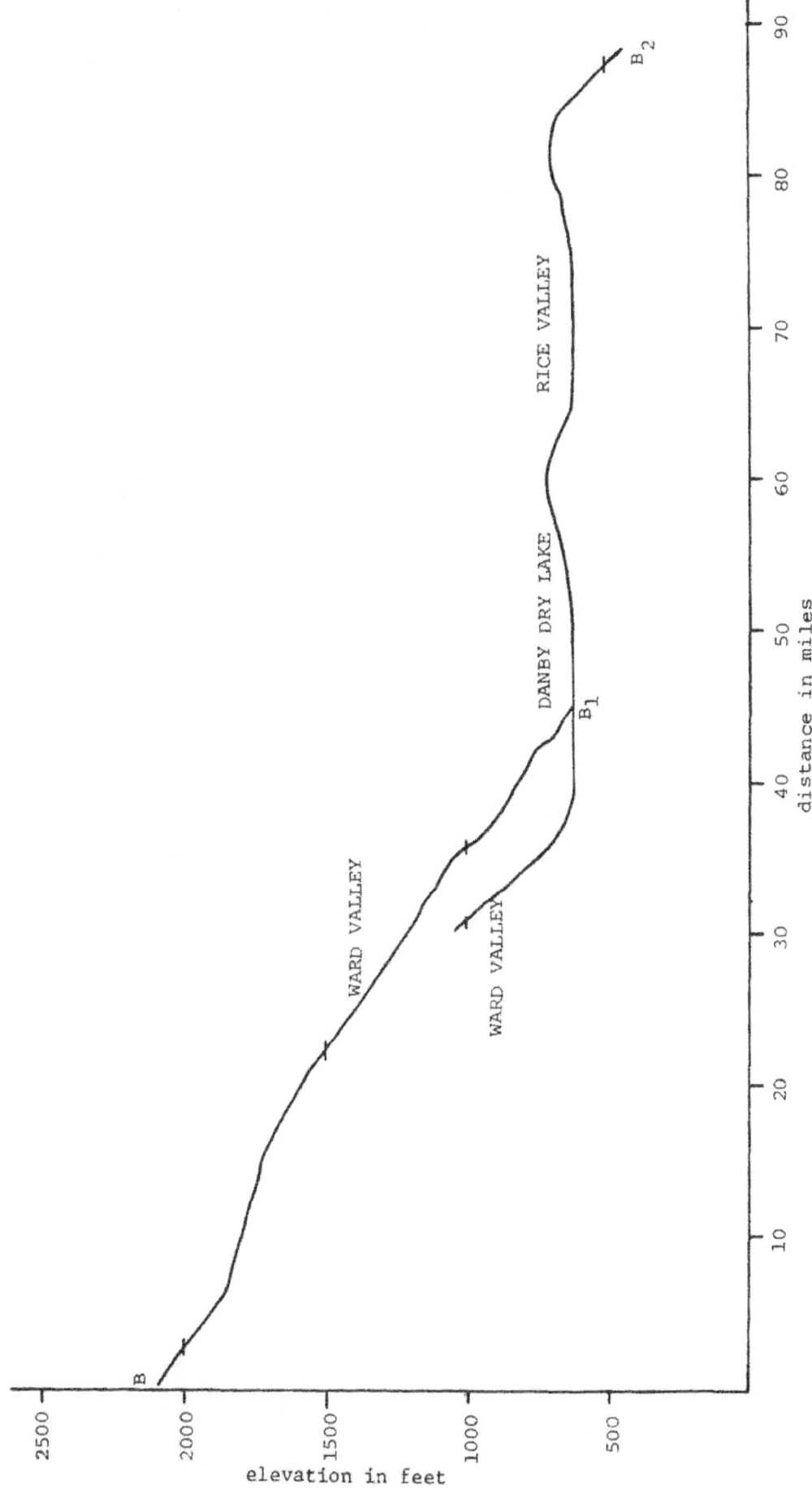

Figure 3c.   Profile of Ward and Rice Valleys

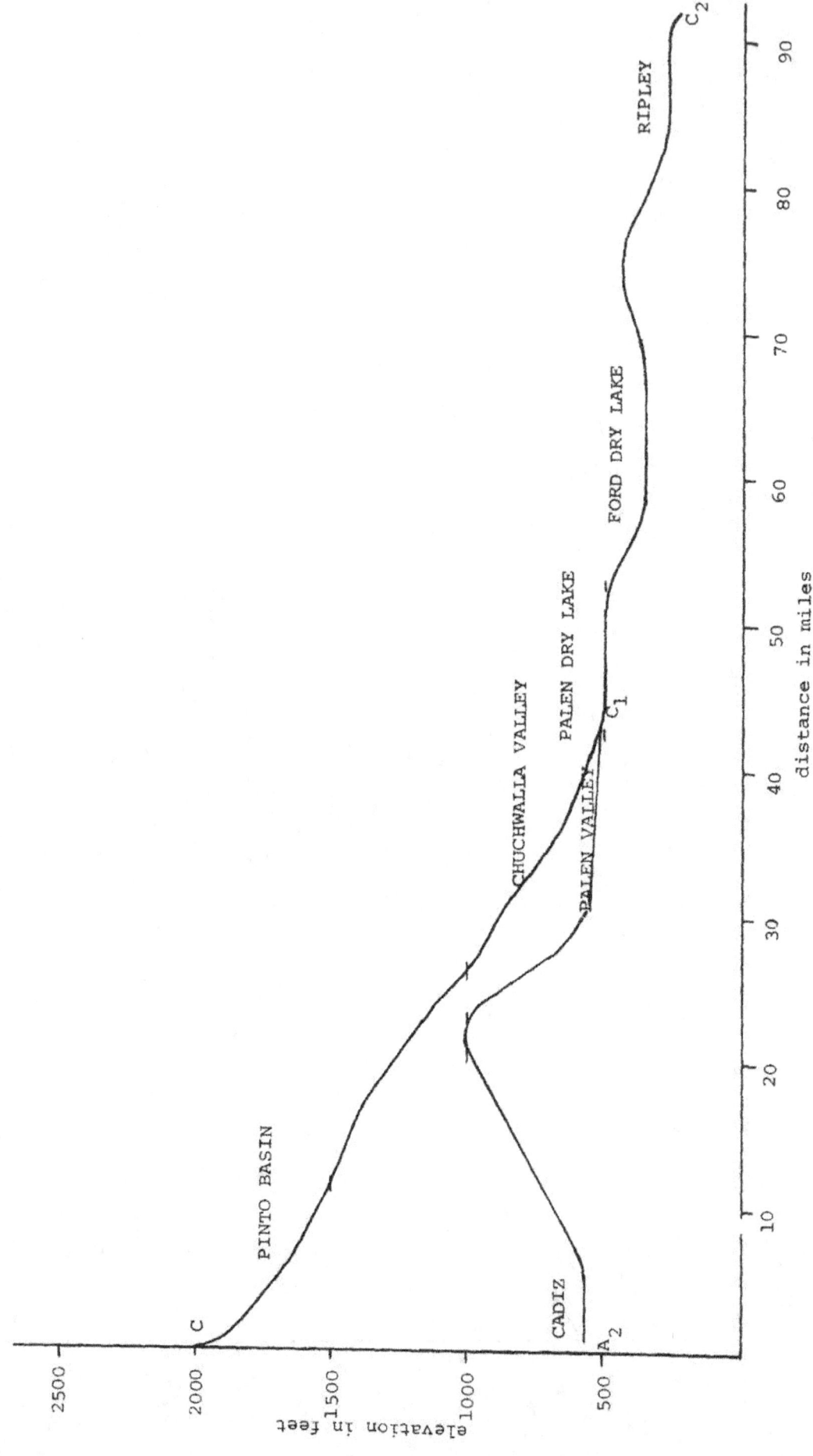

Figure 3d.   Profile of Pinto Basin and Chuckwalla Valley

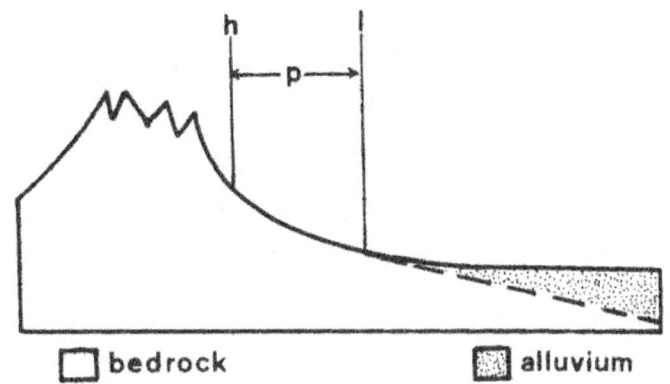

Key

p: pediment
h: high pediment
l: low pediment

Figure 4. Point of Inflex (after Cooke; 1970:27)

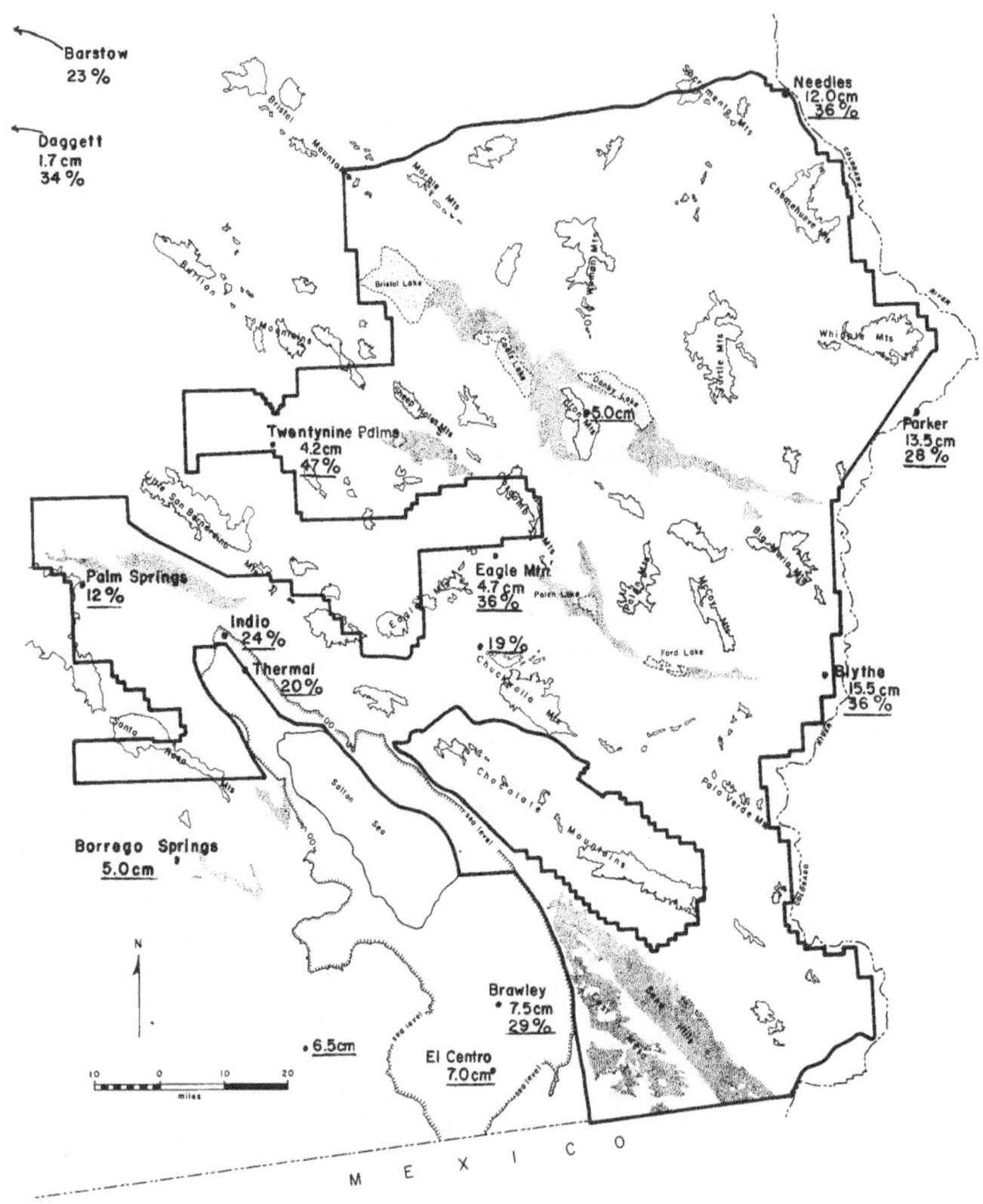

Figure 5. Locations of Sand Dunes (stippled areas)
and Rainfall Averages (in cm. and % of summer precipitation)

Chapter III. ARCHAEOLOGY
Robert H. Crabtree

A. History of Archaeological Research

1. Surveys and Investigations

a. San Diego Museum of Man

Archaeological research in the Colorado Desert began with the work of M.J. Rogers. From the 1920's to the middle of the 1940's Rogers made a number of reconnaissance trips into several parts of the study area, particularly the old shore lines of extinct Lake Cahuilla on the east side of the Salton Trough, in Imperial and Orocopia planning units; along the terraces of the Colorado River and the hilly back county west of the river in the Picacho Planning Unit; briefly in the Santa Rosa Mountains (Santa Rosa Planning Unit); north of old Lake Cahuilla in the Coachella Valley in the Santa Rosa and Orocopia planning units; the Orocopia-Chuckwalla-Eagle Mountains area of eastern Orocopia and western Palen planning units; the basins of Palen and Ford dry lakes, in eastern Palen and western Big Maria planning units; in the general vicinity of Twentynine Palms, Lost Palms and Lost Horse canyons in Joshua Tree National Monument (not in the study area technically--for an overview, see T. F. King 1975); the Colorado River terraces and adjacent Rice and Chemehuevi valleys, in the eastern part of Big Maria and Whipple mountains planning units. Judging from the numbers and extent of sites recorded by Rogers, the old Lake Cahuilla shoreline and the Colorado River terraces received the most intensive investigations, however, it is well to keep in mind that Rogers usually recorded what might be termed "site complexes" or archaeological "zones", which include trails, shrines, lithic and sherd scatters, stone alignments, pictographs, shelters, etc. often scattered over many linear as well as square miles.

Excavation was not usually an element of Rogers' field strategy, but the records provided by the San Diego Museum of Man indicate that some excavation was done in a few instances. Notes, sketches, manuscripts and specimens are available for study at the San Diego Museum of Man. Only very general references to these excavations are contained in Rogers' several publications (cf. Rogers 1939, 1945, 1966).

Rogers never published detailed reports on his research, or at least reports comparable to the standard of contemporaneous reports. Rather, he published articles summarizing his interpretations of various natural and cultural phenomena he had observed in the desert over the years, arranging the cultural material in a rather detailed sequence, which he revised several times, resulting in considerable confusion. Uncritical use of these revisions remains a problem to this time. Rogers' basic contribution was in amassing a large amount of primary data which is still available for evaluation and study. Rogers' evaluation of his data, particularly such natural phenomenon as patination and desert varnish, and to some extent desert pavement and other geomorphic observations are probably still useful. However, his interpretation of cultural data seems to be uncritical and naive, particularly when applied to ceramic and lithic material. This is not to belittle the contribution Rogers made to the data base for these areas. The fault, if there really is any, lies with the tendency to place Rogers and his work in some kind of sacred preserve which does not allow for critical re-evaluation of his work based on more recent field work, including excavations. In addition, methodological procedures and theoretical formulations now exist which were unavailabe to Rogers in his time.

For a summary and eulogy of Rogers' career, see Ezell (1961); for another evaluation of Rogers as an archaeologist see Warren (1966).

b. Elizabeth W.C. and William Campbell

The Campbells were active from the 1920's to at least the 1940's, ranging from Pinto Basin in the south to the west central Great Basin in the north. The Campbells conducted surveys and amassed surface collections which led to the earliest definition of Pinto Basin and Lake Mohave complexes as early man manifestations (1931, 1935, 1936, 1937). A fair amount of controversy was generated over dating old lake terraces and other ancient land surfaces, but the conceptions of these early assemblages is still viable and the dating has received some support. Work was also carried out in the vicinity of Twentynine Palms, but the impact was slight. The Campbells' work in Pinto Basin is reviewed in some detail by T.F. King (1975). An evaluation of the Campbells' work in terms of modern "problem oriented" approaches has been reviewed by C.N. Warren (1970).

c. University of California, Berkeley

A. E. Treganza conducted informal surveys in northern Baja California and western Imperial County. However, Treganza touched on some issues which are still very much alive in the study area, in particular, the development of agriculture and "fish traps" (Treganza 1942, 1945, 1947). A more detailed discussion of Treganza's work is in Weide et al.'s Yuha Desert Overview (1974: 69).

In 1948 Agnes Bierman and Albert Mohr conducted surveys in the eastern part of San Bernardino and Riverside counties. The collections from these surveys are now at the University of California, Los Angeles.

In the 1940's and 50's M. J. Harner was very active with surveys along both sides of the Colorado River and west to Imperial Valley. Harner excavated at the Bouse Site near Parker, Arizona. Only a summary of the sequence at that site has been published (Harner 1958). Harner's collections are at the Lowie Museum, U.C. Berkeley, and site records are on file at the Imperial Valley College Museum, El Centro.

d. San Bernardino County Museum

Since the early 1930's the San Bernardino County Museum, under the direction of Dr. Gerald Smith, has served as an institution for both general public education and active field research. Smith and his co-workers have ranged over a large part of the Mojave Desert with primary emphasis on reconnaissance and recording rock art, although excavations, particularly at Newberry Cave (Smith et al. 1957), have been conducted. In the past decade or so this institution has been very active in the cultural resource sector of archaeological work. The San Bernardino County Museum serves as the archaeological clearing house for San Bernardino County.

e. Archaeological Survey Association of Southern California

In the mid-1950's the Archaeological Survey Association, under the leadership of B.E. McCown conducted extensive surveys around the Salton Trough, concentrating on the old Lake La Conte (or Cahuilla) shorelines. Excavations near Fish Creek on the west side were done and samples for radiocarbon dating collected in a number of localities (B. E. McCown 1954, 1955, 1957). This material is currently being studied and will eventually result in a published report (B. H. McCown 1974). Carl Hubbs, of Scripps Institute, collaborated with the Archaeological Survey Association in the collection and processing of radiocarbon samples (Hubbs, Bien and Seuss 1960, 1963, 1965; Hubbs and Bien 1967). For a listing and evaluation of these dates see D. Weide (in M. Weide et al. 1974: 4-15, 110) and Wilke (1978a).

f. National Park Service

Albert Schroeder, under the auspices of the National Park Service, surveyed along the Colorado River from below Davis Dam in the Mohave Valley to the International Boundary (Schroeder 1952), A major result of this survey was the definition of Lower Colorado Buff Ware, a more systematic attempt at dealing with ceramics than had been done before (Schroeder 1958). Schroeder's excavations and report of the Willow Beach excavations (Schroeder 1961) are also important for the northern portions of the study area.

g. University of California, Los Angeles

The University of California, Los Angeles was active in the study area from 1959 to 1965. Most of their work consisted of brief one to three day surface surveys. Limited excavations at two small rock shelters in the upper Coachella Valley were conducted by Joseph Michels and Jay Ruby in 1962 and 1963 (Michels 1964; Ruby 1964). Lists of the University of California, Los Angeles field work may be found in the UCLA Archeological Survey Annual Reports for the years 1958 through 1968. The collections are housed at the UCLA Museum of Culture History in Haines Hall on the University campus.

h. California State University, Long Beach

William J. Wallace and associates, working out of California State Uniersity, Long Beach, surveyed and excavated in Joshua Tree National Monument, including the Pinto Basin area (Wallace 1964). This region, not included in the study area, has been reported on by T. F. King (1975).

i. University of California, Riverside

Since the late 1960's the University of California, Riverside has been active in various parts of the study area. The momentum of this work accelerated when the Archaeological Research Unit was formed in the early 70's under T. F. King. In subsequent years considerable work has been done by T. F. King, P. Wilke, R. Ambro, J. Barker, T. J. King, C. Rector and others. Much of this work was directly the result of new laws and court decisions both nationally and in the state of California, leading to the now familiar EIR process. The Bureau of Land Management files contain this material. Noteworthy also is the work of P. J.

Wilke on problems connected with the waxing and waning Lake Cahuilla (Wilke 1978a) and the study of post lake adaptations (see also Wilke 1974; Wilke and Lawton 1975).

j. Institute for American Research (Archaeological Research Inc.)

Roger Desautels and Albert McCurdy surveyed various regions adjacent to the study area, particularly in the Providence Mountains north of the study area and on both sides of Imperial Valley. The work was done under contract with both the Bureau of Land Management and the Bureau of Reclamation. In 1973-4 Robert Ellis surveyed a portion of East Mesa near Holtville, in the geothernal area for the Bureau of Reclamation (Ellis 1973; Ellis and Crabtree 1974). A report on the ceramics and settlement patterns is being prepared from this material by Crabtree. The results of the earlier surveys in the form of site records and collections are deposited at the Bureau of Land Management Riverside office.

k. Imperial Valley College Museum

Since the late 1960's this institution has been active in Imperial and southeastern Riverside counties. Excavations at East Mesa were conducted by Michael Barker and Jay von Werlhof. Morlin Childers has been active, especially in the Yuha Desert, investigating possible "pre-projectile point" cultures. Since 1973 Jay von Werlhof has been very active in the field conducting surveys, updating site records, etc. He has focused on rock art, trails, intaglios and fish traps, but has also been responsible for a number of surveys under contract at Sun Desert near Blythe, in the Chocolate Mountains and numerous localities in Imperial Valley.

l. University of Nevada, Las Vegas, Nevada Archaeological Survey

At various times in 1968-70 Richard Brooks, George Kritzman, Michael Moen, Lawrence Alexander and Robert Crabtree surveyed along the Colorado River, from Blythe to Yuma for the National Park Service (Brooks and Kritzman 1968; Brooks 1969; Brooks, Alexander and Crabtree 1970).

Richard Brooks and Daniel Larson evaluated the cultural resources of Tahquitz Canyon (Brooks and Larson 1973). In 1976 Brooks and his fellow workers did limited testing and collecting at Pilot Knob, two localities on East Mesa and one locality on West Mesa (Brooks et al. 1977).

m. Southwest Texas State University

In 1975 Norman Whalen conducted a survey in the southeastern part of Imperial County in seven randomly selected sections in the Chocolate and Cargo Muchacho mountains and the bajadas and intervening wash areas. One hundred eighty-eight sites, including cleared areas, "ceremonial configurations" (intaglios), lithic remains, trails and ceramic scatter were found (Whalen 1976:25-30). Whalen assigns the bulk of this material to "San Dieguito I", although over 75% of the material appears to be non-diagnostic workshop debris. Included is a useful discussion of the function of the cleared circles (128 total sites) and the twelve intaglios. The illustrations and descriptions of the latter are an important addition of primary data to the literature on intaglios (Whalen 1976:47-50 and figs 3 to 8).

n. Other Cultural Resource Surveys

With the advent of "public archaeology" and legal requirements for protection of "significant" cultural resources, considerable effort and literature have been expended in mitigating the effects of various projects which may materially affect the integrity of prehistoric deposits and other related phenomena. The size of the areas in these reports ranges from under an acre to many square miles. Many reports indicate negative or very marginal results, with little in the way of cultural resources present. Others have reported a large amount of material with considerable potential for future research. Most of these reports consist of little more than brief descriptions of sites located with a small amount of background information on local or regional ecology, prehistory and other pertinent information. As they stand they are not a significant contribution to knowledge, nor are they intended to be. Occasionally, however, considerable data is generated and presented in these reports, and it is well worth the time it takes for anyone involved in research of the area to review as many as possible.

Most of these reports exist only as typed manuscripts and an unknown number are not generally available, having been prepared "in house" by private contracting agencies. Although clearing houses have been in existence for a number of years they do not always receive copies of these reports. Since there is no statutory basis they have no legal recourse, especially if private property and firms are involved. Where public lands are involved a report is generally filed with one or another agency. The Bureau of Land Management office in Riverside has a substantial file of these reports, as do the clearing houses.

2. Collections

Individual collections from the Colorado Desert planning units vary considerably in quantity and quality of data. The following survey provides a brief evaluation of these collections. In a few instances the collections were not examined because they were unavailable. In other instances there are already adequate evaluations available and little or nothing could be added by another (expensive) trip to visit the collections involved.

The Riverside Municipal Museum was not visited because the drastic curtailment of its program (due to Proposition 13) made scheduling the visit next to impossible. The Riverside Municipal Museum is said to have ethnographic collections from Cahuilla and Serrano Indians, and these should be evaluated in terms of their importance to the prehistory of the California deserts.

The Museum of Northern Arizona has some collections of pottery types from the California deserts. Collections at the Lowie Museum, University of California, Berkeley, include Treganza's collection from the Colorado Desert. However, these collections are adequately evaluated by Weide et al. (1974). The Campbell collections from the Twentynine Palms area and Pinto Basin are housed at the Joshua Tree National Monument and are discussed in the overview of that Monument (T. F. King 1975). Collections from the west side of Imperial Valley and the Imperial Dunes (Algodones) are housed and currently under study at the Redlands, California headquarters of the Archaeological Survey Association of Southern California. This collection was not evaluated. Other collections in small local museums and in private hands are likely to exist.

a. Colorado River Indian Tribes Museum, Parker, Arizona

This tribal museum has archaeological collections from both sides of the Colorado River, particularly from the area between Needles, California and Yuma, Arizona. The western bank of the river is represented primarily by surface collections, mostly ceramic, from the Palo Verde Valley area secured by the University of Nevada, Las Vegas-National Park Service surveys of 1968-70 (Brooks and Kritzman 1968; Brooks 1969; Brooks, Alexander and Crabtree 1970). Permission to examine these collections must be obtained through the tribal council and Charles Lamb, Director of the Museum.

b. National Park Service, Lake Mead Interpretive Center

The collections from Willow Beach, Arizona, one of the few stratified sites excavated on the lower Colorado River, are housed at the Lake Mead Interpretive Center in Boulder City, Nevada. All of the artifacts, notes, photographic and other records are at the Center. A type collection of Lower Colorado pottery is also kept here, but it has become mixed and the labels do not always match the specimens.

c. Malki Museum, Morongo Indian Reservation, Banning, California

The Malki Museum, the Morongo Indian tribal museum, has a variable collection of archaeological and ethnological materials from the general Cahuilla tribal area. Noteworthy is a documented collection of pottery from the Torres-Martinez Reservation.

d. Palm Springs Desert Museum, Palm Springs, California

The Palm Springs Museum has an important collection of archaeological and ethnographic material from the Cahuilla area, including collections of basketry and whole pottery vessels. This material is available for study to qualified individuals by making appropriate prior arrangements.

e. Museum of Cultural History, University of California, Los Angeles

Desert collections at the University of California, Los Angeles are listed in Appendix I. More detailed information about individual accessions are contained in the Accession Records at the Museum of Cultural History. The accessions listed include sites from outside the study area, and it is likely that most of the material listed is limited to land under federal jurisdiction.

Most of these collections are small; 94 out of 128 collections have ten or fewer items listed, but in the absence of more extensive data from other sources these are important for gaining some familiarity with the range of data in the area. It should be noted that with few exceptions this material was accessioned between 1948 and 1965, reflecting a shift in focus at UCLA and the rise of the University of California, Riverside as a desert research facility.

f. Los Angeles County Museum of Natural History

The County Museum in Los Angeles has several small collections, donated some years ago by the Native Daughters of the Golden West. Precise locations and other documentation is vague. A listing of these collections is given below:

Museum Number	Location	Contents
A.3177	San Bernardino County	Potsherds
A.9464.71	Morongo Valley	Sherds and lithics
A.9464.71	Twentynine Palms	219 potsherds
A.9464.71	Twentynine Palms	Sherds, mano fragments
L.1163	San Bernardino County	Basketry
A.1451C	Twentynine Palms	Lithic materials

These collections could probably best function as teaching materials. Their value, if any, to synchronic and diachronic studies seems rather slight, except for the value of acquainting the researcher with as broad a range of materials as possible.

> g. University of Nevada, Las Vegas, Archaeological Research Center, Museum of Natural History

Collections from three loci in Imperial Valley and one near Pilot Knob are housed at this Las Vegas institution. These resulted from testing and review programs (for eligibility to the National Register) carried out by the Archaeological Research Center under the direction of Richard H. Brooks for the Bureau of Reclamation. A summary of these collections is given below:

Museum Number	Location	Contents
5-496	East Mesa, Lot #1	Includes surface material and specimens from one test pit, including potsherds, lithic artifacts and debris, faunal remains and two charcoal samples.
5-497	West Mesa, Lot #5	All surface material including pottery sherds, lithic debris, cobble tools and various worked lithic items.
5-498	Hell's Half Acre, E. Mesa	This collection comes from the surface and two test pits, including midden and charcoal samples. Included are potsherds, charcoal, lithic debitage, ground stone, fish and mammal bone, mussel and snail shell.
5-499	Pilot Knob Mesa	All surface material including pottery, lithic material, a charcoal sample and two Olivella shells.

h. San Bernardino County Museum, Redlands, California

The San Bernardino County Museum is one of the senior institutions in the Southern California area, with a long standing interest in the cultural and natural history of the desert areas. The recent relocation of the Museum in Redlands and the consequent reorganization of collections has precluded a listing of accessions. However, it should be emphasized that a considerable body of data is controlled by this institution and is worthy of consideration for background research in any cultural resource management program.

i. Archaeological Research Unit, University of California, Riverside

The Archaeological Research Unit at the University of California, Riverside began in 1971, filling the void resulting from the decline in desert oriented field work at the University of California, Los Angeles. Since its inception, the primary focus of the Archaeological Research Unit has been Coachella Valley and certain adjacent areas. However, since 1972, this focus has broadened considerably due to the greatly increased concern for cultural resources resulting from both legislation and litigation on the state and federal levels. Another result has been the accumulation of several important collections, which are among those listed below:

Accession Number	Location	Contents
5	Deep Canyon - housed at the Desert Research Center	66 sherds, 1 mano
14	Deep Canyon - housed at the Desert Research Center	sherds from Riv-422DC, Riv-496DC and Riv-171
15	Martinez Canyon	surface collections, mostly ceramics
22	Tahquitz Canyon and Chino Canyon - housed at Agua Caliente Band, Bureau of Indian Affairs Bldg Palm Springs	sherds, shell beads, lithic materials and flotation material from Riv-513
28	Mecca Hills, Riv-519	one large olla and decomposed mesquite beans
32	Whipple Mountain Cave	small surface collection and material from one test unit; includes perishables
35	Palm Hills, Riv-97, 516, 519, 576, 585	sherds, lithic and faunal material
36	Wadi Beadmaker Site near Dos Palmas Riv-1525, near Travertine Point, Myoma Dunes Riv-1339, near Toro	about 800 catalogued items, particularly ceramics, faunal material and debitage, over 1000 human coprolites, contents of a small burned house including 6 or 7 ollas with burned seeds and misc. historic items.

Accession Number	Location	Contents
40	Riv-150 (southeast of Indian Wells)	Miscellaneous material from one test pit
47	Carnival of Water property (Washington Street)	miscellaneous material from a sand dune
54	Strong Site (Jefferson Street and Avenue III)	miscellaneous material
60	Riv-1315 (Cahuilla village)	miscellaneous items
64	Riv-64, Indian Wells (small excavation by Cabrillo College 1/72)	sherds, debitage and faunal remains
uncatalogued	about 90 sites (recorded)	miscellaneous collections
uncatalogued	Bat Cave Buttes	ceramics and aquatic bird bone

j. San Diego Museum of Man, San Diego, California

The San Diego Museum of Man has large, important and well documented collections. Particularly noteworthy are the M. J. Rogers' ceramic and lithic collections, along with his notes and site sheets. As has been noted here and by others (cf. Weide et al. 1974: 72-73), Rogers' definitions of "site" is rather broad and relates more to the conception of an archaeological zone or district, comprising a variety of cultural materials in varied, but contiguous, natural loci. Rogers apparently collected selectively and this material would lend itself more readily to defining typologies and other variations across a broad geographic range, rather than locational analysis of "activity areas". Also of great importance is a collection of over 4500 whole pottery vessels from the greater Southwest, mostly collected by Rogers (Van Camp 1972: 1). This is in addition to a collection of over 50,000 sherds; truly a collection of great importance to the study area and considerably beyond. The collections at the San Diego Museum of Man are an important resource for background material relevant to the prehistory of the study area.

k. Bureau of Land Management, District Office, Riverside, California

Surface collections obtained by Archaeological Research, Inc. (R. J. Desautels) during several projects for the Bureau of Land Management in 1972 are housed here. A total of 27 sites were recorded and collected, 13 in San Bernardino County, outside the study area, and 14 in Imperial County, seven of which are within the study area. The collections from these latter sites are listed below. The material is catalogued and the catalog and notes are contained in the Bureau of Land Management File N-1,6231.

Imp-68; Boxes 492 and 493 contain 10 stone artifacts, shell, lithic debris and pottery (183 sherds).

Imp-99; Boxes 534 and 535 contain 22 stone artifacts (chopper, cores, scrapers, hammerstones and manos), shell, debitage and pottery (25 sherds).

Imp-100; Box 536 contains 6 stone artifacts and lithic debitage.

Imp-102; Box 538 contains 7 lithic artifacts (cores, hammerstones, choppers, ground stone), debitage and pottery (14 sherds).

Imp-103; Box 539 contains 6 lithic pieces and debitage.

Imp-106; Box 495 contains 31 potsherds

Imp-109; Box 496 contains 10 potsherds.

1. Imperial Valley College Museum

Since 1973, the Imperial Valley College Museum has served as the central clearinghouse for Imperial County site records. A file of published and unpublished papers, reports and other documents relating generally to the prehistory and history of Imperial County and certain adjacent regions has been compiled by the museum staff. The site record file for the county now totals over 4000 historic and prehistoric items. This file has recently been revised and brought up to date, eliminating duplications and generally improving the file. A summary of collections has previously been published (Weide et al. 1974: Appendix 2). The major archaeological collections are from the many years of work by Morlin Childers and from excavations by Jay von Werlhof and the late Michael Barker. Since 1974 this museum has held to a policy of non-collecting on surveys, therefore, the collections have remained substantially the same as they were in the Weide et al. (1974) report. Although this institution has had to undergo cutbacks in staff due to Proposition 13, they have made commendable strides in anthropological research and cultural resource management.

B. Prehistoric Cultural Chronology

The most striking aspect of cultural chronology in the prehistory of southeastern California is the proliferation of chronological schemata and the scarcity of hard data, derived from systematic investigations, which might possibly relate to them. In the following section, questions regarding sequence are reviewed, the data evaluated and a chronological synthesis offered with suggestions for future research problems.

Period I: Pre-Projectile Point Cultures

The question of the antecedants and origins of native cultures of the New World has long been a focus of interest for many archaeologists and other allied scholars, as well as interested laymen. The establishment and virtually unanimous acceptance of early cultures such as Clovis, dating to about 10,000 B.C., is a well documented chapter in the history of Americanist studies. In addition, the development of more reliable dating techniques and more sophisticated approaches to geochronology and palynology in the natural sciences and lithic technology by archaeologists has expanded the scope of Early Man studies enormously. Some of the results of these developments have been: the attempt to push the earliest dating of cultural remains back to at least 30,000 years; the beginnings of studies linking these early industries with Old World antecedants; and a proliferation of hypothesis formulations and outright speculations (cf. Jennings 1978a; Bryan 1978).

Aside from these developments, there is still a body of controversial and poorly or incompletely documented data, interpreted by some as signifying a Pre-Projectile Point Stage. This stage, as formulated by Alex Krieger (1964:42), is characterized as having a lithic technology similar to the Lower Paleolithic Stage of the Old World with core and flake tools, percussion flakes and other large and heavy cobble tools. Beveled and worn bone splinter tools and shallow basin hearths are also a characteristic of this stage. Thin chipped-stone biface forms are absent. Among the sites or proposed culture types specific to Southern California and southern Nevada are the Lake Manix Complex, the Coyote Gulch sites, and the Tule Springs sites, all in the Mohave Desert and near the northern tier of the BLM planning areas being considered in this study. The Lake Manix material has not been adequately dated and its assignment to this stage is debatable on those grounds (Simpson 1976; Glennan 1976; Meighan 1976). Tule Springs has a limited, generalized assemblage dated at 11,000-13,000 B.P. (Shutler 1967; 302).

A fourth cultural complex cited by Krieger is "Playa I". The citation given is "Rogers 1939, 1958" (Krieger 1964: 44), an apparent confusion on Krieger's part, but understandable considering the general confusion over Rogers' terminology and the loose usage which has plagued the archaeological literature of Southern California. Most of this confusion has been cleared up by C. N. Warren in his definitive article on the San Dieguito Complex (Warren 1967). In his 1939 article, Rogers used the term "Malpais" for the earlier "Parental horizon" of the "San Dieguito-Playa" complex (Rogers 1939: Plate 21). Later Rogers discontinued use of the terms "Malpais" and "Playa", combining these under the San Dieguito Complex (Rogers 1958: 3). Thus, Krieger's reference to Playa I, later redefined as San Dieguito II, does not conform to his definition of a Pre-Projectile Stage. It is possible that Krieger confused Playa with the earlier, more limited, definition of Malpais, although the latter was characterized as including "biface ovates" in the assemblage (Rogers 1939: 20). Aside from all this, the term "Malpais" has continued to be used, almost as vernacular, showing up now and then in the literature, undefined. Margaret Weide (Lyneis) has noted this usage of the term in the contemporary situation in the Colorado Desert in much the same sense as Rogers' original definition, and suggests that sites may well exist, in the Colorado Desert, which relate to a Pre-Projectile Point Period, dating prior to 10,000 B.C. (Weide et al. 1974: 76-78).

It is useful to review, briefly, Rogers' original definition of "Malpais", and some more recently discovered materials which have been advanced as possible "Pre-Projectile Point" assemblages, some of which have involved the use of the term "Malpais". As originally defined, the Malpais assemblage included: circular clearings in the desert gravels, sometimes with raw boulder walls, called "house sites" or "sleeping circles" (Rogers 1939: 6-7; 1966: 45-47); gravel pictographs, of both the rock alignment and intaglio type (Rogers 1939: 9-16). Artifacts included in the Malpais Industry were: flake tools made on either "teshoa" flakes (primary decortication flake, derived from rounded cobbles), or "beveled" flakes struck from a prepared core. Core tools included bifacial and unifacial choppers, scraper-planes and biface ovates (Rogers 1939: 17-18). This industry was found mainly on the lowest terrace along the Colorado River and along dry water courses in the Colorado and Mojave deserts from the Colorado River (Rogers 1939: 6). More recently a human skeleton was found under a cairn in the Yuha Desert, west of Imperial Valley, with associated dates derived from caliche (calcium carbonate) adhering to the bones (21,500 + 2,000 - 1,000 B.P.), and associated boulders at 22,125 $\pm$ 400 B.P. (Childers 1974: 2). Two artifacts and several flakes were recovered during the excavation, but association of these with the burial is not clear. The artifacts are described as "beaked scrapers or cores of the 'ridgeback' variety. . ." (Childers 1974: 5). The dates ascribed to this burial have been viewed skeptically by others concerned with the Southern California deserts, in view of the unreliability of dating using calcium carbonate, a ground water precipitate. One team of investigators re-examined the site and has questioned the geomorphic interpretations offered by Childers to the effect that the burial is inclusive within the Yuha Formation (Payen et al. 1978: 450-1). These investigators also note the presence of a thin surface scatter of felsite artifacts (percussion flaked) and waste flakes, the presence of other possible cairn-like features and sherds in the vicinity of the burial. A rim sherd was dated by thermoluminesence at 285 + 100 years B.P. The question is also raised by Payen et al. as to the relevance of the series of dates on other samples of caliche from the burial site (presumbly) to the Yuha Burial (Childers 1974: 9; Payen et al. 1978: 453).

Other criticism has been posed by Wilke on both chronometric and cultural grounds. Wilke notes that cairn burials have been reported in the California deserts at Truckhaven (on the west side of Salton Sea, Imperial County), Death Valley, Panamint and Tecopa, all dating within the past 5,000 years. It is further remarked, as with Payen et al. (1978), that the dating offered for the Yuha Burial is on the caliche, not the burial. Wilke suggests the Yuha Burial is a part of the cairn burial pattern described above (Wilke 1978b: 445-7).

Bischoff, Childers and Shlemon (1978: 747-749) defend the dating of the Yuha Burial, maintaining that the radiometric dates are mutually supportive, and dispute the Payen et al. (1978) interpretation of the stratigraphy of the site. However, the fact is that the dates are not clearly relevant to the burial and the case in favor of the early dating is further marred by inadequate reporting: it is not clear what the physical location of the cairn and burial was in relation to the stratigraphy described by Bischoff et al. (1978). A detailed map would have been helpful. At this point the chronometric data presented is not convincing. Concerning the "ridge back artifacts" found in ambiguous association with the Yuha Burial, Childers has presented information which can be evaluated. In his 1974 article, Childers describes a "uniface tradition" in which cores were trimmed by blows directed in such a way as to produce high angle edges with flake scars converging to a ridge or ridges opposite the striking platform (presumably). The artifacts from the Yuha Burial location are described as "so steep (sided) as to resemble Mexican fluted cores for the striking of blades..." and are not considered to be the oldest lithic material in the Yuha Desert (Childers 1974: 5). The illustration (Childers: 6, Fig. 4, left) on the other hand suggests the artifacts can be duplicated in assemblages in the Encinitas Tradition and Millingstone Horizon of coastal Southern California (e.g. Warren et al. 1961: 21, Figs. 9B and 9C, Plates 6 and 9; Crabtree, Warren & True 1963: 335-336 and 340, Plates 4A - 4D and 4H; C. King 1967: 41-6, Plates 3 and 5, Figs. 6-13). In a more recent article, Childers has provided more details of context and morphology of these tools and the results of replication experiments (Childers 1977). In addition to the core or ridge-back tools, there are concave flakes suggesting spoke shaves, and large blade flakes, triangular in cross section some with small side blows struck near the point, making a sharp curved tip, which he suggests are "graving" tools. Some of the ridge-backs have unifacially retouched edges, also the material "crosses all mineral lines" (Childers 242-3). Included in this "tradition" are tools made with a bi-polar anvil technique including split cobble cores and trimmed flakes derived from these cores. Although Childers discusses the dating of caliche formations in the Pinto-Yuha drainage system in southwestern Imperial County, it is not clear that these dates (30,000-24,000 B.P., depending on elevation) are relevant to dating the ridge-back tool sites. Childers goes on to say that the "relative stage of weathering" suggests Pre-San Dieguito I but later than Malpais dates (Childers: 244-5). The criterion of weathering has never been demonstrated to be valid for relative dating. Also the validity of a San Dieguito I configuration has yet to be verified, and Malpais is a term still without formal definition, as we have already noted. Sites with ridge-back tools are said sometimes to have cleared circles and rock alignments, often partially imbedded in the alluvium within the perimeter of the circular areas. Childers carried out replication experiments duplicating specimens lacking bulbs of percussion. The experiments were successful and Childers interpreted the results as validating these items as genuine artifacts, and not due to natural factors such as thermal fracturing or stream rafting (Childers 1977: 247).

A somewhat more formal and detailed attempt to revive the Malpais concept is a major thrust of Julian Hayden's (1976) discussion of material from the Sierra Pinacate in extreme northwestern Sonora, Mexico, near the head of the Gulf of California and close to the southeastern sector of the study area. Hayden defines Malpais as "an early and distinct basal stage of the San Dieguito Complex..." (1976: 280). The tool assemblage is described as a chopper-scraper industry with percussion flaked (hard hammer), unifacially edged artifacts showing a minimum of effort in manufacture. Preferred materials were suitably sized volcanic rocks, and the Malpais material was generally concentrated near volcanic craters where such material was plentiful. Specific tools include knives, spokeshaves, hollowsided scrapers, notched and beaked tools, and choppers of varying weights and sizes. Disc chopper core tools occur "throughout the period" but are not common. No projectile points have been found. Small knives, scrapers and gouges were made from heavy bivalve shells, especially Dosinia sp., avaiable at Adair Bay near the Pinacate. This assemblage is characterized by Hayden as "especially adapted to woodworking". Included in this complex are "sleeping circles", trail shrines and intaglio figures (1976: 280-2).

Hayden dates this Malpais material by reference to several environmental factors affecting the condition of artifacts and the situations in which they are located. These factors include: 1) Desert pavement, the tightly packed mosaic-like surface of pebbles common in North American deserts, and thought to have formed as the result of the deflation of soils (wind borne in this case) during periods of decreased rainfall (1976: 275-7); 2) Desert varnish, a glossy, dark mineral coating of varying extent and thickness found commonly on exposed surfaces of pebbles in the desert pavement and similar situations. The exact nature of its composition, origin and formation is not well understood, but Hayden suggests that it is a phenomenon associated with the Altithermal, the hypothetical period of hot dry climate in post-Pleistocene times about 7000 to 3000 B.P. The Altithermal is considered by some to have been widespread in the arid west, but it is a concept that is not accepted by all concerned. Hayden goes further, however, and suggests that there may have been an earlier, late-Pleistocene Altithermal (called Malpais Altithermal) preceding the final pluvial period and dating back to about 17,000 B.C. The basis for this is the extent of desert varnish or oxidation on stone tools. It is not entirely clear whether these tools are attributed to early cultures on the basis of these physical phenomena or on the basis of artifact typology. At any rate those artifacts with heavy desert varnish or oxidation are attributed to the Malpais, those with "lighter" desert varnish or oxidation are consigned to San Dieguito I, and those with no desert varnish and only slight or no oxidation are assigned to the post-Altithermal Amargosa cultures (1976: 277-80). In the case of the Amargosa, there appears to be strong typological grounds for this categorization, the data having been presented in an earlier article (Hayden 1967); 3) The third factor, caliche, also referred to as a carbonate (lime) deposit, is found in various degrees on the buried surfaces of stone artifacts (as well as unaltered stone) and has been linked to dry climatic regimes (cf. Daniels et al. 1971: 75). Hayden notes that the post-Altithermal Amargosan tools have very thin deposits of Caliche on their lower surfaces (1976: 280). It is interesting to note that studies of caliche formation in soils near Las Cruces, New Mexico, where conditions are generally similar to but not as extremely arid as the Pinacate, have indicated a four stage sequence in caliche formation. In stages I and II individual pebbles are coated, on the underside, in light to heavy amounts, in stage III the gravels are completely coated and interstices are filled or plugged, forming a more or less solid layer. Stage IV is characterized by the accumulation of layers, or laminae, of lime overlying the stage III layer. Stage II conditions have been found (in New Mexico) in soils dating (by radiocarbon) from older than 7350 years to the terminal Pleistocene about 10,000 years ago (Daniels et al. 1971: 74-5). It remains to be seen how closely analagous the Pinacate situation is to that in New Mexico, but it would appear that caliche formation on the Pinacate material, as described by Hayden, might be comparable to stage I and II caliche formation. It should also be noted that similar observations are in order for the Yuha Burial.

Hayden has arranged a chronolgy for the Pinacate material based on the several criteria listed above and by comparisons with M. J. Rogers' and other investigator's work in the California and Sonora deserts. Hayden begins with Malpais, correlating it with the Pleistocene "Malpais Pluvial", prior to 18,000 B.C. and terminating it (or having it evolve into San Dieguito I) shortly after 16,000 B.C., following the "Malpais Altithermal." San Dieguito I continues in the Pinacate until the onset of the Altithermal around 7000 B.C. The tool kit of San Dieguito I is very similar to Malpais in some respects but is more varied with a wider range of artifact types and manufacturing techniques, and with lighter varnish and patination (1976: 284-5; 286, Fig. 9).

Outside the Pinacate at Ventana Cave (75 miles northeast), San Dieguito I is identified in the Volcanic debris layer and dated at 9350 B.C.(Haury 1950). Hayden further delineates a rather far flung area in which occurs material he identifies with Malpais-San Dieguito cultures. These include (apparently) the material from west of Phoenix, Arizona described by Rogers (1958). Also included are the Panamint Valley data described by E.L. Davis (1970), and some very doubtful material from Death Valley (Clements and Clements 1953) which is disputed by Wallace (1962, 1977). To the south Hayden identifies Malpais material from Tiburon Island and from as far south as Estero Tastiota, north of Guaymas, Sonora (Hayden 1976: 285).

Hayden's discussion while certainly provocative, suffers from the same shortcomings as those found in the work of his mentor, M. J. Rogers. He presents his conclusions in some detail with only very general references to the data upon which it presumably rests. Further the use of desert pavement patination (either desert varnish or oxidation) and caliche as dating criteria are no more verified now than they were when Rogers attempted to use them. Independent verification of the paleoclimatic material might bolster his case, if he could demonstrate a correlation with the cultural remains. When reviewing sometimes ambiguous material such as this, one often wonders if some of this material might not be attributable to specialized activities such as quarry workshop production or seasonal differentiation, regional variations and so on. Lacking clearly definable contexts in undisturbed deposits they remain interesting but speculative and hypothetical interpretations.

Other material has been advanced as relating to a Pre-Projectile Point Horizon, most notably from San Diego County. These sites have yielded (mostly as surface finds) material similar to some of that described by Childers, including putative tools supposedly indicative of bi-polar techniques, and several varieties of crude core and flake tools, some, but not all of which, are unifacial (cf. Minshall 1975; Carter 1957, 1978). Claims of considerable antiquity have been advanced, based in part on geomorphic grounds and partially on typological considerations (Minshall 1975: 46; Carter 1978: 11-14). Unfortunately, the data, as presented, are not compelling and fail on a number of grounds:

1. Radiocarbon dates on caliche have not been demonstrated to be relevant to either cultural or human remains.
2. Some, if not most, of the artifacts for which great antiquity is claimed can be duplicated in assemblages which have been dated post 6000 B.C.
3. Data from Old World assemblages have been cited which are so widely spread in time and space as to severely try one's credulity.
4. The data have been frequently presented inadequately - poorly reproduced photographs, drawings and maps often lacking important details, use of undefined or obsolete terminolgy, misleading use of terminology from the Old World, etc.

Some time has been spent on this question because it is important that those involved in cultural resource management be aware of these issues and be able to evaluate objectively what is valid and what is not. Richard G. Forbis (1974: 15) has set forth the argument against evidence advanced in support of supposedly early cultures of a "Pre-Projectile Point" stage:

1. Many of the sites are surface locations where reliable dating is not possible.
2. Some dated sites have material which may not be the product of human manufacture.
3. Some sites are quarries or workshops where the crudeness of the debris is a result of a manufacturing process, not great antiquity.
4. Some sites seem to be early on the basis of paleontological or geologic evidence, but have not been adequately dated.
5. Some sites are firmly dated to an early period, but have such a small yield of artifacts that Pre-Projectile Point or other affiliations cannot be demonstrated.

None of the material discussed can overcome these objections. Further inquiries along these lines, however, must be continued.

Period II: San Dieguito (ca. 10,000 to 5,000 B.C.)

The San Dieguito Complex is best known from the C. W. Harris site near the coast in San Diego County California (Warren and True 1961), but has been widely reported in the deserts (Warren 1967) where it was originally called Malpais and Playa by M. J. Rogers (1939). He later clarified his interpretations by dropping these terms in favor of the San Dieguito designation (Rogers 1939, 1966). The term "Lake Mojave" is also used by a number of researchers in the Mojave Desert and the Great Basin, and is equally acceptable. The San Dieguito artifact assemblage includes large leaf-shaped knives; points may be leaf-shaped, long wide-stemmed or short wide-stemmed (Lake Mojave or Silver Lake points): lanceolate - similar to early Plains types; also included are crescents (sometimes also referred as amulets, eccentrics or Great Basin transverse points); several types of ovoid and/or domed scrapers, end and side scrapers, engraving tools and drills. The stone technology is somewhat crude. Flaking procedures produced irregular edges, deep bulbs of percussion and step fractures, irregular surfaces, and flat, crushed edges, suggesting support on an anvil (Warren and Ranere 1968: 73-74).

San Dieguito materials are generally found on old beaches and terraces adjacent to remnant dry playas of old lake basins and also on terraces of major water courses, particularly the Colorado River. These settings generally suggest a moister, cooler climatic regime which prevailed during the terminal Pleistocene and early Holocene period some 8000 to 12,000 years ago. Dating of sites attributed to the San Dieguito Complex is not direct, except for the type site (C. W. Harris site) and several others in the San Diego area.

Examination of Malcolm Rogers' site records from the San Diego Museum of Man indicates the widespread occurrence of San Dieguito sites in the study area (also see Rogers 1966: 149-155). Examination of site records at the several clearing houses indicates that nearly 5000 sites in total are now recorded for the study area, with varying degrees of accuracy and clarity. A detailed study of these records should show that many sites with San Dieguito components exist in the study area. The problem is finding sites with undisturbed, buried deposits, not mixed with other later (or earlier) materials. This situation is rare, but is the essential condition for establishing data on dating, seasonality and general cultural relations of the San Dieguito Complex.

Period III: Pinto (ca. 5,000 - 1,500 B.C.)

The Pinto assemblage is best documented in the Mojave Desert, where the widespread occurrence of surface materials has been supplemented and clarified by excavated sites. The complex includes the several varieties of stemmed and notched Pinto points, leaf-shaped points and knives; scrapers and large scraper forms. Also present are drills and graving tools. Milling tools, when present, include manos, metates, and occasionally mortars and pestles.

In the study area, the Pinto Complex is documented in the area north of the Little San Bernardino, Orocopia and Eagle Mountain chain, at Pinto Basin and near Needles, California (Campbell and Campbell 1935; Rogers 1939, 1966; Wallace 1962). Sites with Pinto components have been excavated at Little Lake (Harrington 1957) and at Rose Springs (Lanning 1963) in the southern part of Owens Valley. Pinto materials are widely reported in the Great Basin (cf. Worman 1969; Jennings 1978b); similar materials have been reported in Arizona at Ventana Cave (Haury 1950) and in Baja California (Massey 1966). Pinto is a widespread phenomenon with rather variable associations. However, there are no clear instances of the Pinto Complex from the part of eastern Imperial County within the study area. M. Weide et al. (1974) have discussed a few tantalizing clues from the west side of Imperial Valley, including the as yet poorly reported cairn burial from near Truckhaven. The possible relationship of Pinto Period materials to the presumed periodic innundation of the Salton Trough awaits considerably more data.

Bettinger and Taylor (1974) have suggested two separate styles and distributions for the Pinto points. Points from Pinto Basin are noted by them as being thick and percussion flaked, and the other style, for which they propose the term "Little Lake", is long, thin, extensively pressure flaked, with a deep basal notch. Pinto Basin points are confined to the Colorado Desert and parts of the eastern Mojave Desert. Little Lake varieties are found in the Mojave Desert, Death Valley and north to Owens Valley (Bettinger and Taylor 1974: 13).

Although the Pinto Period is largely defined on the basis of a rather variable point type, it should be made clear that other Great Basin series including Humboldt, Elko and Gypsum appear to overlap in time with various Pinto points, and that there is some taxonomic confusion among these point types.

Period IV: Amargosa (ca. 1,500 B.C. to A.D. 900)

The discussion of this period is based on reasonably well documented material from areas adjacent to the study area. During this period there seems to have been a number of stylistic and adaptational shifts resulting from the cumulative effects of certain gradual ecological changes during the previous period. These shifts are best illustrated from the Rose Spring site in southern Owens Valley (Lanning 1963), where the Rose Spring Period, with three sub-phases, has radiocarbon dates of 950 + 80 B.C. (UCLA 1093B) and 290 + 145 B.C. (UCLA 1093A; Clewlow et al. 1970). Early Rose Springs diagnostics include points of the Humboldt, Elko and Gypsum series, a continuation from the previous period. Middle and Late Rose Springs feature a shift to the Rose Springs and Eastgate series, which appear actually to be a diminution in size of projectile point tips thought to represent the transition from atlatl or hand thrown darts to the bow and arrow. This period is the equivalent of Bettinger and Taylor's (1974) Newberry Period, the Gypsum part of Rogers' (1939) Pinto-Gypsum Complex, and the Price Butte, Nelson and El Dorado phases of Willow Beach (Schroeder 1961), with dates of 250 B.C.+ 250, A.D. 250 + 250 and A.D. 450 + 250 (Schroeder 1961: 82-86). Schroeder equates these phases with Basketmaker II and the Amargosa Culture of the California Desert. At Rose Springs (Lanning 1963), Newberry Cave (Smith et al. 1957) and Gypsum Cave (Harrington 1931), materials associated with the projectile point types cited above, include the mano and metate, several varieties of knives, scrapers and drills, stone and shell beads, incised and painted pebbles and slate plaques. The presence of split-twig figurines and certain zoomorphic petroglyphs at sites dating from this period have been interpreted as suggestive of ritual magic associated with hunting (cf. Smith et al. 1957). In summary, this period appears to represent an adaptational shift in tool types. This shift may reflect a more generalized exploitation of floral resources necessitated, perhaps, by a drop in the populations of larger game animals, such as the desert big-horn sheep.

Within the study area there are no clearly identified finds which could relate to this material although radiocarbon dates exist on as yet unreported archaeological sites from west of Imperial Valley (Weide et al. 1974; Wilke 1978b). This may have been a period of only very slight use of parts of the study area. More likely, however, is that this reflects a very skewed sample - there are still large areas not yet subject to intensive evaluative survey and excavation/collection.

Period V: Late Prehistoric (A.D. 900 - 1900)

The final prehistoric period in the study area is much better documented than the previous periods, but the nature and completeness of the data is quite variable.

It is also quite likely that as more detailed reports are forthcoming at least two sub-phases may be delineated. Several schemes have been advanced which relate to this final period. Various labels have been applied such as "Yuman", Patayan", "Lowland and Upland Patayan", "Hakataya", "Amacava", etc.. All of these designations suffer a serious defect since they are identified with specific ethnic and/or linguistic groups, hence both oversimplifying the situation and neglecting other peoples who may have been present. Several of these terms also refer mainly to data developed in western and central Arizona, rather than the California deserts. I have used the self-explanatory term "Late", but it is useful to review the terminology as it has appeared in the literature relating to the area.

In 1934 Winifred and Harold Gladwin proposed a taxonomic system for major southwestern cultural traditions and their sub-divisions. Major divisions, such as Anasazi, Hohokam and Mogollon are termed "roots"; subdivisions of roots are termed stems; and subdivisions of these are called branches. They included a "Yuman Root", on the same classifactory level as Anasazi, to designate the prehistoric cultures of western Arizona occupied historically by Yuman speaking peoples (W. and H. Gladwin 1934). In 1939 Harold S. Colton proposed using the term "Patayan" in place of "Yuman" to avoid the inference that these prehistoric cultures necessarily spoke Yuman languages or were ancestral to the historic Yumans. This proposal was in line with the policy of using names for prehistoric cultures which have no direct bearing on living peoples (Colton 1939:23). In 1945 Colton further defined the "Patayan Root" concept to include the Laquish Branch at the Colorado River delta, the Cerbat Branch near Needles, California, the previously designated Coconino Branch in northwestern Arizona and the Prescott Branch in northcentral Arizona, west of Verde Valley. These were rather loosely defined, mainly on the basis of pottery similarities and very few other characteristics (Colton 1945).

Following his lower Colorado River survey, Albert Schroeder demonstrated that the pottery from the Needles area (La Paz series) belonged with Lower Colorado Buff Ware rather than Cerbat Ware (Tizon Brown Ware) as Colton had earlier proposed (Schroeder 1952: 32).

In a very general article M. J. Rogers (1945) proposed a three stage sequence for "Yuman" prehistory covering the period from about A.D. 800-900 to the historic period. This sequence is reviewed below:

Yuman I (A.D. 800-900 to 1050), the first shift from the "archaic" pattern (cf. Amargosa III, Rogers 1939), began about A.D. 800 or 900 with an easterly drift of Yumans across the California deserts to occupy the Colorado River Valley from Black Canyon south to the delta. The earliest development of ceramics and agriculture took place at this time and was confined to the area below Blythe, California. Both Anasazi and Hohokam ceramics are intrusive in this and the immediately preceeding periods. Local ceramics included such traits a Red and Red-on-Buff pottery types, shouldered jars, use of red slip or wash, polishing, rim notching, incised decorations, and use of paddle and anvil technique of manufacture (Rogers 1945: 187-9).

Yuman II (A.D. 1050 to 1450) was considered by Rogers to be the time during which Lake Cahuilla (Blake Sea) occupied the Salton Sink. Yuman culture spread east to near the Great Bend of the Gila River and into northwestern Arizona. On the west the occupation extended to near

Barstow and included the extreme southern portion of Nevada. The cultural content is characterized by the disappearance of shouldered jars, rim notching and incised decoration. New elements are stucco finish on pottery, recurved jar rims and tab handles on scoops. Also new in this period are cremations, and domed, circular houses with brush walls appear for the first time (previous types being unknown). Pacific coast shell ornaments appear in this period along with Gulf Coast shell ornaments which were present in previous periods. Yuman II terminates with the dessication and disappearance of Lake Cahuilla (Rogers 1945: 190-2).

Yuman III (A.D. 1450 to 19th century) follows in the wake of the disappearance of Lake Cahuilla with considerable population displacement. Most of the Colorado Desert west of the Colorado River was abandoned. Western Arizona was occupied as far east as the Verde River Valley and in the first several decades of the 19th century the Maricopa, Halchidoma and some Kohuanas moved from west of Gila Bend to reside among the Pima west of Phoenix, Arizona.

In Baja California the Yumans spread as far south as the 30th parallel north and displaced the closely related Seri to the mainland opposite Disemboque Island. The movements in Arizona are partly a matter of historic record, going back to the last decade of the 17th century (cf. Bolton 1916, 1948). Material culture continues much as before with the addition of winter houses of the jacal (wattle and daub) type as well as ramadas. Settlements were semipermanent scatters of houses through the brush adjacent to the flood plains (Rogers 1945: 152-4).

Schroeder re-examined parts of Rogers' scheme in light of his own excavations at Willow Beach (Schroeder 1961) and his survey of the lower Colorado River (Schroeder 1952). This resulted in revisions of some of Rogers' interpretations. After reviewing Rogers' collections and site data at the San Diego Museum of Man, Schroeder found that Rogers' Yuman I (pre-A.D. 1050) ceramic traits (Red and Red-on-Beige shouldered jars, the use of slip and polished surfaces), were most numerous on trails east of the Colorado River passing through the Kofa and Castle Dome mountains in western Arizona. On the River these traits were more common north of Blythe and relatively uncommon below Blythe. This is in agreement with Schroeder's lower Colorado survey data (Schroeder 1952: 49). On that basis, Schroeder rejected Rogers' Yuman I as it had been defined. Schroeder suggests a date of about A.D. 900 for the beginning of indigenous pottery from Black Canyon on the north to the Colorado delta on the south. This is based on the presence of dated Anasazi pottery at Willow Beach, associated with Pyramid Gray pottery and early plainware of the Parker Series, Lower Colorado Buff Ware (Schroeder 1952:55-6), as well as various surface associations both down river and in western Arizona with other dated pottery types, particularly Hohokam types dating prior to A.D. 1150. Subsequent to this work Schroeder proposed using the term "Hakataya Root" to replace "Yuman" as used by Rogers and Gladwin (Schroeder 1957). Later, he expanded on this theme and applied it to the lower Colorado River, western and central Arizona, the California desert, and northern Baja California, in ceramic times only. Schroeder called the Lower Colorado River aspect of this pattern the "Laquish" stem adopting the term originally used by Colton. On the other hand, Colton's term "Patayan" was confined by Schroeder to the Cerbat, Coconino and Prescott of upland Arizona. The Laquish stem was further divided into the "Amacava Branch" centering around Needles, California, the "La Paz Branch" centering around Blythe and the "Palo Verde Branch" occupying the area from the mouth of the Gila River to the delta.

The primary discussion of the Hakataya concerns various manifestations in Arizona and is somewhat removed from the study area. However, it is useful to indicate, briefly, the characteristics Schroeder assigned to the Hakataya: houses were either square, four-posted jacals or round, stone-outlined brush shelters; cremation was practiced; trail shrines and gravel alignments were present; houses were scattered on flats and surrounded by sheet rubbish; and irrigation in farming utilized the innundation method. The gray-brown ceramics were made by paddle and anvil method, firing was uncontrolled and the surface was usually plain and unslipped. Sometimes a poorly executed red design was painted on the vessel, but red ware was rare (Schroeder 1975: 52-56).

M. J. Harner (1958), while accepting the term "Hakataya" in the general sense in which Schroeder intended the term to be used, did not accept the other terminology proposed by Schroeder. Instead he suggested the term "Upland Patayan" to encompass the area where Tizon Brown Ware dominates in upland southern California, northwestern Arizona and Baja California, while the sphere of the Lower Colorado Buff Ware, which included the lower Colorado River from the Mojave Valley to the delta, the lower Gila River Valley and the Colorado Desert was named "Lowland Patayan". Harner rejected the term "Yuman" on the grounds that in historic times both wares were manufactured by both Shoshonean and Yuman speaking groups (Harner 1958: 93). Harner also outlined a sequence for the ceramic period, based on his excavations at the Bouse Site, a short distance southeast of Parker, Arizona. The main features of this sequence are as follows:

Bouse Phase I: A.D. 800 to 1000 (Harner 1958: 94-5). Settlements were located in river bottom lands and near water sources in the desert. Subsistence was "presumably" horticulture with considerable gathering and fishing; hunting was of minor importance. Houses were made of perishable material, probably brush, with little or no stone. Ceramics include polished red-slipped pottery; unpolished, thin white-slipped; red slip over white slip; unslipped buff. Vessel shapes include deep globular bowls and jars with slight or absent necks. Stonework includes an array of scrapers and choppers; slab to oval basin metates with one and two handed manos; polished greenstone ornaments (rare); 3/4 grooved axes (possibly from the Hohokam); projectile points are rare. Bone, shell and wood artifacts are present and include whole Olivella sp. shell beads.

Bouse I is stratigraphically below a component containing Santa Cruz Red-on-Buff (which dates to A.D. 800-1000) and in association with Hohokam Buff Ware. Polished red slip and thin white slip are suggested as possibly a result of contact with Papagueria (southwest Arizona) Hohokam or Mogollon. An association with one sherd of Gila Butte Red-on-Buff (ca. A. D. 600-800) is also noted.

Bouse Phase II: A.D. 1000 to 1300 (Harner 1958: 95-6). Settlements are similar to Bouse I but with a higher frequency in the Colorado Desert, Lake Le Conte (Cahuilla) possibly being in existence at this time. Ceramics represent a continuation of previous styles with the addition of designs in red, painted on an unslipped buff or thin white slipped surface. Some designs resemble those of Gila Butte Red-on-Buff or Hohokam. New vessel shapes include jars with vertical or recurved necks, shallow and deep bowls with slightly flaring lips, and trays.

Painted designs and vessel shapes suggest "acculturative influences" from the Hohokam where they are chronologically earlier. At Bouse this component is stratigraphically above the unit containing Santa Cruz Red-on-Buff (dated at A.D. 800-1000) and in direct association with Verde Black-on-Gray (dated at A.D. 1000-1300) and Gila Red (dated at A.D. 1200-1400). This provides the basis for a date of A.D. 1000-1300 for this phase.

Moon Mountain Phase: A.D. 1300-1700 (Harner 1958-96). This is a tentative phase based largely on surface surveys. Bouse II traits continue except as noted below. Settlements are the same as earlier phases with large scale occupation of the shores of Lake Cahuilla. Ceramic attributes include the absence of neckless globular jars, the addition of stucco surface treatment and molded base jars, slipping declines, red painted designs increase, and scoops are introduced. Vessel shapes gradually differentiate into those of historic times. Coiled basketry occurs.

This phase is seen to be transitional to historic cultures of the lower Colorado River tribes and those of the Imperial Valley.

Confirmation or revisions of the sequence proposed by Harner or the views of Rogers and Schroeder remain a task yet to be accomplished for Colorado Desert prehistory. The question of terminology, as well as chronology, is no closer to resolution than it was when Rogers, Schroeder and Harner were still active in this field.

During the Late Period there appears to have been a continuation of trends begun in earlier periods. The shift to small projectile points, at the expense of earlier types, accompanied the introduction of the bow and arrow and continued with the introduction and wide-spread adoption of a number of variants of the Cottonwood Triangular and Desert Side-Notched points. The distribution of sites from this period also suggests a more balanced exploitative pattern of desert resources with well-defined seasonality. The general configuration from the earlier periods suggests a much stronger emphasis on hunting, with small numbers of people involved. But the cumulative effect of the post-Pleistocene climatic shifts, plus added human factors, may have led to the diminution of hunting as an important subsistence activity and the diversification into seasonal rounds with emphasis on a few plants, such as Mesquite, agave, acorns, etc. Intertwined with these developments in the Late Period was the introduction of ceramics along the Colorado River and adjacent desert areas to the west. Perhaps as early as A.D. 600, this included trade ware from Gila River and Desert Hohokam in the south (Rogers 1945: 185; Harner 1958: 94-5), and various central and northern Arizona wares in the north (Rogers 1945: 175; Schroeder 1961: 41). Sometime prior to A.D. 1000 the local people had begun to manufacture their own pottery (Aikens 1978: 764; Schroeder 1961: 87) of two general, but related varieties, Tizon Brown Ware (Euler and Dobyns 1958) and Lower Colorado Buff Ware (Schroeder 1958), which continued in use until about 1900.

A problem in evaluating the prehistory of at least part of the study area is the dating of recurring high water stands (Lake Cahuilla) in the Salton Basin. Research by Wilke (1978a) at a number of sites at the northern end of Lake Cahuilla, in Coachella Valley, has produced valuable data concerning dietary practices during the last high stand of the lake. Analysis of coprolites found at these sites yielded information on both terrestrial and lacustrine food resources (Wilke 1978a: 103-108). Of equal importance is Wilke's analysis and discussion of radiocarbon dates relating to the last two millenia in the Salton Basin, in which he determined that there were at least three (and probably more) episodes in which shifts in the Colorado River flooded the Salton Basin, with a resulting lacustrine regime becoming established long enough to affect local biota and attract human occupation, at least during the period from A.D. 1000 to 1500 (Wilke 1978a: 57-59). Analysis of the cultural materials is still in process, but Wilke indicates the presence of late types of projectile points, both Pacific Coast and Gulf of California shell ornaments, dating post A.D. 700 and two varieties of Lower Colorado Buff Ware pottery dating from sometime before A.D. 900 to about A.D. 1450 (Wilke 1978a: 57-59). Radiocarbon assays of a number of charcoal and floral samples from several sites along the old shoreline in Coachella Valley yielded apparently modern dates. Wilke reviews these dates and the problems of reconciling them with certain historical records (post 1539) which contain no evidence of a large freshwater lake, such as Lake Cahuilla. Wilke concludes that the samples reflect known fluctuations in atmospheric radiocarbon and for this reason are not, therefore, acceptable in light of the historical records. He concludes that the Lake did not exist (except for brief ephemeral episodes) after A.D. 1539 (Wilke 1978a: 46-57).

Other data from the East Mesa area (southeastern sector of Lake Cahuilla) indicate extensive site areas along high beach lines, bayous and sloughs similar to Wilke's sites, with a similar array of lake-related materials (cf. Brooks et al. 1977; Ellis and Crabtree 1974). Preliminary analysis of ceramic types present suggest a possibly more complex ethnic situation, with use of the southern part of the old lake by peoples from several parts of the Lower Colorado River (Crabtree and Ellis, 1978).

The dessication of Lake Cahuilla would have had a profound effect on the population which had been exploiting the many and varied resources available there. Wilke (1978a) has reviewed data from the Lake Cahuilla hinterland and the west Salton Trough, noting a preponderance of specialized late prehistoric sites relating to the ceramic period and reflecting the restructuring of the settlement pattern (Wilke 1978a: 113-119). Details of the post Lake Cahuilla period are only beginning to be worked out, but available data suggest that such developments as decorated ceramics (mostly red-on-buff or brown types) and some minor elaborations of vessel shapes are largely post-lake developments. Such developments as the adoption of agriculture (cf. Lawton and Bean 1968; Bean and Lawton 1973) in proto-historic times may have been hastened by the post-lacustrine re-adaptations, but solid archaeological evidence is lacking at this time. The relationship of warfare and alliance to population shifts along the Lower Colorado and Gila rivers (White 1974) is a matter for speculation only at this time. Again, archaeological data are lacking.

Most of the data reviewed here which relates to the Late Period can be attributed to the southern part of the study area only, which reflects the almost total lack of organized data north of Coachella Valley in the Palen, Bristol/Cadiz and Twentynine Palms planning areas. Perhaps the research contemplated by the Archaeological Research Unit at Riverside, for the eastern part of San Bernardino County (Wilke, personal communcation 1978) will begin to fill some of the enormous gaps in our knowledge of prehistoric developments in the northern sections of the study area.

Summary

The available archaeological evidence has been reviewed and a five phase development from earliest times to the historic period can be defined. These are, briefly:

Period I: Pre-Projectile Point (pre-10,000 B.C.)

Various data purporting to be relevant to hypothesized cultures of the late-Pleistocene period have yet to meet the test of reliability based on sound dating. This does not mean that evidence will never be found demonstrating this proposed period, but as yet such data as there is, is speculative, subjective or unclear.

Period II: San Dieguito (10,000 - 5,000 B.C.)

A widespread generalized hunting culture with a distinctive stone technology was present in the planning area, but intact sites from this period have yet to be excavated in the study area.

Period III: Pinto Basin (5,000 - 1500 B.C.)

A hunting culture with a distinctive projectile point assemblage, related to widespread cultures of similar age and content in other areas, is known for parts of the study area. However, little detailed information is available. Pinto represents an early transitional culture in which there were the beginnings of a shift from generalized hunting to generalized foraging.

Period IV: Amargosa (1500 B.C. - A.D. 900)

A period very poorly known in the study area, but known for the northern and eastern Mojave Desert. In this period the trend toward generalized foraging (combined hunting and gathering) continues and the bow and arrow replaces the atlatl and dart as the primary larger game hunting weapon. Details of adaptation, settlement, etc. are poorly understood.

Period V: Late Prehistoric (A.D. 900 - 1900)

The Late Period was one in which ceramics were introduced and local types (not yet well defined) arose. The Salton Trough had perhaps two episodes of innundation with subsequent stable lacustrine regimes lasting perhaps 500 years, overall. Adaptation to the lake environment is evident in this period, but the eventual dessication of the lake led to widespread shifts of populations to the hinterland and the development of the historic desert adaptations known for such groups as the Cahuilla in Coachella Valley.

C. Special Studies and the Current Status of Research

Archaeology has become increasingly specialized in the last twenty years or so. New techniques for studying various materials and collateral data have greatly enlarged the scope of archaeological studies, often with very useful results when properly carried out. Some of these are now being applied to data from the Colorado Desert, although some specialized studies have been pursued for many years. In the following section we shall review several of these studies and assess the results and suggest some ways in which more fruitful information may be obtained.

1. Cultural Ecology

The relationships of human populations to their environment, including natural and social factors, have long been a focus of study in the social sciences. However, in archaeology, systematic studies of ecological relationships are comparatively recent. There are some references to these factors in the published writing of Malcolm Rogers, but he was more concerned with chronology as such, and since his studies were primarily based on studies of surface phenomenon, the kinds of data necessary for detailed ecological investigations were not generated. As they are currently conducted these studies have focused on gleaning from the archaeological and geological record, information concerning such factors as seasonality, climate, and the exploitation of flora, fauna and other natural resources by extinct human societies in a great variety of places and times. In the Colorado Desert such studies are in their infancy, but have received an encouraging start with the work of Wilke and others at the University of California, Riverside, in their Perris Reservoir (O'Connell et al. 1974) and Coachella Valley studies (Wilke 1978a). These studies have focused on analyses of faunal and floral remains from excavations in order to answer questions concerning diet, seasonality and climate (or local conditions such as the presence or absence of a body of water in the Salton Sink area). An attempt has also been made to gather information from near Blythe concerning plant and climatic succession by palynological analyses of soils, during and since the terminal Pleistocene (the last 40,000 years). However, results have been very limited or are not yet available (cf. Cross and Bordner 1977). Palynological and rat midden studies in the California deserts have begun to bear fruit (T. J. King Jr. 1975; Mehringer 1967, Wells 1976) as have flotation techniques on hearths in the Las Vegas area (Ferraro and Crabtree 1976). Faunal studies on California coastal shell middens have long been a useful adjunct to more traditional approaches and have become a standard procedure. Sites around old lakes can often yield similar information, as Wilke has demonstrated on the Lake Cahuilla material.

A thorough ecological approach would also include attention to such matters as hydrology and geomorphology, as well as social and cultural matters such as settlement systems and patterns of demography. Studies of these types may lead to a much clearer understanding of processes of adaptation by human groups to the environment and more specific historical events such as migrations, stylistic shifts and so forth. Although a great majority of sites known in the study area consist of scatters of lithic and/or ceramic materials resting either on ancient land surfaces or on unstable shifting dune sand, there are still a respectable number of sites which have stable, intact, buried deposits. Some are open sites and some are shelters and caves. Considering the vast areas virtually unexplored in both the mountains and low desert, a certain amount of optimism is not out of order as we consider the application of ecological studies to the problems of prehistory of the Colorado Desert.

2. Lithic Studies

The experimental lithic studies of Don Crabtree, Francois Bordes and others in the past twenty years have had a strong impact on studies of archaeological materials. As yet none of this has been felt in the Colorado Desert, although some systematic studies have been done in other parts of California (cf. Singer and Gibson 1970, Nance 1970). A recent re-study of the material from the Sayles site in Cajon Pass (Kowta 1969) by J. Brantley Jackson has cast considerable doubt on the presumably ubiquitous scraper plane as a true artifact category (Jackson 1977). Jackson tested four hypotheses offered to explain the existence and function of this class of artifact: 1) they are a functional and morphological reality; 2) they are a series of functionally variable tools which share some morphological features; 3) "scraper planes" are cores; and 4) "scraper planes" are cores that were also used as tools. These hypotheses were tested by: 1) examination of the ethnographic literature for descriptions of tools used in procuring and processing agave and yucca for fibers; 2) technological analysis of the items for processes of manufacture and microscopic examination for traces of use wear; and 3) experiments in fiber extraction and planing wood using "scraper planes". The result of this study did not support the theory that these objects were used for any task, rather the evidence strongly supports the contention that they were cores (Jackson 1977:40).

Such studies as Jackson's suggest a general re-examination and re-orientation of lithic studies and materials not only in the study area, but the far Southwest generally.

3. Settlement Patterns and Systems

Although no settlement studies, as such, have reached print as yet, the work of the BLM California Desert Planning Staff and various BLM contracted studies have resulted in the compilation of considerable archival and field data, with some fairly detailed and sophisticated analyses from the California deserts. These studies were oriented toward resource management problems, but were structured in such a way that ecological variables and their relationship to acchaeological remains were stressed. The resulting data have been placed in a format in which settlement data are readily available. Several of these (Weide 1973, Weide and Barker 1974, Hall and Barker 1975, King and Casebier 1976) and some others not yet available, are either methodological (cf. Weide 1973) or primarily based on archival research. The studies provide background summaries of history and prehistory for the entire Desert region under BLM jurisdiction. Two other studies, Coombs 1979a and Coombs 1979b, are concerned with a 1% field sampling of portions of the western and central ("northeastern" in California) Mojave Desert. The analyses focus on 1) methodological problems of the sampling design (validity and reliability) and 2) matters relating to the data, such as the spatial relationships between site types and densities, and certain environmental factors such as geomorphology, water resources and flora. Similar material has been developed for the study area particularly by Gallegos et al. (1979a) for the Bristol/Cadiz, Turtle Mountain and Palen planning areas; and Gallegos et al. (1979b) for East and West Mesas, in Imperial Valley. True and Townsend (1976) conducted reconnaissance in the Santa Rose Mountains, providing valuable settlement data. A BLM in-house study in the Whipple Mountains, Big Maria and Picacho planning units similar to those of Coombs and Gallegos et al. set the pattern followed (with modifications) by a number of subsequent studies (Ritter 1978, Reed 1979). These studies are invaluable additions to the data base for the California deserts generally, as well as the study area specifically.

4. Rock Art, Gravel Pictographs and Alignments and Intaglios

Designs, pecked or painted on rock outcrops are widespread throughout the world and the study area is no exception. Much of the literature that does exist (cf. Steward 1929; von Werlhof 1965; Heizer and Baumhoff 1962; Hedges 1970; Grant et al. 1968; Grant 1971; Heizer and Clewlow 1973), although very general or somewhat peripheral to the study area, provides valuable background data over a fairly broad part of the farther Southwest. Jay von Werlhof, of Imperial Valley College Museum, has devoted many years to the subject. His work in the study area has also focused on other, perhaps related, forms such as intaglios, gravel pictographs and rock alignments. A publication concerning this material is in the planning stage (von Werlhof, personal communication 1978). Intaglios and rock alignments received considerable attention from M. J. Rogers, and some of his findings are available in print (Rogers 1939, 1966). Others whose observations have been committed to print are Harner (1953), and Davis et al. (Davis and Winslow 1965, Davis True and Sterud 1965). The Archaeological Survey Association of Southern California in Redlands has maintained archival records and continues active in the field (ASA Newsletter, various issues).

Two recently published studies of rock art are of interest to the study area. Carol Rector's study on the BLM "East Mojave Planning Unit" (Rector 1976) in the central Mojave Desert centers around the New York and Providence mountains, just north of the study area. Rector notes some variance from styles and elements present in the other parts of California and the Great Basin, where other investigators have suggested a relationship of certain styles to hunting rituals. Rector stresses certain ecological factors, noting the scarcity of larger game, and suggests that in this area these functioned as territorial markers, trail and spring markers, and perhaps also had some bearing on mythology and shamanistic and initiation ritual (Rector 1976: 243-6).

Ruth Musser (1979) reports on a series of petroglyphs located on four adjacent limestone boulders two miles south of the well-known Blythe intaglios. Musser's analysis is along similar lines to that of Rector cited above, in that the emphasis is on elements of design and areal proximity and placement. Musser notes the lack of elements associated with hunting ritual and suggests that they functioned as trail and/or territorial markers, or as memorials to mythological events. The problem of ethnic affiliation is addressed but could not be resolved (Musser 1979: 42-5).

5. Trade and Trails

The rather remarkable preservation of trails used in prehistoric times in parts of the southwestern deserts, including the study area, have occasioned a number of studies in the past, particularly Johnston and Johnston (1957) and Harner (1951). Rogers used data on artifacts, pottery and shrines, all in association with trails to bolster his discussions of chronology and ethnic movements (Rogers 1939, 1945, 1966). Sample (1950) and J. T. Davis (1961) have gathered considerable data on trails generally in California in conjunction with their studies of trade networks in the greater Southwest.

An impressive amount of data exists in the site records on file at the three repositories (San Diego Museum of Man, Imperial Valley College Museum and UC Riverside) and in numerous unpublished field studies conducted in conjunction with environmental impact reports (cf. von Werlhof n.d.). The von Werlhofs at Imperial Valley College Museum have gathered considerable data on trails in Imperial and

Riverside counties and expect to eventually publish a study of them (J. von Werlhof, personal communication 1979).

6. Fish Traps

On the northwest section of the Salton Trough are a number of areas with numerous so-called "fish traps", "v-shaped" alignments (but with the convergent end left open), constructed of small boulders up to 30 cm. in diameter. There are literally hundreds, if not thousands of these features distributed along old strand lines of the extinct lakes which once occupied the Salton Trough. A. E. Treganza suggested that they were remnants of foundations of devices used to entrap fish from the receding waters of Lake Cahuilla (Traganza 1945). The fish trap hypothesis of Treganza is favorably regarded by current workers in the area. Both von Werlhof and Wilke are working separately on the problem and some results of these studies can be expected in the future. Wilke has discussed the problem to some extent in his recent monograph (Wilke 1978a).

7. Horticulture

The question of agriculture being practiced in the Imperial-Coachella Valley area in late prehistoric or early historic (post Lake Cahuilla) times has been the subject of several brief studies. Treganza (1947) summarized data available after his informal surveys in northern Baja California and the western margins of Imperial Valley (1942). L. J. Bean and H. W. Lawton have examined historic archives and described agricultural practices of the Cahuilla and other local groups in the historic period. They concluded that there is compelling evidence to suggest that in very early historic times people who were engaged in exploitation of resources available about Lake Cahuilla had begun to shift to horticulture: a horticulture patterned after that of the Colorado River Mohave and Quechan (Yuma) peoples. This was essentially an aboriginal practice, in contrast to those practices noted for more westerly peoples such as the Luiseno and others, which were essentially derived from the Spanish (Bean and Lawton 1973; Lawton and Bean 1968). As yet there is no strong archaeological evidence suggesting the practice of agriculture in this area, but some collateral evidence is beginning to be developed (cf. Wilke, Whitaker and Hattori (1977).

8. Ceramic Studies

The single topic of native pottery has received considerable attention by students of the prehistory of California deserts and adjacent areas, however, the results have not always clarified the subject. M. J. Rogers apparently devoted a great deal of time studying specimens of pottery collected on his extensive field trips. He did not publish any definitive studies of this material, but left behind a huge collection and extensive notes (cf. van Camp 1972:1; May 1978:1). The completeness of his notes is variable and their usefulness dubious, as least without extensive restudy using more objective approaches (cf. Schroeder 1952, 1958). Rogers published a study of the techniques of pottery making of the Southern California and Upland Arizona Yumans and adjacent Shoshoneans, including the Chemehuevi (Rogers 1936). In this study Rogers describes the ceramic process from selection of clays through the final firing. He describes and illustrates various techniques, vessel shapes and decorative styles. He describes and compares the variables from group to group (Rogers 1936: 15-42). This is an important and very useful study.

A. L. Kroeber and M. J. Harner published ethnographic notes, gathered by Kroeber in 1906, on historic Mohave pottery. Included in this monograph is a technical description, by Harner, of the historic variants of Parker Buff and Parker Red-on-Buff, which he calls Fort Mojave variant (Kroeber and Harner 1955). Peck (1953) published short notes on pottery from Sand Hills in eastern Imperial County including descriptions of some Buff Ware types.

In an attempt to determine the western limits of the Hohokam, Harold Gladwin surveyed down the Gila River and along the eastern bank of the Colorado River. He identified the Bouse site as the northwestern-most Hohokam site on the basis of polished red and red-on-buff pottery (Gladwin 1930). He was subsequently shown to be incorrect in this assessment (cf. Rogers 1945; Harner 1958), but he did recognize a separate buff pottery ware native to the Lower Colorado River and now called Lower Colorado Buff Ware (Schroeder 1952, 1958).

Harold Colton, dealing with small collections from northwestern Arizona recognized and described Tizon Brown Ware (Colton 1939), but included some material belonging more properly to other wares, a point noted by Rogers (1945) and subsequently clarified by Schroeder (1952, 1958). Tizon Brown Ware was subsequently revised by Euler and Dobyns (1958). A type called Palomar Brown, described by Meighan (1959) and occurring in western San Diego County, as well as other parts of southern and Baja California (in both desert and mountains) was identified by Euler (1959) as a type falling in the Tizon Brown Ware category.

A study of whole vessels in the San Diego Museum of Man, attributed to the Diegueno or Yuman speakers of northern Baja California and San Diego County, has been done by Gena Ruth van Camp. This collection consists of 751 vessels, of which 494 are from the Diegueno. The rest are from neighboring groups in the same region, including the Shoshonean (Takic) speaking Luiseno and the River Yumans (van Camp 1972: 85). This collection was supplemented with an unspecified number of vessels from other institutions and private collections. Much of the Museum of Man collections were gathered by M. J. Rogers. By way of background, van Camp discusses the archaeology and ethnology of the western Yuman area and integrats it into her discussion of the vessels. Matters such as materials, construction procedures, vessel forms and functions, non-vessel forms (pipes, rattles, etc.), decoration and design are all discussed in some detail. van Camp classified Diegueno ceramics with Tizon Brown Ware. A list of Rogers' unpublished pottery types is included and such descriptions as he may have left are included in an appendix (van Camp: 165-169, 208-214). No further descriptions of these proposed types are offered. The value of van Camp's study is in the descriptions of the range of variations of vessel shapes, decorative styles, designs, techniques and motifs. The attempts to impose an ethnic classification are not as useful.

Another recent ceramic study, also making extensive use of Rogers' notes and collections, was published by R. V. May. The collections come from the southern Sierra Nevada Range to Tiburon Island in the Gulf of Mexico, and all west of the Colorado River. The numbers of specimens and the criteria for division into types is not explicitly stated. The material is placed in six series with twenty-two types included in Tizon Brown Ware, and two series with ten types included in Lower Colorado River (sic) Buff Ware (May 1978: 8-10, 15). Procedures of examination are not indicated (i.e. use of binocular microscope). Surface and core colors are given with Munsell values. The only measurements given are for wall thickness.

As they stand these descriptions are incomplete and the differences between types are not clear or seem to be based on a single attribute. May duplicates a name, Salton Series, used by Schroeder (1958) but describes something different. Harold Colton established standards for pottery studies and classification many years ago (Colton and Hargrave 1937, Colton 1953). These standards have been followed with considerable success in the Southwest, with some recent revisions (cf. Madsen 1977) which indicate efforts to increase rigor and description clarity. Californianists could well profit by the example of their Southwestern neighbors. To do otherwise is like the tail trying to wag the dog.

Ceramic studies are sometimes a frustrating and difficult task, but the results can be most fruitful. Standards do exist, as we have pointed out. Several good guides and references exist, particularly Anna O. Shepard's classic "Ceramics for the Archaeologist" (1968), and also Matson (1960, 1965), Colton (1953) and Colton and Hargrave (1937). Ceramic analysis is time consuming and some procedures are expensive, or can be with large samples. Some such procedures are now being utilized at the University of California, Riverside, under the direction of R. E. Taylor. Judiciously selected tests such as x-ray defraction, neutron activation, thermoluminesence, etc. can enhance analysis of the data materially.

In summary a little more effort and attention to current advances in technological analyses of archaeological materials could be a boon to the study of prehistory in southern California. The archaeological record is slender enough as it is, and is rapidly disappearing down the maw of "progress". We can not afford to squander these resources by applying antiquated theory and methods to such data as we have. It is time for Southern California to continue the advance being made by a few individuals at a few institutions and to make it general. Intelligent resource management should insist on it.

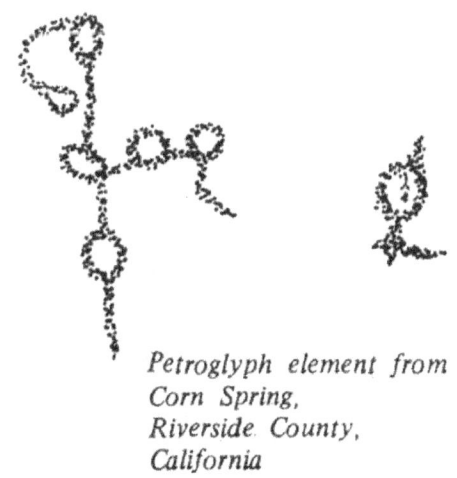

Petroglyph element from
Corn Spring,
Riverside County,
California

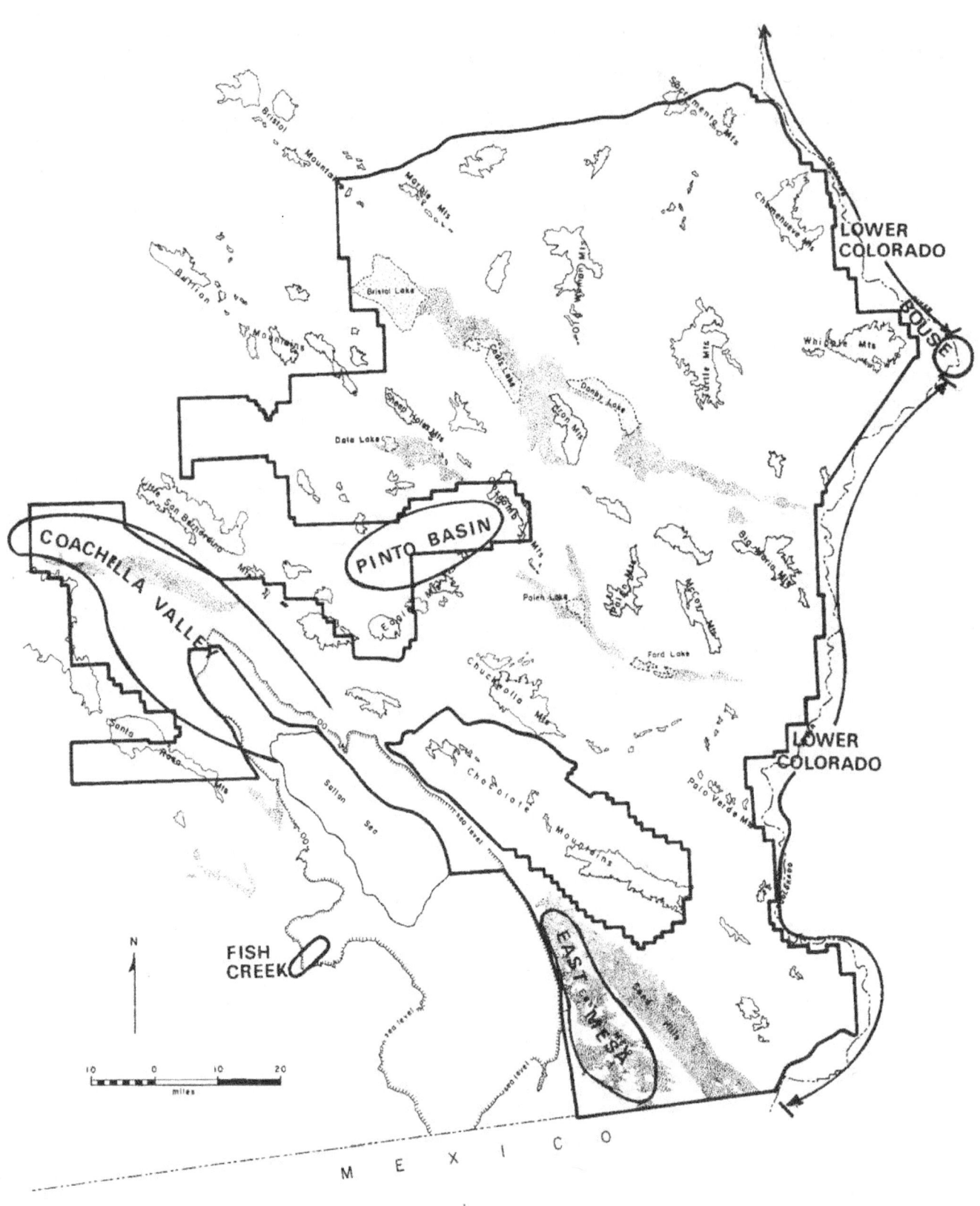

Figure 6. Major Archaeological Areas and Sites

Chapter IV. ETHNOGRAPHY
Martha Knack

A. Introduction

Within the area demarcated by this overview, there were no less than seven distinct Native American cultural groups. Two extensive major linguistic families were represented. The Yuman language family had four representatives: Mohave, Halchidoma, Quechan and Kamia. The Shoshonean branch of the Uto-Aztecan language family had three representatives; Chemehuevi, Serrano, and Cahuilla. Among these groups were three distinct life styles. Mohaves, Halchidomas, and Quechans were riverine agriculturalists, while the Serrano and Cahuilla were Californian hunters and gatherers. The other intermediate groups blended these life styles. Thus the Kamia and Chemehuevi, while basically gatherers, had acquired agriculture and farmed along the riverways in their territories.

The Lower Colorado Desert is a very complex cultural area. In order to simplify this presentation, each of these tribes will be described separately. Much of the basic ethnographic fieldwork dates from the late 1920's and early 1930's, with informant memories extending back probably to about 1880. Data from earlier times must be considered secondary, such as grandparents' narrations to informants in childhood. The Halchidoma data is from historical documents dating from the times described. Laird (1976), the major source on riverine Chemehuevi, received data in an unsystematic manner between 1920 and 1940 from a single informant born in 1871. Bean's Cahuilla work dates from the post-1960 period but to a large extent corroborates and extends earlier sources. Thus none of the sources directly taps the pre-contact period. Information on Halchidoma and Kamia cultures is sketchy. A brief ethnohistorical overview will follow in order to show the interrelationships between these various groups and the changes brought about by contact with foreign cultural entities of Anglo-European derivation.

B. Mohave

The Mohave Indians were Yuman-speaking agriculturalists who lived along the Colorado River. The name "Mohave" is derived from the native self-name, Aha macabe, "people along the river" (Sherer 1967). Their territory extended from Black Canyon in Nevada north of the study area, continuously south down the river valley to Poston. Also, occasionally and intermittently they controlled the territory down river as far as Palo Verde (Kroeber 1953). Their primary settlement area was the floodplain and adjacent low terraces of the Colorado River proper, particularly in those wider parts of the valley where agricultural land extended for considerable distance from the river. They also used adjacent higher terraces for gathering wild foods and ranged widely over the desert in pursuit of a very active international trade. While occupying only a very small portion of the study area, their cultural and historical importance should not be underestimated. The Mohaves were a militarily and culturally aggressive people who strongly influenced the cultures of all the surrounding tribal groups. In turn, they were perceived as a highly prestigious cultural group, especially by the less sedentary desert-dwelling tribes to both the west and east. In military alliance with various tribal groups, they waged active war against tribes on the Colorado and Gila rivers throughout historical times.

Mohaves did not settle in concentrated villages, but rather in small rancherias scattered throughout the floodplains of the Colorado River. Several houses, inhabited by patrilineal kinsmen and friends, were established near the fields. Favorite zones were older terraces in close proximity to the river, enabling the inhabitants to exploit both the riverine and hinterland resources without undue travel. Thus, settlement was nearly continuous but sparse throughout the Mohave territory.

Settlement in any district was subject to modifications depending on the fertility of the soil for agriculture, such as a change of the river channel.

Mohaves built a wide variety of structures, the most substantial of which was the so-called winter house. This was a semi-subterranean house built with a heavy cottonwood log frame, covered with willow and then arrowweed wattling. This, in turn, was mounded with sand to make it air-tight and warm. For summer use an opensided, flattopped ramada was made to provide shade from the fierce summer sun. These were very often placed near the winter house providing year-round dwellings for a family.

Mohaves had patrilineal clans (Spier 1953). Clans were not localized in residence, although component lineages may have existed as a result of the pattern of predominant patrilocal residence. Women carried the name of the lineage as their proper name, informally individualized by nicknames for identification. Men's names did not correspond to clans or clan affiliations. Clans were named after animals and natural phenomena, but were only weakly totemic, with few if any of the clans practicing avoidance of the named animal species. These clans seemed to function only as exogamic units and had no identifiable ritual or land owning functions.

Mohaves did not have chiefs as that term is properly used. There were a series of honorific functions for men in the society, most of which were associated with war or shamanism. The only figure approaching a political leader was the kohota, of whom only one resided in any given district. The kohota was a community leader of the type anthropologists have classically called a "big-man". He gave large and lavish feasts for his neighbors at his home. His advice was sought on traditional matters. He also seems to have had a variety of religious functions, primary of which was the keeping of scalps brought back from war expeditions for use in ceremonial gatherings. The "chief" who appears in historical literature seems to have been an introduced political role resulting from Euroamerican contact. Unlike all other funcionaries who acquire their positions through individual skills, character and the validation of power dreams, the historical chief's position was patrilineally inherited. In addition to the kahota, there were significant men in each neighborhood whose opinions were attended to because of their outstanding character, wisdom, skill and ability. Such local dynamic family heads were sometimes titled pataxam (Fathauer 1954; Stewart 1969a; Drucker 1941: 133).

The Colorado River Valley in which the Mohave lived was subject to annual flooding. In late spring, as the upper river drainage areas thawed, thousands of acre feet of muddy water poured over the flood plain. These spring floods provided the moisture for agriculture in this otherwise extremely arid area, and deposited a thick layer of rich silt which established the fertility of the soil. Mohaves did not practice additional canal irrigation, but rather planted in the low-lying areas directly after the flood's retreat. Thus, plants germinated and began to grow before the soil dried; their roots reaching down to the shallow water table for continued growth and ripening. The fields laid out near the houses were not privately owned but rather were generally acknowledged by surrounding families to belong to those who had cleared and planted them. Fields were occasionally demarcated by stones or other markers which floods were unlikely to wash away. However, disputes did occasionally arise over the use of a particular portion of the land. In that case, a formalized pushing battle was held between the kin groups of the men involved, which could escalate into a club fight.

There was a minimum of clearing to be done, much of the underbrush being already demolished by the flood or buried beneath the thick layer of deposited silt. The Mohaves planted maize, tepary beans (both white and yellow), pumpkins, gourds and sunflowers (see Appendix II for greater detail). In addition, they cultivated a species of tobacco and gathered wild plants (Wallace 1953). With the introduction of European plant species, Mohaves rapidly embraced wheat, barley, muskmelons and cowpeas. Mohaves also cultivated wild species, particularly panic grass, crowfoot grass, curley dock, and several other unidentified species.

More than any other Colorado River group, Mohaves depended on agricultural products for their subsistence, an estimated fifty percent. Maize was dried on the cob and ears stored in large above-ground granaries woven of arrowweed. Dried beans were stored either in shell or removed from the pod. Gourds were valuable as canteens for desert travel, storage containers for a wide variety of products, rattles, bullroarers, and other minor uses. Grass seeds were stored in large crudely-made pottery ollas, or in gourd storage containers. Spiral strips of squashes and melons were sun-dried and stored for future use.

Little ritual and few taboos were associated with any portion of the agricultural cycle. Other than a joyful dance at harvest, the time of plenty, there was little ceremonial involvement. This contrasts with other Southwest agricultural groups such as the Hopis, and may relate to the relative reliability of the fertile Colorado River environment (Stewart 1966a).

However, the floods were not wholly dependable. In some years they came too early or too late, or were not of sufficient height to innundate enough surrounding land. In such years when the agricultural harvest was inadequate the natural products of the surrounding desert were used as a supplement.

Even in normal years, Mohaves exploited a variety of wild plants (see Appendix II). Of these, the most important were the mesquite and screwbean. Often groves of these plants standing eight or ten miles from a home base were regularly visited and harvested. Beans were ground coarsely with a stone pestle in a cottonwood mortar. The resulting flour was made into a baked bread or gruel. Beans were stored whole in large above-ground granaries and were considered a staple food.

A wide variety of other plants growing in the river bottoms were utilized seasonally. The roots and young sprouts of tule were eaten. Pigweed greens were edible in the spring, well-boiled to take out the bitterness. Chia, growing in the sandbars in early summer, was a major source of seeds. This light-weight but highly nutritious food was used by traders travelling on the deserts. Barnyard grass and tansey mustard provided both seeds and greens. Sisymbrium, goosefoot and seepwillow all gave edible greens. Sprangle top, odium bush, yellow nut grass, amannia and evening primrose provided seeds to be prepared like all others, ground to flour on a metate. Children ate ground cherries growing in between the fields. Sow thistle (an introduced species) and spring aster leaves provided greens. A variety of other plants were minor but welcome changes of diet from the ordinary agricultural plants.

In times of crop failure, non-riparian plants which normally provided extremely minor sources of food for groups of travellers along the trails, became major sources of subsistence for entire families. Expeditions of women journeyed several miles into the interior for days at a time to gather these foods. Such foraging expeditions exploited ironwood in the upper arroyos, quailbrush seeds, spring mushrooms, desert thorn berries, yucca fruits and other cactus products, occasionally agave, desert salt brush seeds, yellow and blue palo verde seeds and other desert plants. These were considered famine foods and not elements of the ordinary diet. However, Mohaves could not have utilized these during emergencies if they had not retained familiarity with the desert, the seasonality of its products, their location, and growth patterns. The desert outside the normal settlement areas was a haven in time of failure of the preferred agricultural products (Castetter and Bell 1951; Stewart 1965). However, after a thorough analysis of the literature, Kroeber concluded that no Mohave group lived permanently in the western desert regions or along the Mohave River (Kroeber 1959).

It would seem that any tribe living along a major river would utilize fish to a large extent. However, this was not true of the Mohaves since this area of the Colorado is particularly muddy and few large species of fish are native. Most fishing was accomplished in the sloughs and lagoons rather than in the river proper. Fishing was especially common in late summer as the river receded and before agricultural produce was ripe. Thus, to some extent, the Mohaves utilized the humpbacked sucker, boney-tail minnow and the "Colorado salmon" (see Appendix II). Drag nets, dip nets, basketry scoops and willow wiers with dip nets at their openings were the principal fishing implements. Worms, grasshoppers, sunflower seeds and occasionally corn were used for bait. The use of a curved cactus hook and bean-fiber line may or may not have been aboriginal. Bow and arrow fishing was done by older men but was not a preferred method. Spears and poisons were never used, nor were platforms or rafts. Only men fished and prepared the catch. Fish never provided sufficient surplus to warrant major preservation techniques and contributed only to an estimated 10-15% of the Mohave diet (Kroeber 1925: 737; Stewart 1957).

Mohave depended even less on hunting. Small game was hunted on the river bottoms, throughout the fields, and in the interstitial brush (see Appendix II). However, few large mammals inhabited the Colorado Valley. Rabbits, both jack and cottontail, squirrels, chipmunks, gophers and woodrats constituted the major small game and provided the most frequent form of meat protein. These were shot with a bow and arrow, killed in snares or deadfalls, baited with sunflower seeds, or clubbed. Nets and box traps were used to catch quails. If sighted, an occasional badger or raccoon was killed, but these were not actively sought. Beavers and foxes, it was believed, could only be consumed by the aged (Stewart 1947a: 83). Migratory waterfowl, such as ducks and mudhens, were consumed as well as pigeons. A variety of minor foods such as caterpillars and yellowjack larvae were utilized.

Large birds were usually killed only for feathers, the eagle and hawk being particularly desired. Hawk feathers were the best for arrows; eagle feathers were necessary for the all-important mourning ceremony as well as for military status symbols. Other birds not eaten but plucked were buzzards, crows, pelicans, owls, cranes, blackbirds and roadrunners.

Mohaves believed that many foods, particularly meats, were associated with human physical conditions. Madness or forgetfulness could result from eating a particular food. Foods were associated with luck, swollen glands, early senility, and so on. In short, many meats had magical import.

Big game species were hunted only by a few men, full-time specialists called akwak konik, who had acquired this power through dreams. Such hunters left farming and fishing to other men, and traded their meat products for subsistence foods, since they were under taboo of death not to eat the meat they had themselves killed. There were only twenty to thirty such hunters in the entire Mohave tribe at any one time. Hunting was associated with much ritual and taboo, such as sexual abstinence for four days before and after a hunt. The hunter had to bathe himself ritually for four mornings after his return, while his bow and arrow were left outside of the house to prevent polluting contacts. These specialists brought back one deer or mountain sheep at a time, waiting several days or weeks before hunting again. Such ritualized involvement indicates that this was an unusual food source and not one quantitatively important to the everyday diet (Stewart 1947a; Castetter and Bell 1951: 215). While in the mountains, these hunter specialists occasionally came across other game, such as wildcats and mountain lions, which, while not eaten, were useful for their pelts. Badgers and raccoons also were found and their meat consumed.

One of the outstanding characteristics of the Colorado River culture area was a persistent state of internecine warfare. The Mohaves were justly famous for their militaristic nature and were much feared by other tribes. They usually allied themselves with the Quechans, and were consistently the enemies of the Maricopas, Cocopas, and Halchidomas. The Mohaves, singly or in alliance, periodically fought the Chemehuevis, Utes, Paiutes, Diegueños, Pimas, Kohuanas, or Apaches, intermittent friendships existed with the same tribes. The Mohaves' most consistent peaceful relations were with the Yavapais, Havasupais, and Walapais of the upper Colorado plateau. Thus, Mohaves rarely waged warfare with surrounding hunting and gathering peoples. However, with most other agricultural tribes, their technological and demographical equals, they maintained an endless series of attacks and counter-attacks.

All Mohave men desired fame as warriors and good fighters, and yet they believed this could only come after a validating prophetic dream. Warriors specialized as archers and clubbers, of whom the clubbers were the most feared because they engaged in bloody hand to hand combat.

Mohaves made strict division between a raid and a formal battle. A few local men who desired a particular object - to steal a few horses, to raid for slaves or to gain individual glory - could perform a raid. Without ceremony a small party of such men would leave the valley, travel to another tribal area, make their attack by stealth, and retreat under cover of darkness.

On the contrary, a formal war party was organized for defense or revenge and very often involved men from throughout the Mohave area or allied groups in a joint expedition. Such parties were given a formal leavetaking by the entire community, were preceeded by spies who sought out the enemy, and very often engaged in preplanned, preannounced standing battles between opposing armies. Such a party was always accompanied by the Mohave scalper, of whom only one existed at any one time. This man dreamed the special power to take a scalp without magical repercussions or danger to himself. Shamans accompanied the war party to magically weaken the enemy before battle and to charm advantageous weather conditions. These large war parties took scalps and prisoners, but did not take land, for they attacked areas far too .distant from the Mohave heartland to utilize advantageously. Having to retreat on foot, they did not take crops or other booty (Stewart 1947b; Fathauer 1954).

After their return, the warriors were purified ritually. The community gave them a ceremony of welcome. Prisoners were displayed and taunted. The entire ceremony was repeated at harvest time and carried distinct overtones of fertility. The formalism and ritual elaboration associated with warfare indicates the extreme interest Mohaves took in military expeditions.

The Mohaves fought with tribes along the river whose technologies and products were similar to their own and hence competitive. The plateau and desert tribes produced items the Mohaves desired, and with these they pursued active trade. Wild tobacco, considered superior to domestic varieties, was obtained from the Chemehuevis and Diegueños (Kumeyaay) in trade for corn. Ironwood pods were acquired from Walapais and Chemehuevis. Pinyon nuts and salt came from Southern Paiutes and Chemehuevis and acorns were traded from Diegueños, Walapais, and Kamias (Stewart 1965: 51). Agave was traded in raw unprocessed form from Walapais and later mashed and brewed into a drink (Stewart 1965: 51).

The Mohaves were famous for long expeditions across the desert, through the San Bernardino Mountains to the California coast, where they acquired shells for jewelry. They were middlemen in the trade of Hopi and Zuni products across Arizona and into southern California. Their long distance travels were well known to other tribes. Mohave trade trails stretched across the Mohave Desert, the best known one following the Mohave River and over Cajon Pass. There were numerous subsidiary trails and cut-offs linking this to other routes and leading to various spots along the Colorado River. Major trails paralleled the river on both shores.

As a result of this travel, Mohaves had a very broad knowledge of peoples and places far from their own homeland. Correspondingly, they had a great effect on these other tribes. On the basis of this knowledge, the Mohaves have claimed from time to time that their aboriginal territory extended from the Tehachapis and the San Bernardino Mountains to the Colorado River (BLM California Desert Ethnographic Notes 1978: No. 14). It seems unlikely, however, that the Mohaves occupied such large desert areas permanently to the exclusion of other tribes historically documented to reside in those areas. Rather the individual trading parties, such as those that met Garces, Fremont and other early Anglo-European explorers, passed unmolested through these territories for purposes of trade. It seems that the trade trails were rights of transit across territories occupied by tribes with whom the Mohaves had peaceful relations. Perhaps the lack of warfare with Chemehuevis and the tolerance with which the Mohaves allowed these people to enter the Colorado River Valley had a great deal to do with their need for peaceful access to trade routes across long unprotected desert stretches.

Dreams were very important in Mohave life (Devereaux 1957, 1961). Mohaves believed that acquisition of special knowledge, such as that of a warrior, hunter or shaman, was through dreams. Myths, they believed, were dreamed by the tellers rather than learned from previous narrations. It seems more probable, however, that the incidents, words and songs were in fact learned from hearing myths told in performance, but that the necessary authority to perform these myths in turn had to be gained through a validating dream experience. One outstanding Mohave characteristic of these dreamed myths reflected the strong tribal interest in travel and long distance trade; they are geographically specific. Every event in a myth is told as occurring at a specifically named and described spot. The mythological characters travel long Mohave trade trails through the western deserts, up and down the Gila and Bill Williams rivers, but primarily up and down the Colorado on those numerous historically known trails, side trails, and cut-offs. Each spring and campsite, rock outcrop and playa is specifically mentioned as the mythical beings traverse the real Mohave countryside in dream time. The degree to which Mohaves now hold these stopping points of mythical beings sacred is an issue to be explored by further ethnographic investigation (BLM California Desert Ethnographic Notes 1978: Nos. 14, 18).

The majority of identifiable mythical locations are actually in the Colorado River Valley, some of which are within the eastern edge of the Desert planning units. Several are along the western trade trail to the California coast. The most important mythical location of all Mohave mythology is Mount Newberry in the Dead Mountains, known as Avikwame. This prominent mountain northwest of the Mohave Valley homeland figures in a great number of myths. It is here that spirits dwell and all power dreams have their source. Thus, it is the focal point of the mythical dreamtime, and hence, source of traditional social status for Mohaves. Other spots mentioned in the mythology are the Providence Mountains (no specific point mentioned) in which sacred beings stopped in their travels. The two sacred deer stopped on a mountain peak to the north or northeast of the city of Calico, on another peak just north of the town of Blake, at a spot known in Mohave as Avi waca in the New York Mountains, and at the yellow mountain north of Ibex, as well as at several points and springs in the Paiute Valley. In the myth Kroeber numbers as three, the sacred beings stop at the ridge, Koskilye, which extends west of the Whipple Mountains into the desert, at the spot where the cut-off trade trail leaves the hills and strikes out across the flats. In his myth #7, it is related that the culture hero, Mastamho, created the mountain just south of Ibex. This mountain is called Ohmo and is in the Sacramento Mountains. Within this mountain there are several specified locations which are recorded only by their Mohave names, such as Otahve-k-hunuve, where Dove stopped during one myth. Lake Muroc (Rogers Dry Lake) near the town of Mohave, is the site of several mythical events. Thus, as in Kroeber's myth #7, the two birds stop there on their way to the San Bernardinos. In the Tumanpa myth, the sacred beings stop at Paiute Spring, then at the peak of the Providence Mountains, as well as at a spot just northwest of the sandhills which lie between Kelso and Baker. In the salt trip myth, the Providence Mountains and Muroc Dry Lake are once again mentioned, as well as a spot just southeast of the town of Amboy, and the sandhills south of the Turtle and Riverside mountains. In Kroeber's myth #13, the Chuhueche myth, the following specific additional locations are mentioned: the white sand streak west of Highway 95 where it crosses the California-Nevada state line; a mountain called Kwikantsotka in the Paiute Range; the mesquite grove in the valley near Kelso where the railroad passes through; Screwbean Springs near the south end of the Sacramento Mountains; a point just north of the Riverside Mountains called Aqwaqa-munyo; a mountain in the Chemehuevi Mountains called Setulyku. In the origin myth, a bell-shaped peak in the Turtle Mountains called Taha is specified. In myth #16 of Kroeber, another peak at the western end of the Chemehuevi Mountains about 10-12 miles west of the river is mentioned by the Mohave name Kutsuvave. In myth #18, a cave at the western foot of the Monument Mountain named Tsesaha appears. In the two volumes of myths recorded verbatim by Kroeber and in the two volumes of historical narratives, there are many locations unidentified by English names which need ethnographic verification. These include some known only by their Mohave names, which could probably be identified by Mohave informants. There are also spots that are located only very generally but which may still be recoverable from a knowledgeable raconteur. Particularly the Turtle Tale needs to be investigated further.

Caves and trailside shrines associated with these myth cycles were presented offerings of food, tobacco and arrows by passers-by (Drucker 1941: 164). Such locations, if not looted, should be archaeologically identifiable and protected. The degree to which such sites are now known by informants, and the degree to which offerings are still made, would be an excellent indicator of present feelings about the sacredness of these locations.

Because of the geographically specific nature of Mohave mythology, there are strong indications that traditional, religious Mohave might consider a great number of these spots sacred and desire protection for them. In addition, some of these myths are so specific as to campsites and stopping spots along the Colorado River bottoms, that they might be used as sources for archaeological reconnaissance.

Another area of Mohave religious sensitivity may relate to the final resting place of the dead. Although the Mohave did practice cremation and believed in a specific land of souls (whose entrance was near Needles on the Arizona side of the river), there is apparently still very strong feeling about the resting place of ashes (BLM California Desert Ethnographic Note 1978: No. 14). Cremations usually occurred away from homes very shortly after death (Hall 1903).

The Mohaves practiced an annual mourning ceremony, in which the dead individual was once again honored. In this way the memory of the death and its location, especially that of a chief or other important person, was long kept alive in peoples' minds, even in the absence of fixed graveyards and cemeteries (CSRI 1978: 6-53). Particularly prehistoric cremation sites lack visible markers and leave very few remains identifiable other than by trained archaeologists or Native Americans. As a result, extreme caution should be engaged in with regard to this particular aspect of Mohave culture.

In a recent survey of Mohave residents of the Colorado River Reservation, 88% expressed concern over land use impacts on culture resources, such as archaeological sites, trails and trail shrines, petroglyphs, intaglios and mythically associated locations. Roughly 55% were concerned over plant and animal species and would oppose any policy which they believed to endanger species traditionally utilized (CSRI 1978: 6-51).

C. Halchidoma

The Halchidoma (Halchidhoma, Halchadhoma) tribe was another Yuman-speaking group originally living below the Cocopas near the mouth of the Colorado River. An early Spanish account recounted eight villages and estimated a population of 2,000 (Bolton 1908:276). During historical times they moved north of the Gila River mouth and settled between the Mohaves and Quechan. Early Spanish writers did not remark upon any cultural singularity and the amount of ethnographic detail is therefore small. It can only be presumed that Halchidomas were typical Colorado

River Yumans in culture as well as in speech. This group has since been driven from the Colorado by intertribal warfare as related below in the ethnohistorical section (Dobyns, Ezell and Ezell 1963). They first found refuge in Mexico and later on the Gila among the Maricopas. While they retain a tradition of a unique name, an oral history of residence on the Colorado River, and a slight dialectical difference, they have become acculturated first to Maricopa and later marginal Euro-American life styles. Little remains that is identifiable as aboriginal Halchidoma culture and new data are not available at this time (Kelly 1972). It can only be assumed that they resembled the Mohaves and the Quechans while they resided on the Colorado.

D. Quechan (Yuma)

The literature on the Quechans is much less voluminous than that concerning the Mohaves but it states clearly that these two groups were very similar (Forde 1931: 271; Drucker 1941). Like the Mohaves, the Quechans were agriculturalists, although they appeared to depend on agriculture only for about 40% of their diet. Fifteen percent more was from fishing, and 10% from hunting. The remainder of their diet was from wild plants. Driver (1957) arranged these subsistence foods according to the environment from which they were derived: river bottom, desert and intermediate zones. He concludes that 89% of Quechan subsistence came directly from the river valley. Nine percent was from upper terraces or from both ecological zones, and only 2% was from the desert hinterland. As with the Mohaves, desert foods provided an alternate Quechan resource in case of famine, crop failure, failure of the river to rise, or for sustenance while travelling. Unlike the Mohaves, the Quechans were not major traders: and they did not travel nearly as frequently or as far from their homeland. In most other regards, however, they closely resembled their Mohave neighbors. In particular, the importance of warfare and of dreaming for power and authority are very characteristic of Quechan culture.

The Quechan territory was in the lower portion of the Colorado River section of the study area. The inhabitants lived in scattered settlements rather than centralized villages, each with a population of several hundred. These were scattered along the river bottom, especially near the projecting spurs of the upper terraces (Forde 1931: 102). These rancherias consisted of large permanent semi-subterranean winter houses like those of the Mohaves, and were occupied by more than one family. During summer, each family separated and dwelt under a flat-roofed ramada or in brush shades near their fields. These communities appeared to have had no sib or lineage affiliations and consisted of both related and unrelated individuals.

The Quechans had a very strong concept of tribal identity. This was represented by the leadership of the kwoxot. There was normally only one kwoxot in the tribe at any given time. He was an economic, political and religious leader. He kept the enemy scalps used in funerals and other ceremonial meetings. He looked after the poor and was obliged to provide shelter and food to anyone needing it. He delivered speeches of both ethical and practical import. Further, he performed rituals for the benefit of the entire community. His mere presence was considered beneficial to those nearby. The position of kwoxot was not inherited.

All power was theoretically obtained through dreaming, a vision experience which led to contact with the spirits who lived on Avikwame Mountain. These visions were deemed to be supernatural validation of the claim to terrestrial power. In addition, certain personal characteristics were required. All leaders had to be strong, knowledgeable and capable of getting people to cooperate with them in communal activities. If he were such a person, a man's dreams were considered good, and his suggestions were deemed worthy by the community at large. If a man made poor decisions or if a community failed to follow him, it was ipso facto proof that his dreams were no longer good and that his power had deserted him.

In addition to the kwoxot, there was a military leader called kwanami. It was he who called the warriors to battle and directed the war parties. His position was attained by achievement and proof of his military prowess, tact and ability. His role was situation specific and did not pertain in times of peace.

In addition to these two special roles, there was in each settlement a council of family heads, termed pipa taxan. This group of elders gathered when quarrels threatened the solidarity of the community. They provided runners during war, made decisions over possible movement in times of flood, mediated private disputes, and in general regulated the day-to-day affairs of the community. This was a democratic body, and virtually all families had access to community decision-making processes through participation in it. Thus each rancheria was politically independent (Forde 1931: 133-141).

A great percentage of Quechan diet came from agriculture which depended upon the natural spring floods of the Colorado River. While there was a minor planting of corn and melons in February, before the flood, the main crop was planted in June, after the river had subsided. At this time, more corn and melons, tepary beans, pumpkins, and gourds were planted. Quechans very rapidly adopted the cow pea, watermelon, cantelope and wheat from the Spaniards, all of which are now considered to have been aboriginal crops. There were no canals for irrigation and therefore the technology involved merely a digging stick and a wooden weed cutter. The Quechans also planted several wild grasses as indicated in Appendix II. There was no legendary or ritual associations with the crops, planting, field magic or harvest. In all other regards, Quechan agriculture closely resembled that of the Mohaves, described above.

In addition, a number of wild plants were collected at various times of the year (see Appendix II). Several grass seeds were obtained when ripe, as well as mesquite beans, screwbeans, ironwood tree nuts and chia. These formed an alternative source to fall back upon in years when the spring floods failed to come or, for other reasons, the agricultural crop was insufficient. The large types of beans were stored in large platform granaries standing six feet off the ground on cottonwood poles. Smaller seeds were stored in calabashes and jars. Tobacco was gathered wild but was not cultivated.

Hunting was of very minor importance to the diet. Men went out alone or in the company of a few others, primarily in the winter. Major game sought were deer, antelope, and rarely, mountain sheep. The primary areas hunted were north of the town of Yuma around Castle Dome, Dome Rock, and Tugo. Hunting was not elaborate. They used neither masks nor disguises and did not gather for communal hunts. They shot rabbits, both jack and cottontail, in the valley fields.

Fishing was also of small importance as there were few species in the lower river suitable for eating. Fish sought, however, were the humpback, white salmon and boneytail. Quechans sometimes shot them with unfeathered arrows or caught them with cactus spine hooks, but most often took fish with traps and nets in the sloughs during floods. They used drag nets and scoop nets. Quechan men built wicker weirs out of arrowweed and used watermelon seeds for bait (Forde 1931: 107-120).

The relations between the Quechan and other tribes varied considerably. The Kamias were considered inoffensive and were tolerated in a very friendly fashion. They were permitted to approach Quechan territory in historic times. Quechans occasionally visited Diegueños for ceremonies and also to trade gourds for acorns (Forde 1931: 105). Throughout historic times, Quechans have maintained hostile relations with Pimas and Maricopas, and friendly relations with the Yavapais and Papagos. With Yavapais, they traded dried pumpkins, beans, melons and maize for rabbitskin blankets, baskets, buckskins, mescal and finished leather goods. Quechans traded with Hopis for woven blankets, particularly of wool. The Mohaves and the Havasupais were intermediaries in this trade. Relations with Mohaves were uniformly friendly and the Quechan received eagle feathers in trade with them. These two tribes were often military allies against others in the district. To the Cahuillas, Quechans traded gourd rattles for acorns, and from the Kamias, tobacco. From the Pimas, they traded martynia pods for weaving the black patterns in baskets (Forde 1931: 124; Davis 1974: 45).

Many Quechan men were dreamers. Through these dreams, the leaders, singers, funeral orators, and doctors all acquired power. These dreams nearly universally included a visit to Avikwame, the holy mountain wherein the spirits of the world were believed to dwell. There a particular spirit befriended the dreamer and granted him specific powers. Very often these included the power to cure specific diseases, arrow wounds, snake bite, soul loss or contact with ghosts. Quechans believed that when the world was created, the culture hero, Kumastamxo, presented to mankind the skills and technology they would need to survive. He made his home at Avikwame, after the destruction of the first spirit home at Axavolypo. Thus, during aboriginal times, Avikwame was the source for all mystical and terrestrial power. This mountain was the same as that held sacred by the Mohaves (Forde 1931: 176-179).

The boys' initiation rite, which involved endurance running to the four directions on four subsequent days, apparently had no geographically specific locale. The girls' puberty rites were held at the homestead of her family and also involved no centralized location (Forde 1931: 150-155).

Quechan dead are cremated. Formerly this occurred near the house of the deceased, closely following death, preferably that same night. Beginning some time prior to 1930 and continuing at present, cremation was performed at a specialized cremation ground on the reservation, where a permanent mourning shelter has been constructed (Forde 1931: 208). The keruk, the main Quechan ritual in ethnographic times, is a four day ceremony of mourning which re-enacts the events which had originally taken place on Avikwame in the myth time. This ceremony is now performed annually at a specific place (not geographically identified by Forde) on the reservation, probably as a result of agency pressure. In former times, the keruk was not an annual ceremony, but took place sporadically depending on the availability of labor, community incentive, and food to sustain the participants. Since approximately 1890, the Diegueño practice of making death images has been absorbed in a rudimentary form by Quechans (Forde 1931: 221). The myth upon which the keruk is based has clear parallels with the Mohave one. The sacred mountain and the events of the creation cycle are all those of the Mohave myths (Forde 1931: 176-179). Undoubtedly, like its Mohave antecedent, the Quechan myth has intense and specific geographical correlates. However, the form in which it has been published is not specific enough to identify the location of the various mythical events. It is not unlikely, therefore, that other closely associated Mohave locations, both in Mohave territory and in Quechan territory, were associated with the supernatural for Quechans as well. Because of the fragmentary nature of our knowledge of Quechan ritual, this is a question that clearly needs immediate field investigation.

E. Kamia

Information on Kamia culture is very sparse, consisting primarily of one monograph of memory ethnography from six informants then long residents on the Yuma reservation (Gifford 1931). On the basis of this limited information the following sketch of Kamia culture is offered.

The Kamias were a semi-sendentary group of agricultural Yuman speakers, living along the waterways of the Alamo and New rivers, and the territory south of the Salton Sea. Linguistically, they spoke a sub-dialect of the Eastern (Southern) Diegueño. Culturally, their Diegueño lifestyle was modified by agricultural practices learned from the Quechan. Kamia had particularly strong friendly relations and trade with the Quechans and Diegueños. Estimates of aboriginal Kamia population are limited to a single census in 1850 which showed 254 persons. The scarcity of historical mention of residents in this area hints that the native population was at all times very small. Occupation of the Imperial Valley was also intermittent, depending on the availability of water in the rivers. As these marginal resources increased or decreased depending on long-term weather patterns, the population either occupied this area or sought residence in other, more dependable, areas. Thus, during the historical period between 1829 and 1849, the Kamias retreated from their upper areas around Brawley to the lower New River and eventually to Algodones on the Colorado. This movement was caused by a decline in spring flooding. This denied the all-important agricultural resources and made the area no longer inhabitable for Kamias.

Settlement was scattered along the waterways. Individual houses were occupied by nuclear or extended family households and spaced 100 yards or more from each other. There were no nucleated villages, nor were settlements permanent. Although housing was substantial, consisting of semi-subterranean dwellings of the Colorado River type (cottonwood frames, willow substructure, arrowweed thatching and sand-covered), these were not occupied year round. Square, flat-topped ramada-like sun shades covered with arrowweed were usually built for summer use. In addition, small separate dwellings were built for older people. There may have been specialized sweat houses. Kamias built granaries of arrowweed and willow elevated on pole frames close to their houses for food storage. When wild plants were available elsewhere in the valley, Kamias made a series of temporary camps in the gathering locations, which have not been described in detail in the literature.

Kamias, as a group, claimed to have had one single chief, whose functions were to organize the food quest of the various groups and to perform ritual functions, as well as to lead in war. Gifford has expressed a doubt that these leaders were in fact aboriginal, but were rather a result of historical contact with Europeans (Gifford 1931: 26-27, 31, 50-51). Such chieftainship was not hereditary. Rather the leading men of an area agreed through informal means that a given man had the wisdom, knowledge and foresight to make decisions for the group. The primary qualities for leadership were knowledge of the available food resources, effective public speaking and reliability in social relations with all the members of the group.

In social organization, the Kamia tribe was divided into patrilineal lineages. The names of some of these lineages show close correlation with those of Kumeyaay (Southern Diegueño). While there was some temporary patrilocal residence after marriage, this did not lead to the development of localized lineage villages. There seems to be no subdivision of the land into lineage territories or usufruct areas. Lineages seem to have served only to control marriage and not as a means to organize ritual organization or to structure political relations in any way.

Kamias practiced floodwater irrigation, based on the seasonal flooding of the overflow outlets of the lower Colorado. The seasonal flood crested in May or June. As soon as the water receded, they planted corn, beans, melons, squash, pumpkins and gourds in the still-wet soil. Canal irrigation was not practiced. The plants received minimal additional attention, only a little weeding and some hilling to prevent wind damage. The primary locations for agriculture were along the Alamo River from south of Brawley to Holtville, and in the area of Indian Wells, and along the New River (to the west of the study area). Farming may also have taken place at a spring near the sandhills northeast of Brawley, possibly Sunset Spring. Kamias did not plant or artificially stimulate the growth of wild species.

Once crops were planted and well-started, they needed little further tending and the population was free to gather now-ripening wild foods. Foremost among these were mesquite and screwbean, which ripened in June, July and August. The beans were either stored whole in the granaries or pounded to flour in a mortar and pestle and kept in this form. Mesquite roots were used for weaving, the inner bark for string, and the gum for dying both weaving fibers and human hair. Its wood was used for a variety of purposes, such as bows, clubs and digging-sticks (Gifford 1931: 42). Mesquite was thus a very important plant.

Tule was important for both pollen and roots were eaten. Yerba mansa, Atriplex torreyi and a wide variety of other seeds were gathered. Leaves and tubers were collected from plants of uncertain identification. Akwil nuts were gathered during occasional trips to Cocopa territory. Acorns were traded from the Kumeyaay (Diegueño) in exchange for watermelons (Gifford 1931: 23). Yucca fiber for sandals and finished baskets were also obtained from Kumeyaay. Mescal (Agave) was gathered in Kumeyaay territory either on expeditions for this purpose or received in trade for agricultural products (Gifford 1931: 23). Much of this trade took place near Mountain Springs(Kroeber 1925: 601). Salt was collected along the southern edge of the Salton Sea and formed an important Kamia trade item. Other mineral resources also were utilized, particularly granite for pestles and metates acquired near Jacumba. Steatite from the same area in Kumeyaay territory was manufactured into arrow straighteners. Manganese dioxide, again from near Jacumba, was used for face paint. Clamshells for jewelry were imported from Cocopa territory (Gifford 1931: 27).

The Kamias fished in the rivers and sloughs of their territory. A hook made out of cactus spine and fiber from bean vines and wild plants was used in hand. In addition, Kamias used a basketry scoop similar to that of the Quechans. They made seine nets but usually simply shot the fish with a bow and arrow.

F. Chemehuevi

The basic pattern of Chemehuevi settlement and social organization can be extended to their Colorado Desert territory from the better documented Southern Paiute sub-groups. This pattern depended upon several characteristics of the plants upon which these people depended for subsistence. Vegetation grew in localized areas, rather than being evenly distributed throughout the territory. Secondly, these plants tended to produce during short seasons only. Thus the human groups were small, mobile, fragmenting and congregating in a flexible manner. The usual production and consumption unit was a small band of bilaterally related persons. During periods of plentiful plant growth, groups of twenty-five to fifty could congregate near productive sites. At other times, when food was more scant, human population would fragment into groups as small as single nuclear families. This minimal unit contained the necessary labor balance to utilize the environment, including as it did an adult female and an adult male.

Human group mobility was determined more by altitude than any other single factor. Foods were gathered from several ecozones and stored at a central location, very often at a point where various ecozones abutted. This central location was the most frequently used camping site and was near a reliable spring, stream or other water source (Steward 1938: 180-186, 230-236). Two or three of such base camps might be located around the countryside for seasonal use. From such base camps small gathering expeditions sought out the currently productive plant growth. After two or three days, these foraging parties would return to camp. If a particular area was known to be producing well in a given year, news of this would spread rapidly among the nearby bands. They would gather to share the rich seasonal surplus before it could be usurped by competing animals such as squirrels, woodrats and so on. The territory each band used was flexibly defined and groups passed back and forth fairly freely for seasonal gathering activities (Kelly 1934; Stewart 1939).

Membership of the band was probably unstable. The group which wintered together might vary from year to year since the wide spreading bilateral kinship ties permitted a person access to more than one group. This flexibility most likely also characterized riverine Chemehuevi communities.

Like band membership itself, leadership was flexible and kinship based. During those portions of the year when very small groups or even individual families were the sole social unit, the head of the family, the eldest male, was the unquestioned leader. His duties were diffuse, but centered upon the subsistence needs of the group as a whole. During these periods there were no community leaders at all. Each family was responsible for and to itself for its own actions.

When larger groups gathered around temporarily rich resources, a more elaborate form of leadership was made manifest. The headman of such groups was the senior, most able and most respected male member and was usually the geneological focal point of a substantial network of kinsmen. In addition, he was expected to be calm, nonaggressive, well-informed, and senior but not senile. These required personal characteristics usually assured that the role was not inherited automatically from father to son. However, the need to have widespread kinship ties meant that a succeeding headman was often related to his predecessor. It was also believed that a brother, son, or other close relative was more likely to have learned the things that a headman should know than was a stranger. The headman was neither formally elected nor placed into office. His position was an outgrowth of community respect and the voluntary acknowledgement of the sound leadership of a particular man. Thus headmanship was a transitory phenomena, informal and fluctuating.

These characteristics of headmanship related directly to the duties expected of this leader. "His task was principally to keep informed about the villagers, and if all the families travelled to the same pine nut area, to manage the trip and to arrange where each was to harvest" (Steward 1938: 247). Thus the headman was an economic manager, with knowledge of the best gathering areas for each season, and the responsibility of leading the group to them. As such he was responsible for the success or failure of the whole group to procure subsistence. If a neighboring group desired to enter the usufruct area of another, it was the headman who was customarily contacted for permission. He would then direct them to areas where their activities would not interfere with those of the home group. Such permission was never refused, for it was well-recognized that the unpredictability of wild food production assured that the host group itself would need the temporary use of the visitor's terrain someday in turn. Thus periodic surplus was cheerfully shared with neighboring groups as a form of insurance for reciprocality at a later date. This permitted a flexible adjustment of the human population to the waxing and waning of localized food resources, redistributing the population over the landscape.

The headman also had social functions to perform. He arose early in the morning and expounded to all within hearing on their moral duties of hard work, marital faithfulness, economic cooperation and other community-held values. In cases of dispute, the headman was sought to mediate and to offer advice since he was a kinsman whose opinion was valued, often having ties to both parties. He was a man of respected wisdom and of great moral standing. His role was as an interpreter of community traditions. His advice could either be accepted by the parties or rejected. In this as in all things, an individual retained the right to agree with the headman, conform to his advice, and therefore stay in the community in peaceful cooperation, or he could leave the group, and utilize his kinship ties in other groups to affiliate under another leader. The authority of the headman was not absolute and did not constitute political power. The number of occasions in which a headman could mediate were strictly limited. He did so only as a respected member of the community, rather than as a commander or ruler of any kind (Steward 1938: 246-260).

There were other men who also had special social roles, most notably the game drive leader. This man had received visions in which the supernatural spirits of rabbits or antelopes had granted him power over them. When the abundance of game indicated that it would be profitable, several bands gathered to hold a communal drive. An individual with the power over animals directed the activities according to the dictates of his particular spiritual guardian. Ritual preparation was believed to be as important to the success of the drive as was physical action, for ritual violations would result in withdrawal of the game by the spirit and hunger among the people. Thus, the game drive leader controlled the behavior of the group during the drive, but as soon as it was over his power terminated.

Like that of the shaman, the game drive leader's power was limited to specific situations. Leadership in game drives, headmanship, or other leadership roles, brought little or no ecomonic reward. Headmen hunted for their own families and were given no subsidy by the community in return for their services. Respect and social status were the only rewards while the responsibilities were many (Driver 1937: 91-94; Drucker 1937: 28-30; Steward 1938: 246-248). Thus, Chemehuevi leadership was situation specific, seasonal, flexible, and limited only to the social group of which the particular leader was a part.

Laird (1976: 24-30, 168-173) claims that among riverine Chemehuevis there was a more formalized leadership pattern involving a hierarchical relationship among band and supra-band headmen who she calls chiefs and paramount chiefs. She maintains that the major chiefs periodically met in confederation, used a special esoteric language amongst themselves and had other unique behavioral patterns. It seems likely that this was a product of historical contact with both the riverine Mohaves and the hierarchically-oriented Anglos.

Chemehuevi population distribution within their territory was strongly effected by the local desert environment upon which they depended, particularly groups just west of the Colorado River. In desert areas, plant growth is sparse and unreliable, depending strongly upon the pattern of that particular year's rainfall. Further, plant resources are localized, with some areas being vastly more productive than others. As a result, human population utilizing such flora were mobile, flexibly readjusting to the fluctuation of available food plants. People moved to successive locations throughout the year depending on which plant was ripening. Social groups were consequently small due to the scant production of food in any one area at any one time. Desert Chemehuevis depended more heavily upon flora than faunal resources since animal meat availability was even less reliable.

Major Chemehuevi food plants were Joshua trees, mesquite, screwbean, Mohave yucca, agave, beavertail cactus, buckhorn cholla, prickly pear and other cacti, crucifers, pepper grass, desert thorn, chia and blazing star, with pinyon and rice grass used where available (Laird 1976: 107-109). A wide variety of minor plants were used as indicated in Appendix II. The technology for gathering and storing this harvest was common among all Chemehuevi groups (Drucker 1937: 9; Knack 1978b).

The major basketry fiber, willow, was indispensible in Chemehuevi technology. Wild hemp, milkweed, and agave provided fiber for string (Laird 1976: 108). Bows were made of willow or juniper (Drucker 1937: 20). Arrows were often simply a pointed willow but occasionally had stone tips added (Drucker 1937: 201; Laird 1976: 106). Compound arrows were also made with a Phragmites vulgaris (reed or cane) shank and a sagebrush foreshaft (Laird 1976: 107). Any wood was used for digging sticks. Houses were often of willow, arrowweed or sagebrush in simple dome-shaped karnees (Laird 1976: 106).

As previously stated, animals provided very little food, compared to plants, and were relatively unreliable. Chemehuevis highly valued deer, mountain sheep, and antelope but such game was very rare (Laird 1976:112; Knack Interviews 1978a). These animals produced not only great quantities of meat but also large hides for clothing, a rare commodity. Their sinews were used for backing bows and for sewing. Horns were boiled for glue; bone was used for awls and other tools. Of far greater dietary importance than large mammals was small game, particularly jack rabbits and cottontails. Often community hunts and game drives were used to harvest large numbers. Rabbits were not only a major source of meat but their fur was cut into strips and woven into robes, the primary garment for winter. Important though rabbits were, smaller game was also actively pursued. Woodrats, kangaroo rats, chipmunks and gophers were hunted using deadfalls and snares. Lizards of various kinds, particularly chuckwallas, and desert tortoises were hunted. Birds, especially quail and doves, were shot with bow and arrows (Drucker 1937: 7-8; Laird 1976: 112-116; Appendix II).

For the most part women were responsible for plant food gathering, processing and storing. They were in charge of household tasks, child care and cooking, while men aided with house building and meat storage (Knack 1978b). Women processed most seeds by parching them in a basketry tray. When ready for use, seeds were ground to flour on a metate, and then baked or prepared as soup or gruel. Fleshy plants such as agave were shorn of leaves and then pit-cooked for several days, producing a pastey mass that was then sundried. Mesquite beans and screwbeans were the major storable products in this area and provided the bulk of the winter diet.

Men shot game with bow and arrows and dug burrowing animals from their holes with short sticks. Cooperative hunting drives were used against rabbits, the animals being chased into an extended net. Clubs and simple sticks were often used against small game in a very informal manner. Small game also was caught with snares, nooses, deadfalls and other traps by both men and women (Drucker 1937: 7). Once acquired, game was roasted and any surplus was either distributed to neighbors or sundried for future use.

Surplus foods of all kinds were kept in earth caches lined with grass or broken basketry fragments, and covered with earth. In such a way food could be stored for a season or years, depending on the needs of the family.

Once Chemehuevi groups had acquired access to land on the Colorado River, they quickly shifted to at least partial dependence upon floodwater farming. In this regard they very closely resembled Mohaves in both crops and technology. They undoubtedly continued to rely upon desert flora and fauna to a far greater degree than Mohaves and were apparently more mobile, moving frequently into the desert. In technology and many other regards, the riverine Chemehuevis seem to have adopted cultural traits from the Mohaves.

The association between religion and land use in this area is difficult because even the most practical and mundane activities had a ritual overcast. For this reason, any separation of religious activities from others is purely artificial.

Chemehuevis practiced what has been called a "fall festival" associated with the pinyon harvest. At this time large groups of people came together in the most productive groves. Surrounded by luxurious food resources, social dances and intergroup activities were intense. These were times of great joy. Occasionally, the memorial mourning ceremony was celebrated then as well (Steward 1938: 45-46, 55, 122, 184, 237).

Game drives also had ceremonial overtones. The material preparation of the nets, runners and beaters was considered ineffective without the accompanying ritual. The leader of the game drive was a man of shamanistic powers, and his preparation included chants and prayers (Steward 1938: 40).

There were a number of rituals involving individual life events which had ecological significance. For instance, when a boy killed his first large animal of the most important species, the meat was taboo to him and his family. It had to be given away to other members of the group (Driver 1937: 63; Drucker 1937: 8). Women also had ritualistic limitations, particularly during their first menstruation. The menstruant's physical mobility was restricted to either her home or to a special hut. Her gathering production was decreased and she experienced dietary taboos.

Subsequently, for four or five days each month, she could not eat meats or oil, including pinyon nuts: she was forbidden salt and the consumption of hot substances. During the month following child birth, these same taboos were extended to her husband as well (Drucker 1937: 34; Driver 1937: 97-98). These restrictions eased the pressure on limited meat production by decreasing their consumption by the female half of the population.

There are other ritual associations with land, particularly in the area of myths and narratives. Laird maintains that at least riverine Chemehuevis inherited, in a loose patrilateral fashion, a series of songs grouped into either mountain sheep or deer cycles, each with subdivisions and minor subcycles. She stated that these songs related the travels of mythical personages and animals over particular named locations of the Chemehuevi landscape. Interestingly enough, a great number seem to follow Mohave trade trails up and down the river, rather than crossing the traditional Chemehuevi desert homeland. This may indicate a late historical source for these songs stemming from Mohave contact, and dating from the period of riverine occupation. Laird asserts that each cycle describes, in great detail, a trip from a particular mountain range to the desert floor. This would, of course, parallel the traditional Chemehuevi pattern of annual use of altitudinally separated ecological zones. However, the songs remembered by her informant described the Whipple Mountain range to the New York Mountains, Providence Mountains, and Granite Mountains at minimum, but she offers no greater details. The inheritance of one of these song cycles, she maintains, permitted a man to hunt in the area described by the song. This would appear to be a pragmatic Chemehuevi utilization of an acculturated myth cycle, applying esoteric Mohave trails to a very practical need in Chemehuevi life. However, there is no indication that these hunting territories were defended or exclusively held, but may perhaps have been a description of the usufruct right of different men's band hunting territories (Laird 1976: 1-20, 32).

One myth relates that the mythic being, Southern Fox, travelled from the Whipple Mountains to Death Valley, stopping at West Wells, the Dead Mountains and Paiute Springs, traversing the New York Mountains and the Ivanpah Mountains, visiting Pahrump and eventually ending at Furnace Creek. Other stories are too imperfectly related to identify specific locations. She does say that the riverine Chemehuevis considered all the Panamint Mountains to be sacred and Mount Newberry in the Dead Mountains to be the source of all mythical power, again showing very strong Mohave influence (Laird 1976: 159-60, Map I).

Laird also records that petroglyph sites were ritually associated. She states that Chemehuevis interpreted them as having been created by the supernatural helpers of shamans (Laird 1976: 123).

The Chemehuevis exchanged basketry caps and burden baskets for mountain products from Cahuillas (Davis 1974: 18). Chemehuevis also traded various unspecified products with Yavapais (Davis 1974: 27). Mohaves exchanged eagle down and chicken hawk feathers for Chemehuevis rabbitskin blankets (Davis 1974: 27).

A recent survey of twenty-nine Chemehuevis showed that 59% are concerned about the continuing availability of medicinal, basketry, and food plants and would be concerned if policy changes endangered any of these. Petroglyphs need protection according to 48% and trail shrines and intaglios by 14%. Animals traditionally hunted were seen as of importance by 17% of the respondents (CSRI 1978: 6-36).

G. Cahuilla and Serrano

Cahuilla and Serrano settlement was characterized by a relatively high degree of stability for desert dwelling groups. Camps consisted of approximately 75 to 100 persons and were located near permanent sources of water, usually mountain streams or reliable springs and wells. Palm oases were favorites and include Thousand Palms, Willis Palms, Biskra Palms, Hidden Palms, Macomber Palms, Willow Hole Oasis and Seven Palms Valley. Such locations provided not only palm fruit but other plant resources, such as mesquite, which cluster near water sources. These villages were located near rich resource gathering points. The Cahuillas' favorite camping spots were along the lower edges of alluvial fans, where water from springs was available and yet desert resources easily could be exploited. From these base camps, gathering excursions of fairly limited extent spread out in all directions.

Often base camps included traits implying permanence such as community houses, sweat lodges, localized lineages with place name affiliations, ritual reciprocity between lineage groups, and geographic intermarriage patterns (Strong 1929: 12-25). Each village contained the core membership of a patrilineage. It was said that these lineages were grouped together into two exogamous moieties, Wildcat and Coyote (Drucker 1937: 28; Strong 1929: 20-25). Since marriage was patrilocal, women of the village were primarily inmarried from more distant areas. The gathering sites related to each village were fairly clearly specified, much more so than in the case of the desert-dwellers to the north and east. Rights to utilize these resources were inherited through the patriline (Drucker 1937: 27; Bean 1972: 90-91). Furthermore, such social statuses as leadership, ritual positions, possession of a sacred bundle, or use of community ceremonial hall, were inherited patrilineally. Moieties controlled intermarriage and the reciprocal exchange of ritual services. For instance, funeral rites for the members of one moiety were performed by the members of the opposite. Feasts were hosted on the moiety level. The annual mourning ceremony was sponsored by each moiety in alternate years. Thus, fundamental social functions were lodged ritually in the moieties, themselves with geographical correlates and mutual interdependence.

The material investment in the village was quite substantial. Houses were semi-excavated. Large cottonwood poles supported heavy, flat roofs.

Like social organization, political organization in the Cahuilla-Serrano area was more explicit than in other sectors of the study area. Localized lineage villages were headed by a functionary called the kika or net who fulfilled both economic and ritual functions. Most often the geneological head of the lineage, his position was said to be inherited, although the community always retained the right to veto an heir on grounds of personality qualifications (Strong 1929: 17; Drucker 1937: 28). The kika served as an economic leader, deciding where, when, and who should leave the village to gather wild plants. He was also a ritual figure and managed the first fruits ceremonies which initiated the harvest of major staples. He was the nominal owner of that tract of territory to which the group claimed customary use rights (Drucker 1937: 28). Any other group desiring to share the products of this region had to apply to the kika for formal permission to enter the area. The kika also mediated disputes within his group on a wide variety of issues, basing his decision on traditional values and on consensual agreement of the community elders (Strong 1929: 17; Drucker 1937: 28; Bean 1972: 104-105).

In addition to this headmanship, there were other regularized positions of authority. Primary among these was the ritual leader called the paha (paxaa?). This position also was conditionally inherited from father to son, although further qualifications were considered important. The paha was the keeper of the bundle of sacred paraphernalia communally owned by the lineage. This bundle was a symbol of lineage unity and a source of spiritual protection. It was used in nearly all lineage-based rituals (Strong 1929: 18). The paha was the kika's messenger, announcer and ritual assistant. He also may have been a rabbit drive boss and thus involved instrumentally in the food quest (Drucker 1937: 29; Bean 1972: 105).

There was a hereditary officer called a singer, tcaka or takwa. The singer was a ritual specialist charged with remembering the oral traditions, chants, songs and myths of the group. These were sung at the annual mourning ceremony and funerals and had to be word-perfect in their recitation. As the keeper of the spiritual esoterica of the group, the singer was very highly respected (Strong 1929: 18-19; Drucker 1937: 28; Bean 1972: 106-107).

There is evidence that the eastern desert villages of both Cahuillas and Serranos experienced some simplifications of the classic patterns just described. The major ethnographies of both these groups were based primarily on evidence from the mountain-dwelling villagers to the west; however, they also contain hints of a more elementary desert pattern. Often attributed to historical break-down or post-contact contamination of the data (Strong 1929: 19), this simplification may have been the result of lower population density and the necessities of desert living. Thus, for instance, near Twentynine Palms, a Serrano oasis, the paha of one moiety kept the ritual paraphernalia of the other. There was only one kika for all the Serranos living here regardless of lineage. These and other data indicate to me a simplification of social organization in the face of more stringent environmental circumstances, where the population was not able to culturally "afford" the structural overhead.

The Cahuillas and Serranos were not agriculturalists in pre-contact times, but hunted and gathered in the areas surrounding their villages. Mesquite beans and screwbeans were major plant products, providing a subsistence base.

Mesquite was particularly prevalent in the Thousand Palms and Seven Palms areas and the northern Borrego Desert where groups congregated from as far away as Coyote Canyon to gather and trade mesquite products for acorns and pinyon from elsewhere. The Coyote Canyon mouth, Borrego Springs, Rockhouse Canyon, Palm Springs, One Thousand Springs and Chino Canyon were also major gathering areas. Mesquite provided wood for building material, logs for houses, limbs for bows and arrows, shoots for compound arrows, gum for adhesive for arrowpoints, and other uses (Bean and Saubel 1963). Screwbeans are found in the same general areas as mesquite, especially in the Coyote Canyon area and northern Borrego. Its wood is heavy and dense and most useful for such things as the mescal (agave) cutter, a sharp-edged beam used for lopping off the stout mescal leaves from the juicy heads.

In the deserts a variety of cacti were used: barrel, beavertail, chollas of various kinds, prickly pears, and other species. Many favorite gathering spots were near Desert Hot Springs (CSRI 1978: 6-14). Leaves, stalks, fruits, and seeds were utilized. Agave or mescal was a particularly important plant. Once the leaves were removed, the main head provided a substantial mass of food while the flowers, leaves and stalks were also utilized. Various yucca species were used in similar ways. The smaller seasonal plants such as catclaw, locoweed, palo verde and desert willow provided edible seeds. Palm trees were sought everywhere; their groves provided camp sites, particularly in the foothills on the edge of the Borrego Desert, Palm Canyon, and other locales. The trees provided fruit and building materials. Cahuillas ate a variety of tubers, including wild onions and desert lilies. Seasonal plants used for greens were wild celery, milkweed, sage, pepper grass, sea blight, and others. Chia, pigweed, palo verde, ocotillo, boxthorn, tidy tips, desert dandelion, blazing star, tansey mustard, sea blight and many other desert plants provided seeds which were valued. Like most wild seeds, these were prepared by parching and grinding them into flour; the resultant meal was used to make bread or gruel. Surpluses were stored in their whole form for later milling. Extra dates, fruits, and berries were sun-dried and stored in caches or granaries. Of course, major surplus products were mesquite beans and screwbean, kept in large woven granaries near the houses. Favorite gathering areas were the Mecca Hills, Thousand Palms, and Martinez, Sheep and Pushawalla canyons.

Cane was a source of compound arrow staves. Palm fronds were used for roofs, as were arrowweeds. Cactus thorns gave needles and pins for tatooing. Mistletoe berries were eaten and the leaves produced a black basketry dye.

Both cottontail and jackrabbits provided meat supplies, with woodrats, kangaroo rats, mice, chipmunks and squirrels as minor sources. Quail were the favorite fowl. Deer and antelope were preferred but very rarely found. A variety of smaller desert game such as chuckwallas, desert tortoises, rattlesnakes, ants, grasshoppers, cicadas, crickets and moth larvae were utilized whenever available. Flickers and eagles were sought primarily for their feathers, which were necessary for ritual purposes (Drucker 1937: 7-11; Bean 1972: 36-67).

A great number of the recorded Cahuilla and Serrano rituals had ecological importance. Game drives were under the control of the paha (Drucker 1937: 29; Bean 1972: 105,147). The Serrano practiced first fruits ceremonies for mesquite, agave, and in some areas, pinyon and acorns. These rituals acknowledged the dependence of the human population on supernatural beings who controlled the fertility of these food resources. By giving thanks in this way it was believed that productivity could be assured for the following year. Most of these ceremonies followed a pattern in which the paha announced that each family was to pick a limited amount of the fruit. Without eating this, they returned to the village. There a ceremony took place involving singing, chanting and dancing for as many as three days. Then there was a ritual eating of this carefully gathered small portion. Only then did the paha announce that the harvest was open and that the food could be freely gathered (Drucker 1937: 40-41; Benedict 1924: 24, 142-143).

All social gatherings regardless of purpose were initiated by a communal sharing of food in the form of a feast. Each family brought a basket of prepared mesquite meal; from these contributions a feast was prepared in which all took part (Benedict 1924).

Some anthropologists see events such as these to be of great ecological importance. Bean, for instance, states that in the case of the Cahuilla, "The ritual activity kept the environment in proper balance" (Bean 1972: 105). The argument is that such rituals were primary means of redistributing localized surpluses by bringing large numbers of people together during peak periods of productivity, and ethically demanding an exchange of food in feasts and gifts.

The Cahuilla and Serrano also practiced male initiation rites involving the Jimson weed plant, Datura meteloides. In specific sites such as Devil's Canyon and the Mecca Hills, the paha gave each boy a drink of the liquid made from datura (also known in California by its Mexican name, toloache) which induced the visions believed to presage the boy's future life. Dancing and chanting followed, publicly announcing his initiation into manhood (Benedict 1924: 383; Strong 1929: 31-132; Drucker 1937: 35-36).

The killing of a deer was a time of community celebration. Throughout the night each member of the lineage gathered and sang. In the morning the meat was distributed to all (Benedict 1924: 379; Strong 1929: 135; Bean 1972: 147). This sort of investment in time and effort could hardly have taken place if venison were an ordinary part of the diet.

Shamans had other economic functions. Spiritual helpers, acquired through dreams after drinking the datura decoction, granted power to shamans and often taught them songs and dances to be used in particular rituals. Most commonly this was power to cure illness, often of a specific type. Other shamans had the power to find lost objects or foretell the future, while still others could charm antelope or rabbits. Some were believed to control rain, being able to both bring it or drive it away. Such powers were used to protect the harvest when a cloudburst might ruin the crop. Cahuillas believed that some shamans could aid in the fertility of certain wild plant and animals, and thus could "create food". There were also ritual beliefs associated with first menstruation, birth, and a young hunter's first kill. These seem to have been of little geographic significance (Bean 1972: 135-159).

Petroglyphs and arranged-rock sites, especially in Palm, Painted, Martinez, Andreas, and Rainbow canyons, and the Torres Hills, at Travertine Point, and Indian Wells, still have sacred associations for living members (CSRI 1978: 6-14). Pushawalla, Palm, and Martinez canyons, the Mecca Hills, and the Mule Mountains are considered highly significant in their entirety (CSRI 1978: 6-64, 7-24). Edam Hill, Indian Wells, and Tahquitz Canyon have unspecified but clearly felt mythical associations, as does a ring-shaped rock alignment on the Agua Caliente Reservation (CSRI 1978: 6-15). Grinding rocks such as those in the Painted Hills, Martinez Canyon, in the hills west of Whitewater Canyon and along the south side of Highway 86, are also important to contemporary Cahuillas (CSRI 1978: 6-24).

Nearly all Cahuilla informants on the Devers-Palo Verde powerline investigation indicated that cemeteries, historic and prehistoric, and hence all village sites and palm oases, were rendered sacred by the souls of the dead. They should not be desecrated or exposed to profane view (CSRI 1978: 6-14, 15, 26, 31).

Trade relations were particularly close between Cahuillas and Kamias to the southeast. Desert Cahuillas and Serranos traded with their linguistic affiliates in the mountains for the specialized products of each area. Cahuillas and Serranos do not appear to have taken part in as extensive long-range trade as did the Mohaves; however, trails are remembered and considered culturally important today. Most writers (Bean 1972: 68) consider the Colorado Desert to be a territorial boundary for the Cahuillas, an area of little use and forbidding access. This would not indicate strong or persistent trade involving social or commercial ties betwen Cahuillas and riverine tribes.

A recent survey of Cahuillas living in the study area shows that 46% believe that traditionally-used plant species should be protected and 70% believe the same of animals traditionally hunted. Nearly 60% feel that arranged-rock, pictograph, and petroglyph sites should be preserved; 40% believe that there are other unspecified natural "power" sites with continuing sacred significance. Trails and ceremonial sites are held important by 47% of the interviewed individuals, and 42% said that there are other traditional use sites, such as initiation camps, with sacra-secular importance. Nearly 55% believe that all burial locations, including previously occupied camp sites, are sacred and should not be profaned, because of the continuing association with the souls of the dead residents. Fully 80% of those interviewed believed that there were some sites in the desert that require protection. Thus it seems very clear that Cahuillas today continue to feel a close personal and spiritual connection with the desert landscape. Therefore the implications of land management policy decisions will be of interest and concern to many of them (CSRI 1978: 6-12, 22).

H. Ethnohistory.

Throughout the historical period, the Lower Colorado River area has been characterized by intertribal warfare. Some alliances were stable - Quechans and Mohaves together against Halchidomas and their allies on the Gila River. Other affiliations were unstable - Chemehuevis were, at one point, associated with Mohaves, and at other times stood against them.

During the earliest known historical period, in the late Seventeenth century, Halchidomas were living below the Gila-Colorado confluence (Dobyns et al. 1963: 197), but in approximately 1700 they moved up the Colorado to the area around Parker. Here they held the northern terminus of the Spanish Road from Sonora. As such they became critically important to Spanish trade and travel, and consequently the Spaniards rapidly cultivated a lasting friendship with them. Halchidomas desired access to Spanish trade goods, while other tribes, desiring the same object, feared favoritism (Dobyns et al. 1963: 198-201). The Yuman-speaking tribes, in general, had little to offer Spaniards in return for manufactured and exotic goods, other than their traditional war captives. Formerly a minor result of warfare, slave raiding became a major motivation and took on new meaning (Dobyns et al. 1957; Malouf and Malouf 1945; Smith and Walker 1965) as the Spanish market opened up for human labor. The Papagos were ideally located to serve as middlemen and they soon took on this role, increasing military pressure against the Halchidomas, their traditional enemies. In order to facilitate their own trade, the Spaniards made every effort to prevent the intertribal warfare, often interfering via negotiators or making overt threats (Dobyns et al. 1963: 200-205).

Throughout the Spanish period relations were for the most part amicable between Spaniards and the tribes in the Lower Colorado River region. Overt hostility was rare. Spanish explorers and missionaries visited the area only occasionally and instituted minimal culture change. However, in 1779, they did attempt to found a mission at Yuma on their southern route from Mexico to California to be headed by the veteran missionary and explorer, Garces. This was probably an attempt to pacify and secure this area for travel, as there was an unusually large armed escort at the mission. Less than two years later, for reasons that remain unclear, the Quechans attacked and killed all the missionaries. This massacre ended the Pax Espana in the area and renewed warfare between Quechans and other groups, particularly Halchidomas (Stewart 1967; Dobyns et al. 1963).

Beginning in 1826, Euro-American fur trappers entered the Lower Colorado River. Tribal relationships with these fur trappers were not nearly as amicable as they had been with the Spaniards and frequent small skirmishes took place. James O. Pattie and Jedidiah Smith both had minor fights with the Mohaves (Stewart 1966b).

At the same time, the intensified Yuman warfare had reduced the Halchidomas in population. This small tribe was further depopulated by several epidemics of European introduced diseases, all within a short period of time. Mohave anger at incursions which they associated with Halchidoma-European friendship and the weakening of the Halchidoma tribe itself, created the opportunity for a renewed Mohave-Quechan alliance against them. Some time betwen 1826 and 1829, these two powerful tribes managed to defeat the small intervening group. The entire Halchidoma population was dislodged, left the river, and fled to Mexico. From there, in 1833, they travelled again to join their previous allies on the Gila. There they co-resided, especially with the Maricopa, and to a large extent acculturated with them (Dobyns et al. 1963: 205-213).

This left an unoccupied space along the river, and according to Chemehuevi tradition, the Mohaves invited them to live here. By 1859, they were in the Chemehuevi Valley and in the Colorado Valley proper (Stewart 1967). They also occupied the northernmost end of the Palo Verde Valley before 1880 (Roth 1977: 1). They claimed that Mohaves invited them to use Cottonwood Island (Van Valkenberg 1934). This tribal shift had removed Halchidomas from the Colorado and introduced Chemehuevis to a new riverine agricultural lifestyle, to which they very rapidly adapted. They absorbed not only subsistence techniques but also concepts about chieftainship, the power of dreams, an entire religious complex, and other markedly Mohave culture traits.

The Kamia also underwent tribal relocation at this time. Their mixed farming-hunting-gathering economy in the Imperial Valley was precarious at best. Between 1824 and 1849, there was apparently a naturally caused, long-term water shortage and little water overflowed into the basin. This made continued agriculture impossible and upset the tenuous Kamia adjustment. With the New River drying, Kamias left, retreating to Huerta along the Alamo River. There they shortly had trouble with Mexican troops and moved again to Algodones on the Colorado, between the Cocopas and Quechans. Quechans tolerated their entry and made no effort to dislodge this small remnant (Gifford 1931: 7-9).

With the advent of the period of United States' control, great changes took place on the Lower Colorado River in terms of the balance of power between the tribes and the cultural autonomy of all tribes. After gold was discovered in California in 1849, travel increased tremendously along the wagon roads. Established trails were used, one passing through southern Quechan territory, crossing the southern Colorado Desert, and entering San Diego. A second crossed the river at Fort Mohave and followed the Old Mohave (trade) Trail to Cajon Pass and into the Los Angeles basin. In 1850, Fort Yuma was built in order to pacify the southern tribes and protect this wagon travel. During the 1850's, several railroad surveys traversed the area and engaged in minor frays with local tribes, especially the expeditions led by Sitgreaves and Whipple.

In 1854, the Mohaves waged a major war against the Cocopas on the Gila River, continuing the traditional pattern of intertribal warfare. Again in 1857, the Quechans and Mohaves allied against the Gila River peoples, particularly the Pimas and the Maricopas. In this case, the Colorado River groups lost severely. This was the beginning of their military decline (Spicer 1962: 269).

During the 1850's, Mormons feared that Utah would soon be attacked by the United States. They actively cultivated the friendship of the tribes in the study area lying to the south, which worried the United States military (Stewart 1969b). When Mohaves attacked a wagon train passing through their territory in 1858, the United States took this opportunity to retaliate in full measure. The Mohaves lost bitterly. With over half their men dead, they sued for peace. Fort Mohave was established in order to control this area and to suppress Indian warfare. It was not until 1865 that the Colorado River Reservation was set aside with the intent that Mohaves should move to this southern edge of their traditional territory and take up peaceful farming. In that same year, however, warfare broke out between the Mohaves and Chemehuevis (Stewart 1969b). The Chemehuevis lost these battles and retreated into the desert. They returned again only two years later, taking up residence on the Colorado River Reservation. Meanwhile a splinter group of Mohaves, desiring the benefits of cooperation with the now militarily dominant Americans, moved to farmland on the reserve. The construction of an irrigation system by the BIA in 1915 made this option even more attractive and population grew steadily. The numerically predominant progressive faction has since then been consistently more amenable to BIA programs and policies than the more conservative groups. These stayed in the Mohave Valley territory and eked out a scanty traditional living subsidized by annuities from the military (Devereux 1951).

As with other Native American tribes, the Mohaves, and probably also Quechans and Chemehuevis, experienced an increase in the power of chiefs and other community leaders at this point. The United States civil and military authorities found it more convenient if tribes could be represented by a single individual with the authority to make decisions committing the entire native group. Rather than trying to negotiate with each rancheria headman separately, they favored strong "chiefs" and backed up the decisions made by the more cooperative leaders. Annuities and other goods were made available to these men for distribution to "their" people, providing a powerful new political tactic unavailable under the traditional economy. "Chiefs" were given special treatment, such as trips to Washington, in order to curry their favor. They were presented with tokens such as uniforms to indicate their position of superiority. During the period between the military defeat of 1859 and approximately 1874, there was a florescence of the power of chiefs. Eventually, their cooperation became cooptation and they lost the ability to make decisions independent of United States wishes. The reservation period had set in (Kroeber 1965).

In the 1870's, the major non-Indian presence in the Colorado River area was the mining industry. Large mines operated, as at La Paz and Ivanpah, where Chemehuevis were employed as laborers (Roth 1977: 5). It was only comparatively late in the 1870's that Americans began to invade the river valleys themselves for agricultural lands. In 1877, a major irrigation project was initiated to open Palo Verde Valley to Anglo farming methods. The chief engineer was a man named Calloway. Three years later, Indians, fearing that their homelands would be lost through the completion of this and similar projects and irritated by Calloway's personality, shot him. In retaliation, the military was called out and placed on the Colorado River Reservation. It was only after six or seven years that they were once again permitted to spread out and to reclaim those of their scattered traditional farming areas which had not since been usurped. Chemehuevis returned to the Chemehuevi Valley, but never re-established in the Palo Verde Valley (Roth

1977).

In 1890, the military decided that the Lower Colorado River area was in fact pacified. They gave Fort Mohave to the BIA for a boarding school for Mohave Indian children. This school operated until 1931. In 1910, the land surrounding Fort Mohave was made into a reservation in recognition of the de facto existence of a concentrated traditionalist Mohave population which had persisted nearly continuously in this area since aboriginal times.

In 1935, the construction of Hoover Dam dramatically changed Indian life on the Lower Colorado River. The annual overflow of the river, which had provided irrigation water and fertilizing silt, ceased. The Bureau of Reclamation did not build the large-scale and expensive canal irrigation needed to compensate for its loss in the area below the dam. This meant essentially that traditional Indian subsistence techniques were, in one sudden movement, destroyed. Unable to use the land any longer, the Indians in the study area turned to wage labor more than ever before. They depended upon working for other people instead of being self-sufficient on their own land. This dependence was complicated by the Depression and several changes in the local industrial structure at this time. There was a decline in mining which threw many Indians out of work. Others had, for years, worked as wood cutters for steamships plying the Colorado. In the 1930's, these boats ceased operation and the Indians lost this independent form of employment. Another long standing area of Indian wage labor had been in the railroad roundhouse at Blythe, which closed. Indian unemployment was extremely high by 1940.

In 1938, the construction of Parker Dam and the filling of Lake Havasu flooded much of the Chemehuevi Valley, further reducing the agricultural land base.

In 1950, more land was removed from the control of those tribes who believed it to be their reserve. The BIA relocated here some 150 Navajo and Hopi families. This created a permanent ethnically based factional block within tribal government.

In 1937, the Colorado River Reservation tribes had organized a tribal council under the Wheeler-Howard Act. This body filed suit against the federal government for damages incurred in the filling of Lake Havasu and won a settlement of some $80,000. The award of this money created another major factional dispute among the tribes. Chemehuevis claimed that they alone had exclusively occupied the valley and therefore deserved to divide the money only amongst their own members. The Mohaves claimed that since they were part of the congregated Colorado River Reservation tribal government, the Chemehuevis had to share it with all the groups. Later, when the affiliated tribes filed suit under the Indian Claims Commission Act, the Chemehuevis again tried to divide the suit. With the increasing value of lake-front property, this dispute over control of the now-innundated Chemehuevi Valley continues to cause tribal dissension (Roth 1976).

In recent years the recreational development of Lake Havasu and the Southwest in general has led to booming tourist housing, boating and water sports facilities, and other tourist service industries on and near the reservations. Major irrigation projects have been constructed by the BIA to substitute for the now-lost annual flooding of the river, but agriculture has not been successfully re-established as a subsistence base. The tribal economies of the study area are now dependent upon serving Anglo economy and Anglo-owned industry (Stewart 1969b; Bee in press). In December 1978, some 25,000 acres of land, once part of the Fort Yuma Reservation and held in trust by the BLM and other government agencies since 1893, was returned to the Quechan tribe by administrative action (Wassaja 7:1:8, Jan. 1979). The associated water rights, while apparently dating from the original 1884 reservation, remain in practical doubt (Bee 1979).

Petroglyph element from Corn Spring, Riverside County, California

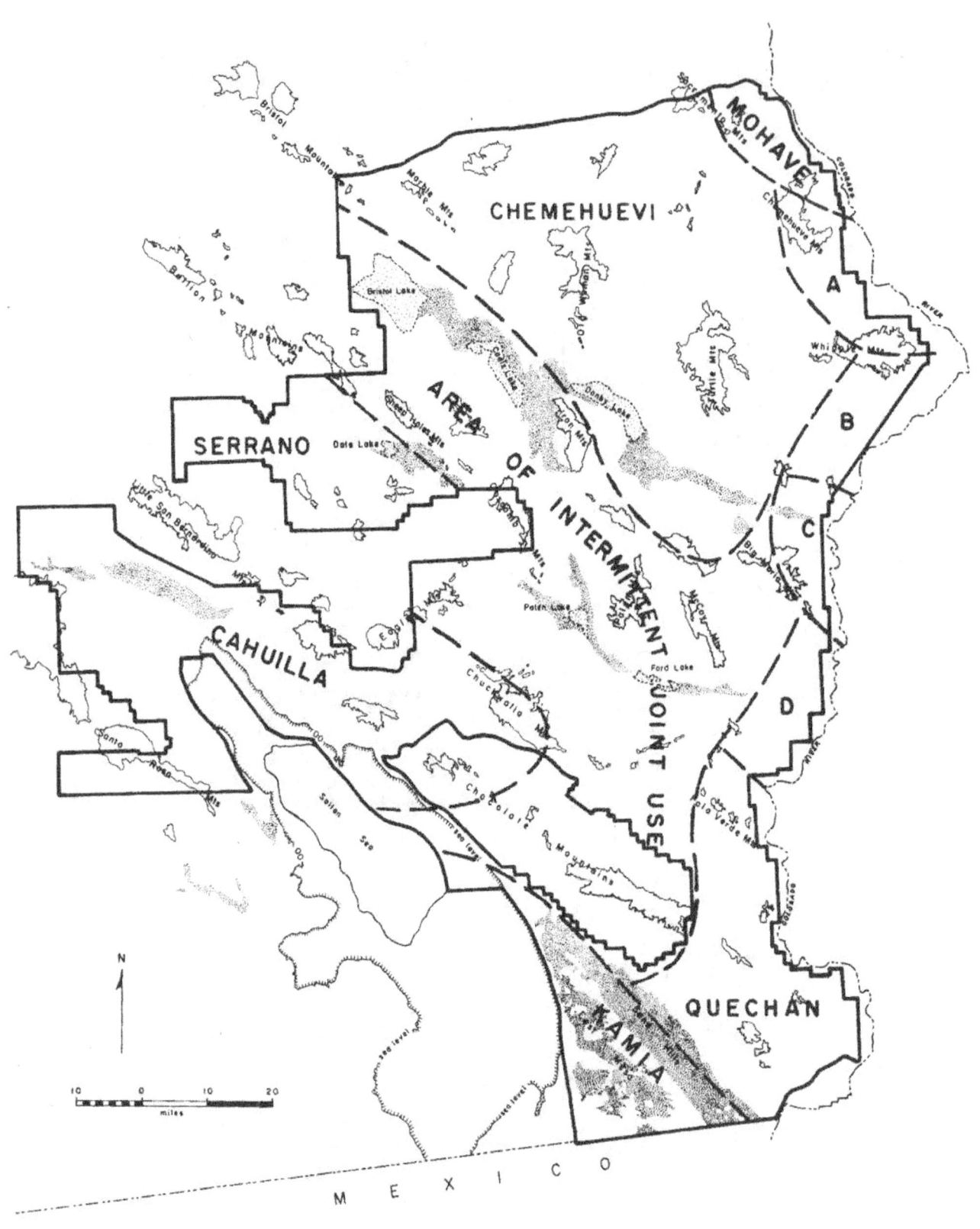

Figure 7.   Tribal Boundaries in the Colorado Desert

Chapter V. HISTORY
Elizabeth von Till Warren

The Colorado Desert portion of the California Desert Conservation Area (CDCA)
has remained one of the most sparsely populated regions of the American West.
The desolate landscape provides little in the way of natural water supply and
dependent food plants.   Until the development of the Imperial Valley irrigation
system, virtually no permanent settlement took place except on the better-watered
fringes of the desert, along the Colorado River on the east or the mountain chains
dividing the desert from the coastal plains. Despite 130 years of statehood, this
immense segment of California has retained its wild and primitive landscape, and
remains an unknown wilderness to most of the American public.

The uses to which this vast land has been put since Europeans first penetrated
California reflect the intransigent nature of the land and its climate. The story of
the Colorado Desert is embodied in two major themes: Communication and
Exploitation.   Only in the last fifty years has there been any awareness aroused of
the value of this land for its very nature: raw wilderness. Throughout most of the
modern history of human relationship to it, the land has been an obstacle to travel
and communication, and a place to exploit for its resources that can by put to use
elsewhere. Exceptions to this pattern are few: Imperial Valley irrigation (exploited
by agri-business, however, at the expense of the small farmer), national parklands
and scientific research.

These two major themes will be utilized in this report to organize the
developments in the unfolding story of the Colorado Desert. Virtually all important
historical activities can be related directly to one or the other concept.

This narrative overview is intended to provide the broad historical context of the
development of the Colorado Desert. Resources cited do not, in most cases, exhaust
the literature in a particular subject; some themes in this history have received far
more attention than others by historical researchers and writers, while others have
been virtually ignored.   At least some literature has been identified for all the
major areas of concern here.

A. Communication

    1. Trails and Wagon Roads

The history of the Colorado River itself has been well researched. Many good
publications focus upon it. A valuable, lesser known resource is Melvin T. Smith's
unpublished doctoral dissertation for Brigham Young University, "The Colorado River:
Its History in the Lower Canyon Area" (1972). Smith's comprehensive work on the
lower reaches of the river is an excellent source for the study of the eastern
boundary of the Colorado Desert.

However, the early thrust of modern history of the Colorado Desert is the story of the development of lines of communication across it. The history of the region throughout the Spanish/Mexican period from 1540 to 1848 is the history of its trails, including the few small settlements that were attempted at key spots along the way. The Spanish/Mexican period ended with the Mexican War and the signing of the treaty of Guadalupe-Hidalgo. In all the 348 years of Spanish/Mexican claim to the region, the dry and forbidding deserts of the interior were obstacles to expansion of the agricultural economy. Had it not been for the need to find an overland route between Sonora and the coastal missions which were founded beginning in 1769, even the paltry information learned in the Spanish/Mexican period would not have been accumulated.

The story commences with the first exploration of the Colorado River in 1540, when Hernando de Alarcon journeyed up the Gulf of California from Acapulco and entered the Colorado River (Cline 1963). He was apparently able to penetrate as far as the Gila River (Bolton 1949) before giving up and returning to Mexico. Melchior Diaz also travelled to the same area later in 1540, attempting to rendezvous with Alarcon, but failed (Forbes 1964; Sykes 1970). Alarcon and Diaz' reports on the bleak nature of the country, added to Coronado's failure to find the mythical Seven Cities of Cibola with their fantastic treasures, discouraged the Spanish from further exploration of the northern desert regions (Cline 1963).

The mysteries of the far northwestern frontier of New Spain were but slightly penetrated by Juan de Onate in 1604-05, travelling down the Colorado to its mouth. Despite his recommendation that a presidio be established there, no action was ever taken (Forbes 1964). Interest in this unproductive region waned until 1701 and 1702, when Father Eusebio Kino explored the area of Sonora and reached the Colorado River on two exploring trips. Kino's report that California was not an island but attached to the mainland rekindled interest in an overland route to California (Forbes 1964; Norris and Carrico 1978). However, continual Indian wars in Arizona checked this plan until 1771 (Cline 1963). With order finally restored by a new governor, Jose de Galvez, northward advance was possible once again.

A second impulse to northward expansion came from the Franciscans, who had replaced the Jesuits in New Spain in 1767. They wished to make a good showing in their new missionary field. With the founding of four coastal California missions between 1769 and 1771, it became increasingly important to establish an overland route between Sonora and Alta California (Cline 1963). The man who first demonstrated the feasibility of such a route was Fr. Francisco Hermenegildo Tomas Garces, a Franciscan monk who was in the vanguard of exploration of the area. His success was greatly due to phenomenal ability to relate to the Indians, an ability well documented by Garces' diarist, Pedro Font (Coues 1900). Garces was able to persuade many different Indians to share with him their knowledge of the routes and watering holes they used in their extensive commerce across the deserts.

In 1771, Garces led an exploring expedition from Tucson to the Colorado River, made friends with the Yumas and opened a trail between Sonora and the California frontier at Calexico (Cline 1963). A better trail was discovered in 1774 (Forbes 1964) by an expedition commanded by Juan Bautista de Anza and guided by Garces.

The de Anza party crossed from Tubac, Arizona to San Gabriel, first entering California at the mouth of the Gila River. From this point, near Yuma and Pilot Knob, the explorers pushed south into Baja California to avoid the impassable sand dunes of the area. Their trail did not cross again into California until considerably west of the planning units included in this review. Indians were vital to the success of the journey (Forbes 1964; Weinman-Roberts 1979).

De Anza and Garces led an emigrant party over the same route in 1775-76, providing much needed strength for the weak mission outposts (Forbes 1964). Garces accompanied the second expedition only as far as the mouth of the Gila. Here he separated from the party, and accompanied by Pedro Font and Sebastian Taraval, de Anza's guide of the previous year, journeyed up the Colorado to the Mohave Indian villages north of Needles. They subsequently crossed the Mojave Desert to San Gabriel and the San Joaquin Valley (Coues 1900; Van Dyke 1927). A few months later they returned by the same route, demonstrating the feasibility of contact between San Gabriel and Tubac by this circuitous route.

The Garces/de Anza successes led to the establishment of two small settlements at the Colorado River crossing. Puerto de la Concepcion (Bolton 1966) or Mision la Purisma Concepcion (Chapman 1921; Hoover, Rensch and Rensch 1966), and Mision San Pedro y San Pablo de Bicuner. These two pioneer hamlets, established in 1779, survived only a scant two years. The first mining by Europeans in the Colorado Desert was done by men based at these settlements. One mining site was at the Potholes, near the recent site of Laguna Dam, and the other was in the Cargo Muchacho Mountains (Shumway, Vredenburgh and Hartill 1980). In 1781, the Yumas rebelled against the harsh life of the missions' stations, destroyed the buildings and massacred all the men but five. Women and children were made captive. Garces was killed in the uprising (Forbes 1964; Roske 1968; Weinman-Roberts 1979). For the next two years, Spanish soldiers under Pedro Fages attempted to ransom the captives and subdue the Yumas (Priestley 1913), but finally, in 1783, use of the Yuma route was discontinued. In 1786, the route was made officially off-limits to any one (Forbes 1964).

Minor excursions were made into the CDCA in the years following the closure of the trail. No significant entradas were made, however, until the 1820's, and then a second route was opened up. By this time, also, the governing of the California frontier had passed to Mexico, which had thrown off Spanish rule in 1821.

In 1821, a party of Cocomaricopa Indians arrived at San Gabriel and announced they had come in only six days' journey from the Colorado. The new (to the Spanish) trail was known as the Halchidoma Trail (Forbes 1964) or the Cocomaricopa Trail (Norris and Carrico 1978). It began east of Blythe and approximated Interstate 10 across the Chuckwalla Valley, through the Mecca-Indio area and Coachella Valley to San Gorgonio Pass. The Mexican authorities in California immediately saw the possibilities of this trail for a safe mail route, and sent Jose Romero and Jose Maria Estudillo to scout it in 1823 (Bean and Mason 1962). They penetrated deep into the Imperial Valley, but were turned back because the trail was only suitable for foot traffic and lacked sufficient forage for horses. In late 1824, Romero and Estudillo again set out for the Colorado and were successful in reaching the river near Blythe (Forbes 1964). Subsequently, it was adjudged that the Yuma Road was superior and little further interest developed in the Maricopa Trail during the Mexican period. The westernmost end of the trail was utilized by the Mexicans as a way to the Salton Sea salt beds, where there were some salt mining operations (GLO plate 1856, Norris and Carrico 1978).

Activity increased along the Yuma Route following its reopening by Romero in 1823 (Forbes 1964). In 1824-25, Santiago Arguello discovered a short cut via Carrizo Corridor that significantly reduced the length of the road (Norris and Carrico 1978), and by 1827 a route from New Mexico and northern Sonora to California had opened up. Expeditions along the trail included trapping, government couriers, mail, and overland emigrants. In an effort to provide support to travellers, the Mexican government in 1826 established a small outpost called Laguna Chapala. The post, located near Brawley, lasted only four months. It is significant as the first attempt to establish a European outpost in the Colorado Desert away from the river (Farris 1977; Norris and Carrico 1979; Warren and Roske 1978).

Throughout the remaining years of Mexican hegemony, the Yuma Road was used heavily for overland immigration and commerce (Warren 1974), conducted primarily by pack train. The Mexican period came to an abrupt close when the U.S. defeated Mexico in Alta California in 1846 and gained half of Mexico's territory by the Treaty of Guadalupe-Hidalgo in 1848. American military forces guided by Kit Carson and commanded by General Stephen Kearney crossed the Colorado Desert en route to Southern California in 1846 and 1847, marching by way of the Yuma Crossing and Pilot Knob through Mexico and re-entering at approximately Calexico. They proceeded to Vallecito via the Sacketts Well area and Carrizo Corridor (Norris and Carrico 1978). Two months later, the Mormon Battalion rolled in, bringing very large wagons which had necessitated some changes in the original Sonora Road (Tyler 1964). The new road was heavily used beginning in 1849, the first year of the California Gold Rush (Foreman 1939).

The job of surveying and marking the boundary between the U.S. and Mexico began in 1849. The portion from San Diego to the Gila River took one year, beginning in June 1849 (Bartlett 1854; U.S. Government 1857). His assignment to the Boundary Survey brought Lt. William H. Emory into direct, personal contact with the thousands of overland emigrants who began to pour into California from the east via the Yuma route. Emory's graphic accounts contained in his correspondence depict the extreme hardships encountered by the unprepared, eager gold seekers. The U.S. government was finally forced to detail soldiers to escort the people through the worst portions of the trail, and establish two camps along the way as well. Camp Calhoun was a temporary camp on the California side of the Colorado River crossing at the mouth of the Gila River; later it was named Camp Yuma and finally, Fort Yuma, in 1852 (Conkling and Conkling 1947). The second outpost was named Camp Salvation, and its precise locality is obscure. It was at or near Calexico, where the Yuma Road from the east recrossed the border from Mexico into the U.S. (Conkling and Conkling 1947; Foreman 1939; Hoover, Rensch and Rensch 1966).

Lt. R. B. Marcy was assigned to escort overland parties to California; this fascinating story is found in Foreman (1939). So much use of the trail was made following 1848 that within a few years stages began to ply the route between California and Arizona and points east. Early stage lines include Swacaffer and Warner's of 1854, the San Diego and San Antonio Mail Line with its "Jackass Mail" route, 1857, and the Butterfield Overland, 1858. The stage lines maintained their own relay stations, freeing the army from this unwelcome obligation. Only Fort Yuma became a permanent post, with troops also maintained at the California end at Vallecito in San Diego County until 1854 (Heilbron 1936).

The only other early American outpost in the Colorado Desert was at the Colorado River, at Pilot Knob, south of the Gila crossing. Here the road veered south into Mexico to avoid the extensive sand dunes along the border. Pilot Knob or Pilot Peak (Cowperthwait Map 1850) was the site of an 1848 ferry station called Fort Defiance (Conkling and Conkling 1947). The station survived but a short time.

The men operating it angered the local Indians, were massacred and the ferry returned to Indian control. In 1850, Louis Jaeger (or Yaeger, Yager) bought the franchise from the Indians, and moved the ferry five miles upstream, where he operated the ferry for nearly 30 years.

Impact on the desert from the emigration activity up to this time was strong along the trail and minimal to none elsewhere. Animals ate off the vegetation and any wood available was used for fires. A few wells were dug, but for the most part, the activities of the people were not nearly as devastating as the natural forces the people encountered. Wells were often completely and quickly obscured by sifting sands or flash floods. The New River of the early accounts was an overflow channel of the Colorado River which headed northward into the Salton Sink. Periodically this channel would be active, washing away some sites or changing the topography in their vicinity. In 1849, the river flooded, providing much water in standing ponds, which were utilized by overland emigrants. By 1853, however, these pools were already drying up (Farris 1977).

The Butterfield Stage Lines, in an attempt to provide a chain of reliable water sources and relay stations on the desert between Vallecito and Yuma, excavated several wells, but outside the boundaries of the planning units under discussion here.

A second route to Yuma was discovered early in the American period. Dr. Isaac W. Smith of San Gorgonio Pass and a small party surveyed a route down the east shore of the Salton Sink in 1857, for San Bernardino County. The road went via El Toro (Torres), Indian Wells, Palm Desert, Palm Springs, Windy Point (Whitewater), and Cabezon. This route would in time become very popular because it was much shorter between Los Angeles and Yuma. Eventually, it would take away most of the traffic from the Vallecito route. However, in the early years of the American period, the Smith road was not feasible because of the paucity of water between Dos Palmas and Yuma. Development of water sources did not occur until the construction of the railroad in 1876-77 (Warren and Roske 1978).

A very important trans-desert route was developed via the Mojave River and a chain of springs extending to the Needles area. However, this trail was north of the Colorado Desert boundaries of this project, and only Needles itself was involved. It is therefore excluded from this report.

A different destination for the second major cross-Colorado Desert trail was the Bradshaw Route (Warren and Roske 1978). Francis Johnston has written extensively on the development of this route, which parallels the old Cocomaricopa Trail of the Spanish/Mexican period (Johnston 1972 and 1976). The route as developed by Bradshaw served the mining camps developing near La Paz, Arizona. Bradshaw opened a ferry near Providence Point, opposite Olivia and Olive City (later Ehrenburg), Arizona. The Bradshaw route used sections of road pioneered earlier by Brown and Frink in supplying the Washington Survey of the 1850's (Warren and Roske 1978).

The Frink Brothers also developed a trail that was well used in the early mining days of La Paz, connecting that remote area with supply points in California. This route, more northerly than the Bradshaw Road although also using the Salt Creek Pass between the Orocopia and Chocolate mountains, did not turn toward Tabeseca Tank as did the Bradshaw Road. Frink's road ended six miles north of La Paz, at another ferry which was begun by Frink but became known as the Hamilton Ferry. A description of the route and stops along it is contained in Warren and Roske

(1978).

Another route was known across the Colorado Desert in the early 1860's, but its secret was so well kept that it did not become an effective route for desert travel. Paulino Weaver, who lived in San Gorgonio Pass, was apparently shown a route by friendly Morongo Valley Indians among whom he lived for many years. The road headed up the Morongo Valley to Yucca Valley, to Twentynine Palms, and then apparently in a more or less direct easterly line to the Colorado River. The trail is not well represented in the literature (Belden 1956; Bancroft Maps, 1863 and 1868).

Minor roads connecting the eastern ends of these trails were put into use early (Warren and Roske 1978). The discovery of mineral resources and their subsequent development also provided stimulus to lesser roads, connecting the deposits with the major overland routes and/or the Colorado River. Good early maps detailing these data are: Bancroft's Maps of California 1863 and 1868; Map of the Colorado Mines 1863; Map of California and Nevada 1887, General Land Office maps, various dates; McAllister 1905; Rand McNally's California and Nevada Map from their Business Atlas of 1876; Rueger's Automobile and Mines Road Map of Southern California 1903; Thurston's Desert Map 1915, and Automobile Club of Southern California (ACSC) maps of various dates. A summary of these is contained in Warren and Roske 1978.

2. Steamboating

Prior to the actual construction of railroads across the desert, a great deal of attention was given to the possibility of providing supplies to the remote interior via the Colorado River. The story of steamboating began with the assembling of the Uncle Sam at Port Isabel in 1852 and her use over the next two years between Yuma and the mouth of the river. The side-wheeler General Jessup was next brought to the river by Capt. George A. Johnson, and plied the river as far as Black Canyon by 1854. Johnson developed the trade, serving upriver points such as Castle Dome, Ehrenberg, Aubry, Camp Mohave and Hardyville. In January 1858, the General Jessup unexpectedly met up with Beale's party working on the road that crossed from Arizona to California at the Needles. Johnson ferried Beale across the river, a service that undoubtedly saved Beale many hours of hard work. Beale described this extraordinary scene:

> ...our party was transported at once, with all our baggage, to the other side....I brought the camels with me, and as they stood on the bank, surrounded by hundreds of wild unclad savages, and mixed with these the dragoons of my escort, and the steamer slowly revolving her wheels preparatory to a start, it was a curious and interesting picture (Beale in Drago 1967:210).

The opening of the river to steam navigation brought a new spate of activity at landing sites along the river. Remote mines could now be worked profitably, with their ores shipped via steam packet to smelters in industrial centers. The landings began to grow into important supply centers, but the entire enterprise was doomed to only a brief place in the sun. Railroads were operated by men determined to stamp out any competition. The Colorado River steamers definitely were competitive, and in 1869 the Colorado Steam Navigation Company became part of the Southern Pacific holdings (Drago 1967; Harrington 1962; Roske 1968). For a few years following completion of the railroad in 1877, the line delivered goods at Yuma for shipment upriver, but not enough traffic was generated to keep the steamers busy. Boats no longer brought supplies to Port Isabel, and that shipping point completely died out. The railroads built branch lines to remote parts of the desert, and when the Laguna Dam was built on the Colorado in 1908, the steamer traffic ended forever.

The significance of steamboating to the history of the Colorado Desert lies in the brief stimulus to road and mining camp development in the interior that was served by Colorado River boat landing sites. Once steamboating was discontinued, much of this impetus to development was deflected to connections between the mines and the railheads, changing the pattern of road development in the desert. Development of new ore bodies was retarded until well into the 20th century, when short line railroads made remoter desert area accessible (Norris and Carrico 1978).

3. Railroads

During the 1850's, a great battle waged in Congress to adopt a route for a railroad to connect the east and west coasts. Congress ordered the U.S. Army to conduct surveys along selected geographical parallels to evaluate possible routes. In the Colorado Desert planning units, surveys were run along the 32nd and 35th parallels. Most of the work along the 35th parallel was conducted north of the boundaries of this portion of the CDCA, following the line of the Mohave Indian Trail. In a few instances, however, portions of these surveys penetrated areas under study here.

Lt. R.S. Williamson of the U.S. Corps of Topographical Engineers in 1853 explored the route to the Yuma area from Vallecito. Lt. Parke was a member of a side party sent out by Williamson to explore the San Gorgonio Pass area. Parke penetrated as far as San Felipe Creek, despite lack of Indian guides beyond Point of Rocks, and returned to the main party at Warner's Ranch. W.P. Blake, geologist, accompanied the Williamson expedition and named many geographical points. He also recognized the extinct Lake Cahuilla from the evidence of ancient shore lines and high water marks. The report of the Williamson survey constituted Volume V of the Railroad Surveys. Very valuable data concerning the country, climate and Native American population are found in these accounts (Parke 1854, 1855; Williamson 1856).

The 32nd parallel route was explored in 1854 by Lt. Parke, between San Diego and Yuma, and is found in Volume VII of the Railroad Surveys. No railroad was built along either of these routes for many years. Competing economic interests and political considerations tied up construction in the region. It was not until 1877 that the Colorado Desert was transsected by steel rails, and then the line was built from San Gorgonio Pass to Yuma via the eastern shore of the Salton Sink, along the line of the Isaac Smith survey of the 1850s. The railroad ended at Yuma and was not built farther east until 1882, when a land deal was worked out with the Texas and Pacific Railroad and the line was then built as far as El Paso. Information on this railroad construction project is found in Bancroft 1890; Daggett 1922; and LaFuze 1971.

A mailroad corresponding to the 35th parallel route was completed by the Atlantic and Pacific Railroad Company in 1883. The line was constructed along a route surveyed in 1868 by Gen. William J. Palmer for the eastern division of the Union Pacific Railroad. Palmer discovered the natural passage for a railroad to be twenty to thirty miles south of the Old Government Road across the Mojave Desert. The line passes through the Colorado Desert along only a small portion of the northern boundary of the planning units. Palmer also surveyed a line connecting San Diego with this route via Amboy, southwesterly to Morongo and San Gorgonio passes. This line was never built. Sources for this railroad include Bell 1870; Palmer's report 1869; and Myrick 1963. Myrick contains a detailed account of the problems that plagued railroad construction because of rival bids for the commerce and the privilege of opening up new territory to rail traffic.

The 32nd parallel route, between San Diego and Yuma, remained unused until the 20th century. In 1854, a San Diego and Gila River route was surveyed via the San Dieguito River, and in 1867 a proposal was made to join up with Fremont's Memphis and El Paso route via the 32nd parallel. In 1870, the San Diego and Fort Yuma Railroad was surveyed through Jacumba, but no action was taken. A rail connection between San Diego and Yuma was finally constructed by the San Diego and Arizona Railroad via Carrizo Gorge. Construction began in 1908 but was not completed until 1919. Virgil Wyatt's essay on railroad construction in San Diego County is the source of these details (Heilbron 1936).

A network of branch lines and spurs gradually grew up between the main transcontinental routes and important mining camps. After the irrigation of Imperial Valley, spurs for agricultural communities also were constructed. These short lines more properly belong in the section below on Exploitation of the Desert. The impact of the trans-desert routes was immediate and vital to the development of other modes of travel (automobile). The watering stops constructed every few miles, the maintainance crews stationed on the remote desert, all provided havens of safety for the venturesome auto traveller of the early 20th century. Prior to the invention of the horseless carriage, even wagon traffic moved to roads paralleling the rails, since the water and assistance available there greatly decreased the hazards of desert travel. Only as automobiles became capable of travelling longer distances with less gasoline, could the early automobile roads begin to develop short cuts between railroad stops. Sources of information on these early railroad towns include: Myrick 1963; Bard 1973; Croffut's Guides to Travel, various dates; many maps, both ACSC and others; and Warren and Roske 1978 (to 1880).

4. Military Outposts

Military outposts connected with communication in the Colorado Desert declined in the late 19th century. The post at Fort Yuma was maintained until 1861, then abandoned temporarily at the outbreak of the Civil War. In April 1862 it was briefly regarrisoned by Col. James E. Carleton (Conkling and Conkling 1947) during his campaign with the California column. Following the war, small detachments were assigned to Fort Yuma until 1877, when the Southern Pacific Railroad (SPRR) extended its line to Yuma. A few soldiers remained at the Fort until 1884, when the reservation was turned over to the Interior Department. Later it became part of the Yuma Reservation and was used for an Indian school (Conkling and Conkling 1947).

5. Telegraph Line

In 1873, a military telegraph line was run from San Diego to Fort Yuma, by a direct route through the mountains rather than by way of the established roads to Yuma. This line closely followed the boundary with Mexico, running through via Mountain Springs paralleling a pack route that had been in use since 1851 (Heilbron 1936). The military telegraph used the old tollhouse at Mountain Springs that had been constructed in 1865 in connection with road building. A military road was also constructed at the same time, paralleling the telegraph line (Heilbron 1936).

A second telegraph line also was constructed paralleling the railroad to Yuma in 1877. This line was built to serve the railroad but also was available for public use.

6. Mail Service

Non-military federal activities in the 1850-70s in the Colorado Desert focused on mail carrying and distribution. Mail routes were subcontractd to private carriers during this period. Mail lines which ran through the Colorado Desert planning units in the early years of the American period included the short-lived Swacaffer and Warner of San Diego (1854), the San Antonio and San Diego Mail of 1857, and the Butterfield Overland route of 1858 (Conkling and Conkling 1947). The Butterfield Stage carried the mails through the desert via the Yuma route until 1861, when the operation was suspended because of the Civil War. Thereafter, the mails were carried by stage over the central route until after the war. In 1869-70, mails were again routed by stage over the southern routes. Fort Yuma was again a distribution point, but the days were numbered for this mode of transport for the mails. In 1877, after the SPRR extended its line to Yuma, the mails were moved by rail and not by wagon or stage (Conkling and Conkling 1947),

Local mail delivery developed as the area became settled. The paucity of settlements is reflected in the designation of official routes for mail carriers. The first routes in the planning units discussed here are described in Frickstad (1955). A map of the postal system in California and Nevada was published by the Postmaster General of the U.S. on March 1, 1910 (Von Haake, 1910), and is interesting for a picture of the sparse population reflected for the Colorado Desert. Mails and the telegraph were the only means of rapid message communication across the desert until the development of the long distance telephone system. Originally this was accomplished by cable, and the first lines did not cross the Colorado, but the Mojave Desert (Davenport 1963). Recent technology using microwave relays has now been instituted, with long distance telecommunications (both telephone and television) available throughout the desert (Norris and Carrico 1978). These methods of communication represent the culmination of the 200 years of effort expended in bridging the Colorado desert with communication networks.

7. Automobile Roads

Automobile travel across and within the Colorado Desert area first developed using existing wagon roads. These roads, by turns rutted, sandy, muddy or rocky, proved too difficult for the more restricted capabilities of the horseless carriages of the period. Consequently, automobile roads were demanded by the touring public early in the 20th century.

In Southern California, motorists banded together in 1900 to form a club of automobile owners. The club issued maps to members, and published a monthly magazine, Touring Topics (1909), now renamed Westways. These magazines provide an invaluable resource for understanding the hazards of early auto travel, the routes recommended to points of interest, and the equipment available to the motorist. Edna Perkin's adventures chronicled in White Heart of Mojave (1922) is a good portrayal of the difficulties of auto travel of the period.

The Automobile Club of Southern California maintains a good archive of its old maps at its headquarters in Los Angeles. The earliest map especially for automobiles that this author is aware of is an independent map published in 1903 by Henry Rueger. The ACSC first tour book was issued in 1909, and contained nearly 100 maps (Mathison 1968). Each county also issued maps, as did private parties. County roads were surveyed by county road crews and construction of county road systems was accomplished by means of local taxes. The California Department of Engineering paved its first auto road in 1912 and began to issue maps as early as 1918, and state funds were expended for highway construction for wagons even earlier (Cleland 1918). Federal funds had been used in construction of the Old Government Road through the Mojave Desert, north of the planning units that comprise the Colorado Desert. The federal interstate road network began to develop prior to World War I, although the roads were little more than dirt tracks crossing the desert that bore ambitious names: Ocean to Ocean Highway, Midland Trail, etc. As roads were broken through away from the railroad tracks, providing shortcuts between small railroad communities, service areas were sometimes constructed especially to provide automobile assistance (Norris and Carrico 1978). By the mid-1920s, these communities were growing in number and size, although travel along the roads was still relatively hazardous. The U.S. government helped to make travel safer by publishing at various times Water-Supply Papers that detailed the routes between water holes and documented the conditions of the roadways (Brown 1920; Mendenhall 1909; Thompson 1927).

One of the most unique stories of motoring across the Colorado Desert revolves around construction of a roadway across the sand dunes in the eastern end of Imperial County near the Mexican border. These dunes were impassable for animals and wheeled traffic alike, and had caused the diversion into Mexico of the old roads of the Spanish/Mexican and early American period that connected Yuma with the California coast. Since the construction of the Southern Pacific Railroad, and the construction of a road paralleling those tracks along the eastern shore of the Salton Sink, most traffic had been directed into Los Angeles. San Diego, at the turn of the century, cast about for ways of attracting more business, and the lack of a good road between San Diego and the Colorado River was one of the more obvious problems.

In 1901, San Diego Chamber of Commerce members determined to do something about this situation. They raised $60,000 to construct a road by way of the old Star Mail Route through Devil's Canyon to Imperial Valley. Only $47,000 was ultimately used, and the remainder was returned to the subscribers. The Mountain Spring Grade was constructed with these funds, and some miles of primitive plank roads across the sand dunes.

By 1910, owners of the growing number of automobiles demanded some improvements to the plank road over the dunes. The county then constructed a "brush road," by spreading brush over the worst spots of the trail to keep the wheels from sinking into the sand. In 1913, the Automobile Club of Southern California called a convention to consider a better road from El Centro to Yuma. When San Diego agreed to furnish the lumber for a new plank road across the dunes, the road was then designed to serve San Diego. Imperial County furnished food for the workers and paid the freight for the materials. Towns along the way sent workers to a central labor camp constructed at Gray's Well; the daily labor crew varied from 10 to 50, but the work was completed in six months.

The plank road then consisted of two parallel tracks of 2" X 8" pine planks spiked to 2" X 6" ties 8" long. The result was a wooden track providing two feet of width for each tire. Occasional turnouts were constructed so cars could pass. By 1916, this road had worn out and was replaced by a solid plank road nailed to heavy cross ties and bound with strips of iron. The surface was coated with asphalt and sand, making a corduroy road. The plank road this time was built in sections, twenty or thirty feet long. There was no excavation for this roadway, and the sections could be moved at will with a four-horse team, so that the planks could follow the constantly changing contour of the dunes. If the road was about to be covered with sand, the maintenance crews would move the road.

In 1917, the road had to be replaced again. This road lasted until 1924, when a redwood road was constructed. As time went on, the road became so corrugated it resembled a washboard. Tires blew out frequently on it, despite the maximum speed of 12 miles per hour. Maintenance of the road became very costly, averaging $35,000 a year in the 1920's.

Finally, in 1926, state engineers developed a blow-over design. This roadway was built on an embankment that allowed the sand to blow over it. The highway surface itself was paved but would not be covered by the sand because of the elevation of the roadbed. Highway 80 was then paved with asphaltic concrete on this elevated bed. By 1926, the new highway was completed. Some portions of the old plank road were used as a frontage road for a while, but the old wooden highway passed into memory (Warren and Roske 1978: 11-88,9).

In the 1930s, one of the first interstate highways to be paved was U.S. 66 (now Interstate 40), along the northern edge of the Colorado Desert planning units. U.S. 60-70 (later I-10) between Indio and Blythe was paved in 1936 (Norris and Carrico 1978). Sources for the federal highway information are cited by Norris and Carrico; California State Highways construction and development can be found in Fenzke (1980). Bard (1973) details the impact of the growth in interstate highways on local service area; Norris and Carrico (1978) also include some of these data. Mathison (1968) documents the development of the ACSC.

   8. Airports

Air travel in and over the Colorado Desert has not developed as a significant aspect of communication. Most of the important airports have been constructed in conjuction with 20th century military bases in the area (see below, Exploitation). Small facilities serve the various communities of the desert, with Palm Springs particularly generating a fair amount of traffic because of its status as a health and recreational resort for upper income people. However, major airports for interstate and international travel developed in better populated area: Yuma, Mexicali (Mexico), San Diego, and Los Angeles. No major airports have developed in the desert.

B. Exploitation

Exploitation of the desert has taken a variety of forms, some extractive and some non-extractive: mining, farming/ranching, water control and distribution, energy production, military training grounds and weapons testing, scientific research, recreation/health spas, and small tract development. Management of these multiple uses has generated increasing response on the part of the federal agencies responsible for the desert. This section will outline these developments.

1. Federal Management

The federal government, in 1850 in control of the vast area of former Mexican lands in the west, first had to define the boundaries of the new territory and then survey and map it. These two major tasks represent the first actions on the part of the U.S. government to manage the resource today labelled the Colorado Desert. These activities were essential to providing for the orderly transfer of the land from public to private ownership. The Mexican boundary survey has been discussed above in Section I. The eastern border of California in the Colorado Desert area was the Colorado River, and therefore no boundary surveys were necessary. Because no land grants from the Spanish and Mexican periods impinged on the Colorado Desert planning units, the activities of the Land Claims Commission in the early 1850s also had no bearing on this region.

The process of surveying and mapping the Colorado Desert began in 1852, when Henry Washington and a small party of surveyors ascended the San Bernardino Mountains and established the San Bernardino Base and Meridian. In 1854 and 1857, Washington extended this line to the Colorado River, working his way through uncharted territory all the way. In the process, he passed through the northern half of the Colorado Desert planning units, and named several places. Washington used wagons in his work, and was assisted by Hank Brown, who later became an important resident of the San Gorgonio Pass area (Haenszel 1974). Brown later began a road across the desert toward Blythe, and apparently made good use of the knowledge he gained in working with the Washington survey party (Warren and Roske 1978).

Contracts were also let to other surveyors to map the California desert. GLO maps (on file in the BLM office in Riverside) detail the area and were the first official maps produced for the desert. Later, however, surveyors had trouble finding the monuments and stakes set up by these first parties. Even at the time many questions were raised regarding whether or not the work had actually been done in the field (Harrington 1962; Warren and Roske 1978).

Also in the early 1850s, the U.S. government sent Indian Commissioners into the field. Although not authorized to make any commitments to the Native Americans, the Commissioner set aside (illegally) large tracts of land for reservations (Norris and Carrico 1978). One such tract covers part of the western portion of the planning units of concern here. However, these areas were never fully developed as rerservations, although the Torres-Martinez and Agua Caliente (Palm Springs) reservations were eventually set aside from the larger reserves delineated by the Indian Commission. Once the Indian population was confined to reservations, the remainder of the lands could be made available for mining, ranching, and other uses

(Roske 1968).

A piece of federal legislation that had far-reaching effect on California was the Railroad Act of 1866, providing land grants to the Southern Pacific Railroad which was supposed to build a rail line linking up with the Atlantic and Pacific Railroad that was laying track from the east. Alternate sections for 20 miles on either side of the track were bestowed on the railroad in return for constructing the lines. This checkerboard pattern of land ownership has greatly affected the utilization of these lands in the period since these land grants were made (Lavender 1972).

Water resource management was addressed early by the federal government. Following the disastrous floods of 1905 which bankrupted the privately-owned California Development Company, the federal government was asked to resolve arguments over how much water could be removed from the river by any state. There were not only interstate but international ramifications, the supply to Mexico being a prime consideration as well. The federally sponsored Colorado River Compact of 1922 recognized the division of the Colorado River Basin into an upper and a lower region, and limited the consumption of the water in each basin. While the intent was to provide for orderly management of this limited resource, the negotiators of the compact have over-appropriated the available waters. The potential for law suits and reallocation is significant, as projects upstream from the Imperial Valley come on line and remove their allotment from the stream. The quality of the water provided is also of continuing concern; irrigation results in highly polluted return streamflows, making the water less and less usable without significant treatment   (BLM Imported Water Report, n.d.; Lavender 1972).

The Newlands Act of 1902 should have had more impact on the development of the state's irrigated lands than it has had. Under provisions of the act, lands irrigated by public reclamation projects could only be claimed up to 160 acres for individual or company ownership; 320 acres was permitted under community property laws for married couples. This law was very unpopular with developers of the irrigated lands, and in the years before the construction of the Boulder Canyon Project, Californians pressured the Department of the Interior to waive this rule. In 1933 they succeeded (Lavender 1972). The result has been the shouldering aside of small businesses in favor of corporate farms of giant size. A suit was brought in the courts to force the Imperial Valley landowners to comply with the regulations of the Newlands Act, but the decision handed down in 1980 supports the large landholder.

Management of the land itself was the province of first the General Land Office, and later the Department of Agriculture's Grazing Administration. Until the passage of the Taylor Grazing Act of 1934, however, no control was exercised over the Colorado Desert lands. This act had virtually no impact on the region either; it was not until the responsibility for managing the desert came under the control of the Bureau of Land Management in 1946 that the first attempts were made at range management. Since that time, the BLM also has been engaged, by order of Congress, in evaluating lands for their "uses,", and classifying them for different types of management based upon the values recognized. The current project of producing a plan for management of the entire California Desert Conserevation Area is the latest in a series of management alternatives sought by Congress (BLM Draft Plan 1980).

Other federal legislation that has had great impact on the desert lands is the Small Tract Act of 1938. This Act authorized the sale or lease of not more than five acres of public lands classified as chiefly valuable for home, cabin, health, convalescent, recreational or business sites, subject only to the reservation to the U.S. of all oil, gas and other mineral deposits. This is the legislation responsible for the small tract booms of the '40s and '50s, the so-called "Jackrabbit" housing (Lavender 1972; Norris and Carrico 1978).

Mineral resources had been overlooked by the Congress in specifying disposal procedure for public lands. Consequently the Gold Rush of 1849 was held in a wide-open field, and the forty-niners and their successors framed their own regulations (Dana and Krueger 1958). These regulations were incorporated into the federal acts of 1866, 1870 and 1872 providing for the sale of placer claims at $2.50 per acre and of lode claims at $5.00 per acre. In 1920, the Mineral Leasing Act stopped the sale of lands containing coal, phosphate, sodium, oil, oil shale or gas, and placed them under a leasing procedure instead. Potash and sulfur were added later to this list. The Materials Disposal Act of 1947 provided for the disposal of lands containing sand, gravel, clay and timber.

The Boulder Canyon Project, authorized by Congress in 1928, has had the most significant and direct impact on the Colorado Desert. It provided for the damming of the river at Boulder Canyon, construction of the All-American and Coachella canals, an extensive subsidiary irrigation system for the desert, and the delivery of Colorado River water via aqueduct to Los Angeles (Lavender 1972).

2. Mining

An excellent, well documented survey of the mining resources of the entire California Desert Conservation Area is contained in Shumway, Vredenburgh and Hartill, 1980. Only highlights of the developments in the Colorado Desert are incorporated here; readers are referred to this monograph for more detailed discussion.

Exploitation of the Colorado Desert mineral resources began very early, in 1780-81 at Cargo Muchacho and Potholes districts along the Colorado River. These gold mining activities were associated with the missions at the Gila River crossing. With the destruction of these outposts, the mining activities also were suspended until the late 1870s.

Salt was recovered from the Salton Sink in the 1820s, but little is known of the operation (Norris and Carrico 1978). In the planning units that comprise the Colorado Desert, no documented instances of other mining activities in the Spanish/Mexican period have been found, although there are numerous accounts of early arrastres and shafts representing Mexican or Spanish mining techniques (Shumway, Vredenburgh and Hartill 1980).

In the American period, discovery of the first claims usually was incidental to travel across the desert to rich diggings elsewhere. The La Paz and Castle Dome booms in western Arizona attracted large numbers of miners from California and up from Sonora, Mexico in the early 1860s. These areas were poorly known at the time and travelling to the mines constituted a great adventure. Interesting information on the state of knowledge of the time is contained in maps published by Bancroft and DeGroot in 1863 depicting the routes to the mines. Fairchild (1933) documented a trip to the Colorado Mines in 1862 that provides a fine portrayal of travel across the desert.

Prospects recognized in the first two decades of travel and exploration in the desert include the Mule Mountains (1861), McCoy and Maria Mountains (1862), the Turtle Mountains (1862-65), Eagle Mountain District (1865), the Paymaster (1867), Old Woman Mountains (1873), the area around Twentynine Palms (1873), the Cargo Muchacho (1877), and the Picacho (1879). The Dale and Virginia Dale claims were discovered about a decade later. In some instances, the mines may have been worked earlier, possibly by Mexican or Spanish miners, but authentication is lacking (Shumway, Vredenburgh and Hartill 1980).

The big boom years in the Colorado Desert were between 1870 and 1890. The slow start is undoubtedly due in great measure to the lack of accessibilty of the mines, a condition that partly reflects the control over the growth of the region that was exercised by the railroad interests. Many of the previously listed mining areas continued to be worked, and major new finds were made. Of these, Tumco (Hedges) is probably the most significant in terms of values recovered, although Stedman, Orange Blossom and Bagdad were also important gold properties. Eagle Mountain provided and continues to yield valuable iron deposits.

20th century finds of continuing value included other non-precious minerals. Gypsum at the Midland site was developed by U.S. Gypsum from claims made as early as 1904. The boom years for the plant were the 1920s and 1930s. Other deposits of value include fluorite (Red Bluff), manganese (McCoy Mountains), uranium (Maria Mountains), and copper (McCoy). Gypsum and salt were taken from Bristol Dry Lake in operations that began at the turn of the century. Salt mining continues today at the site (Myrick 1963).

The impact of these activities on the desert ranges and valleys has been great. Some of the most significant historic sites of the Colorado Desert are the remains of mining camps. The evidence of the mining can be clearly seen despite the decades that have elapsed since many of these properties were worked. Vegetative changes occurred where activities disrupted the typical plant communities, but the most long-lasting effect has been the excavation of miles of tunnels, the construction of headframes and other facilities, the residences and water systems, and the roads and railroads constructed to serve the needs of mining.

Railroad branches and spurs built to serve the mines in the Colorado Desert planning units include the Cadiz-Parker line from the Santa Fe road, completed in 1910, the Ludlow and Southern, serving Stedman and the Bagdad-Chase properties, and the Amboy-Saltus line (Myrick 1963). This line actually was composed of two short spurs that brought gypsum and salt from the collecting ponds at Bristol Dry Lake to the main line of the Santa Fe. The gypsum operation shut down in 1924, and U.S. Gypsum Company moved the equipment and rails to the Midland site on the Blythe-Ripley Branch of the Santa Fe. A 1-1/2 mile long rail line was constructed there to carry the gypsum to the main line.

3. Farming/Ranching

Although cattle and sheep were moved through the area as early as 1776 with the De Anza expedition, and the Yuma route was heavily used in the Mexican period for the movement of animals between California and Sonora, Arizona and New Mexico (Warren 1974), no ranches were established in the area until the American period. The only exception to this picture is the abortive settlement at Yuma between 1779 and 1781. Some farms were established then in the bottomlands along the river, but with the destruction of the settlement, this activity ceased (Roske 1968). The paucity of water on the desert itself discouraged any thought of farming. Agricultural development would only flourish when water could be imported in significant quantities. The Coachella Valley, however, began to develop an agricultural industry, prior to importation of water, by means of drilling artesian wells (Harrington 1962; Norris and Carrico 1978).

Beginning in the first decade of the 20th century, the Coachella Valley's farmers planted extensive date, fig, and grape acreage (Harrington 1962). Towns that developed apace with the agricultural growth were Thermal, Mecca, Indio and Coachella. By 1918, however, the water table was seriously depleted, stimulating the formation of the Coachella Valley County Water District to promote water conservation and replenish the underground basin. This organization cooperated with the Imperial Irrigation District to develop the All-American Canal (see below) and the Coachella Valley extension. Now, the high salinity of the Colorado River waters used in the Coachella Valley has become a problem. This situation is expected to be alleviated with the delivery of State Water Project allotments in 1990 (BLM Report on Imported Water, 1978).

4. Water control and distribution

Exploitation of the desert's agricultural potential was dependent upon major irrigation schemes. The Colorado River was regarded very early in the American period as a possible source for the necessary water. In 1859, Dr. Oliver M. Wozencraft planned reclamation of the desert by importing water to the Salton Sink area, then dry. He secured from the California State Legislature all state rights to 1600 square miles of land, patents to be issued on completion of the reclamation work. The project was sidetracked by the Civil War, but his engineer, Ebenezer Hadley, county surveyor for San Diego County, recommended a canal location practically identical to one adopted 40 years later (de Stanley 1966). In 1873, Dr. J.P. Widney, an army surgeon, published some articles in Overland Monthly urging the flooding of the Salton Sea area, but he was not taken seriously (de Stanley 1966).

The army, however, did investigate the possibility of irrigating the desert with Colorado River water. In 1876, Lt. Eric Bergland arrived in the Colorado Desert from the east, crossed the river at Yuma and travelled to Algodon Stage Station. There he split his command, sending one party to the mud volcanoes near Mt. Purdy, below the border, and the other along the regular stage road toward Los Angeles. His duties included evaluation of potential for irrigation. The parties rendezvoused at New River or Indian Station, and did not return to the planning units under discussion here (Bergland 1876; Wheeler 1876). No official action was taken at the time of this investigation.

Throughout the decades from 1880 to 1900, the area that later would become Imperial Valley was used for cattle grazing. According to de Stanley (1966), the animals fed on pepper grass and watered at seven ponds or lakes left over from earlier overflows of the Colorado River: Pelican Lake, west of Imperial; Mesquite Lake, northwest of Imperial; Blue Lake, west of Seeley; Cameron and Diamond lakes, south of Blue Lake and toward the border; Laguna Lake, near Calexico. These were all "cut out" by the 1906 floods, except for Mesquite Lake which was drained for farming (de Stanley 1966).

In 1896, the California Development Company was organized to conduct water from the Colorado River to this area. Because of the contraints of the regional topography, the first canal was excavated partly in the U.S. and partly in Mexico, re-entering the U.S. near Calexico. Water first flowed through the canal in 1901, providing support for about 1500 to 2000 people, a large number of them in the employ of the irrigation company (Harrington 1962). Agricultural production mushroomed; small towns sprang up and by 1905, Imperial, Silsbee, Calexico, Heber, Holtville, Brawley and El Centro were all in existence (Norris and Carrico 1978). Imperial County was then carved out of San Diego County and home rule came to these people so far removed from coastal California.

The Colorado River carried a staggering amoung of silt in its flood waters. Now much of the silt is removed before it reaches the lower Colorado, but in the early days of the 20th century, the Colorado was described as "too thick to drink and too thin to plow." Annually this silt was once deposited at the mouth of the river, and depending on the size of the annual flood and the runoff upstream, many tons of silt and debris were added to the delta at the Gulf of California (Sykes 1970). The first canal of the California Development Company became silted in within a few years of its opening. In 1904, in order to avoid a shortage of water during low stages of the river, one of the intake ditches was cut. This cut was not repaired in time to divert the spring 1905 flood, and water poured through this cut into the old overflow channels of the Alamo and New rivers, by which it was carried to the Salton Sink. The lake in the old sink grew rapidly, forcing the Southern Pacific Railroad to built a series of "shoo-fly" tracks to keep above the advancing flood waters (Harrington 1962). The New Liverpool Salt Works on the east side of the sink, and other facilities were flooded out at this time (Harrington 1962; Lee 1963).

This disaster was only the first in a series that continued throughout 1906, forcing the California Development Company to turn to the federal government and the Southern Pacific Railroad Company for help. Since the canal was constructed partly in Mexico, the federal government could not offer direct aid, but the railroad was in a position to do so (Harrington 1962). Finally, with assistance from Bureau of Reclamation funds provided by Congress, the railroad succeeded in turning the Colorado from its ancient overflow channel back to the main stream bed, but not before 1907, and not before the Salton Sea had expended to cover over 400 square miles (Lee 1963). Subsequently, an "All-American Canal" was authorized as part of the Boulder Canyon Project. This canal was constructed entirely in the limits of the U.S., avoiding any potential international problems as had threatened during the 1905-07 crisis (Norris and Carrico 1978). The canal was completed in 1940; the Imperial Dam, necessary to the project, was completed earlier, in 1935. Another part of the project was the delivery of water to Coachella Valley by way of the Coachella Canal. Due to wartime delays, the valley did not receive its water until 1948 (Norris and Carrico 1978).

Other irrigated areas that were developing agriculture with Colorado River water include Bard, near Yuma, which benefitted from the construction of the Laguna Dam in 1908, and the Palo Verde Valley, whose irrigation system originated northeast of Blythe (Norris and Carrico 1978). Both of these areas suffered from the 1905-07 floods, but Palo Verde received no federal reclamation funds. Both areas were unable to develop their full potential until the Boulder Canyon Project solved the flooding problems in the lower river channel.

The first recorded water appropriation on the lower Colorado was made in 1877 by Thomas H. Blythe for the Palo Verde area. The early development of the region and Blythe's role in it are spelled out in Dekens (1962). A combination of factors prevented the successful culmination of the irrigation project after the death of Blythe in 1883. The Colorado floods were one problem. Another was that the affairs of the Blythe estate were in disarray from 1883 until 1904, when finally his daughter was able to take control (Dekens 1962). An act of the State Legislature created the Palo Verde Irrigation District in 1923. This district covers a thirty mile stretch along the Colorado, and has first priority rights to use California's share of the Colorado. About 90,000 acres are currently irrigated, producing alfalfa, cotton, lettuce, melons and livestock (BLM Imported Water Report, 1978).

The future of agricultural and domestic water allocation in California is at present clouded. The Boulder Canyon Project required that California limit the amount of water it could withdraw from the Colorado, but gave the state the right to use one-half of any excess or surplus water unapportioned by other legislation (BLM Imported Water Report, 1978). When the Central Arizona Project comes on line in 1983, surplus waters will be sharply reduced. It has been proposed to take water from the Columbia River drainage and add it to the Colorado River basin, but no studies have been accomplished to determine the feasibility of this idea (Imported Water Report, 1978). A moratorium on such studies was imposed in 1968 by the Colorado River Basin Project Act.

The Los Angeles Aqueduct was the second major construction project connected with the Boulder Canyon Project that directly passed through the Colorado Desert. The aqueduct was constructed between 1934 and 1941 (Norris and Carrico 1978). Parker Dam was constructed first, as part of the scheme (Lavender 1972). The Aqueduct construction was larger in scale than the All-American Canal system, but has less direct value to the desert itself. The aqueduct delivers water to Lake Mathews, near Riverside, and then to cities in the Los Angeles metropolitan area. Four pumping plants were constructed in the desert (Parker Dam, Iron Mountain, Eagle Mountain and Hayfield), and long power transmission lines were also fabricated. This mammoth project has had some permanent impact on the Colorado Desert, at the sites selected for permanent installation and in changing the visual landscape through the construction of above-ground transmission lines. Temporary impact was very intense. Rice (formerly Blythe Junction on the Santa Fe Cadiz-Parker line) became an important supply point and mushroomed (Dekens 1962; Norris and Carrico 1978). Desert Center, a small community established to serve motorists between Indio and Blythe (Jennings 1979) boomed temporarily (Gallegos et al. 1979a). Long range impact is also felt in the addition of the small maintenance crews at each permanent facility and there are proposals to divert some aquaduct water into desert basins for ground storage.

5. Energy Production

The desert itself has not benefitted from the generation of power. Its role has been as an obstacle which transmission lines had to cross from hydroelectric sites on the Colorado. With the advent of newer technology, the desert is now being explored for its potential in the production of nuclear energy, as at Sun Desert site near Blythe. Again, the desert would only function in this instance as terrain over which transmission lines would run. Geothermal and solar capability also are now being explored, however, and for the first time qualities possessed by the desert itself would be utilized. The area around Niland, at the southest corner of the Salton Sea, is being investigated at the "youthful volcanic knobs, hot springs and mud pots" of the area (Sharp 1976). (Sharp also reports that at one time carbon dioxide was produced from shallow wells in the area.) Coal firing plant sites are being explored as well, for instance near Rice and Cadiz.

6. Military training grounds and weapons testing

World War II brought about a new appreciation of the desert for its basic qualities that could be of assistance in the war effort: open spaces, low population density, and lack of dense vegetative cover. All of these characteristics were favorable for the need to train large numbers of men to serve in the deserts of Africa, and to develop accuracy in airborne and long range bombing and ordinance missions. The eastern Colorado Desert provided conditions similar to the anticipated African campaign, and in March 1942, General Patton selected the site for the Desert Training Center (DTC). Initially, this center, 10,000 plus square miles, was selected rather than a similar parcel in Arizona because of its better water supply, better rail transportation, larger area for maneuvers, and more land under government ownership. Within a year, so many troops were involved that the land area had to be expanded to include the Arizona area as well as another small parcel northeast of the original site. The concept of the DTC had also expanded to provide the U.S. its first simulated theater of operations. Its new purpose was to train all types of units in combat and service, under combat conditions. The DTC name was changed to the California-Arizona Maneuver Area (CAMA) to reflect the alterations of size and purpose.

The CAMA was closed down on April 30, 1944, because the service units were being shipped out very rapidly, especially transport and communication specialists. Over 130,000 troops and nearly 27,000 vehicles had passed through the area between January 1 and April 30, 1944 (Meller 1946). The land has reverted to its original owners (BLM and the Santa Fe Railroad), but it still bears the scars of the extensive maneuvers, camp sites and connecting roads.

Other subsidiary sites temporarily used during World War II include Camp Young, between Indio and Desert Center; Camps Granite and Coxcomb between Rice and Desert Center; Camp Essex, near Danby, Camp Ibis, near Searchlight Junction; and a camp for POWs and deserters near the latter. The Clipper, Dead and Eagle mountains were used as artillery ranges, and the Anza-Borrego Desert was used briefly for weekend tank training maneuvers (Norris and Carrico 1978). An air field was established at Blythe (Heald 1960; Norris and Carrico 1978), at Rice and at Condor Field near Twentynine Palms (Norris and Carrico 1978). Subsequently, this latter base was also used for armored division training. Patton's headquarters were located at a site just south of the Iron Mountain Pumping Plant.

A 750,000 Naval Ordinance Test Station was established in Indian Wells Valley, outside the study area, and Camp Dunlap Aerial Gunnery Range was set up in the Chocolate Mountains east of the Salton Sea. Of all the World War II bases in the study area, only the Chocolate Mountain Gunnery Range remains. A Marine Corps base was established at Twentynine Palms in 1952 and remains in use today (Norris and Carrico 1978).

prevented the successful culmination of the irrigation project area. At Blythe in 1883. The Colorado floods were one problem. Another was that the affairs of the Blythe estate were in disarray from 1883 until 1904, when finally his daughter was able to take control (Dekens 1962). An act of the State Legislature created the Palo Verde Irrigation District in 1923. This district covers a thirty mile stretch along the Colorado, and has first priority rights to use California's share of the Colorado. About 90,000 acres are currently irrigated, producing alfalfa, cotton, lettuce, melons and livestock (BLM Imported Water Report, 1978).

The future of agricultural and domestic water allocation in California is at present clouded. The Boulder Canyon Project required that California limit the amount of water it could withdraw from the Colorado, but gave the state the right to use one-half of any excess or surplus water unapportioned by other legislation (BLM Imported Water Report, 1978). When the Central Arizona Project comes on line, Arizona is prepared to take

HISTORY - E. Warren

7. Scientific Research

Research into the nature of the desert itself, of its plant, animal and human populations, is exploitative but in a largely non-extractive sense. The desert has fascinated many people, and research into its characteristics has been going on since the region came under the control of the U.S. Among the best materials available for study of the nature of the desert in the early years of American intrusion are the works completed by the U.S. Topographical Corps, and the Railroad Surveys. The U.S.G.S. has provided an important source of data for the developing knowledge of the area's geology, water supplies, and mineral resources. Studies of the animals, vegetation and human populations were conducted under the auspices of the U.S. Department of Agriculture, the Bureau of American Ethnology, the Bureau of Land Management and by private institutions such as the Carnegie Institution. Over the years, many universities and museums have sponsored desert research.

Salient publications are included in this report in each section: Ecology, Archaeology, Ethnology, History. The only purpose of mentioning this type of activity here is to present a complete list of exploitative projects that have been conducted in the Colorado Desert.

8. Small Tract development: Homesteads, Resorts

Small Tract development was especially encouraged by the Act of 1938 (Lavender 1972). However, in many cases, the uses spelled out in that act were begun long before this particular legislation was enacted.

In the 1880s, Palm Desert and Palm Springs began to open up as health resorts and small agricultural areas. The irrigation system established for Palm Springs was very inadequate, and the growth of the region was retarded for several decades (Norris and Carrico 1978; Harrington 1962). For the first fifty years of its existence, Palm Springs was a wintertime health resort with modest accommodations (Harrington 1962). It was not until after World War II that the town became a desert playground for the wealthy. Palm Desert and other nearby communities grew as people became aware of the beneficial effects of the dry desert air.

Yucca Valley, Morongo Valley and Twentynine Palms are localities that had earlier roots in ranching, but developed rapidly after the passage of the Small Tracts Act. Twentynine Palms boomed especially after the establishment of the various military bases during and after World War II. The Small Tract Act has encouraged a sizeable community of retired persons to live there (Ryan et al 1978). The Keys al. 1978).

The resort, second home and vacation communities, as well as the small tracts that were homesteaded, have frequently proven to be unsuccessful developments (Douglas and Wallace 1978). The pattern of land use and especially the transfer of land into private hands, has caused a great deal of damage to the ecology of the desert lands that were so developed. The term "Jackrabbit" homesteads is often used to describe these plots; the derogatory dimensions of the term relate to the proliferation of the small tract homesteads, and their damaging effect on the land.

9. Recreation

Recreational uses of the desert have increased significantly in the past several decades. Early devotees of the desert had a lot of explaining to do, and usually puzzled people by their insistence of the beauty of the land, its attractiveness and other positive reactions. Poetic accounts of these characteristics were published by Mary Austin, John Van Dyke and others, and their perceptions have finally begun to be shared by a large number of visitors to the desert (Russell and Lotridge 1978).

Parklands were set aside in the 1930s, as non-exploitative values began to be recognized officially. The first in the lower CDCA was Joshua Tree National Monument, 800,000 acres, dedicated in 1936 (Norris and Carrico 1978). Visitation remained low until following World War II.

Recreational use of the desert boomed after the war, and Picacho State Park and Salton Sea State Park were established. Coincident with the availabilty of money and leisure time to pursue exploring the desert, came the development of heavy duty vehicles which could take the punishment of off road driving. This combination has raised the problems of management of the desert to a critical level. The BLM is faced with the nearly impossible task of managing lands for multiple uses. In the Colorado Desert, the land is brittle--the ecology shatters easily. Multiple uses may be easy for Congress to mandate, but impossible for the BLM to implement without destroying the very resource it is asked to manage.

In the mid 1970s, the BLM began a crash study program designed to inventory the desert resources, the varying origins of impacts on them, and the kinds of impacts that can be identified. This work is preliminary to developing a management plan for the vast acreage that constitutes the CDCA. As of 1980, a preliminary plan was ready for public review, with final action to be taken by Congress at a later date. It is hoped that in the political tug-of-war sure to come, the desert itself is not forgotten.

Petroglyph element from
Corn Spring,
Riverside County,
California

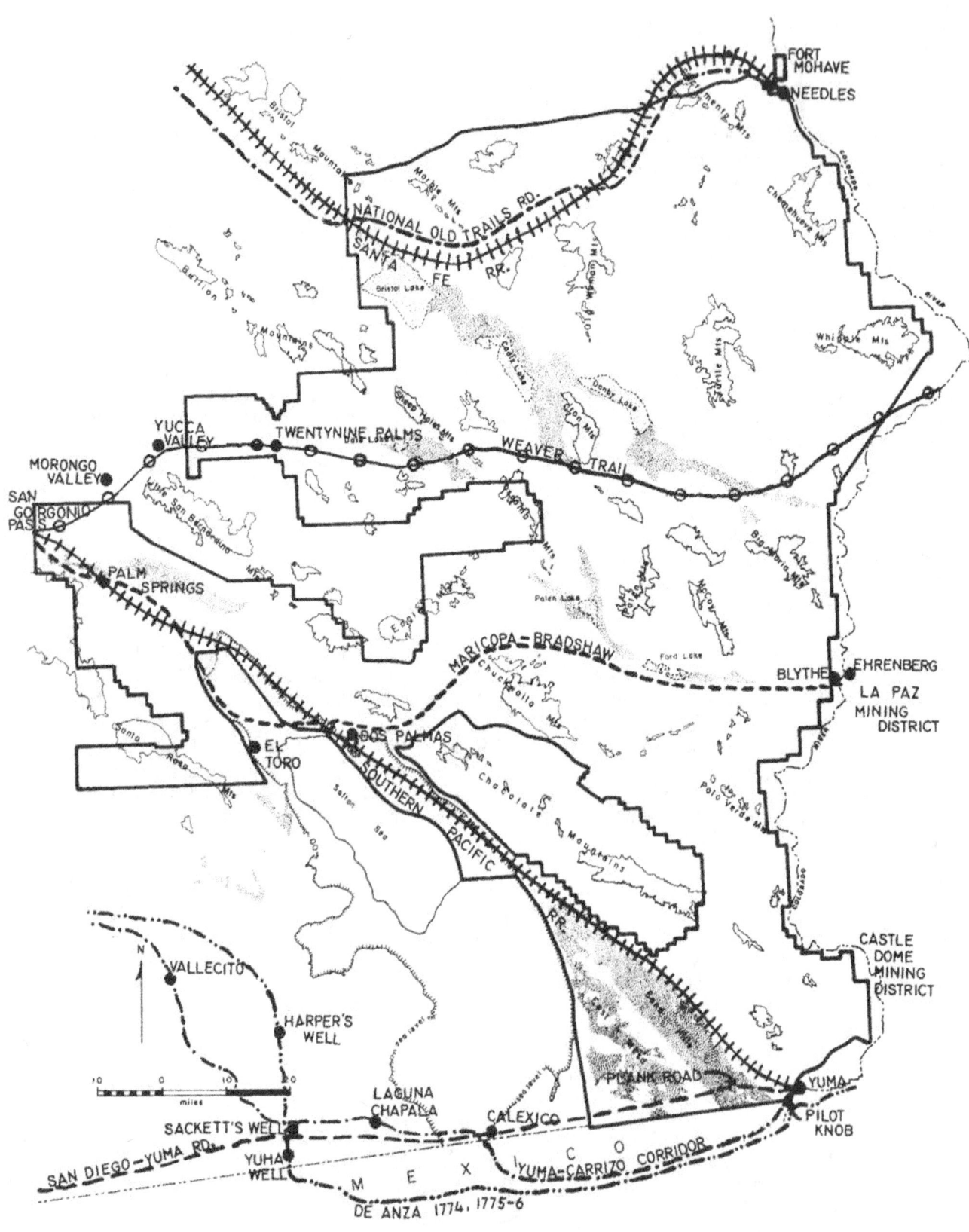

Figure 8. Historical Resources: Communication

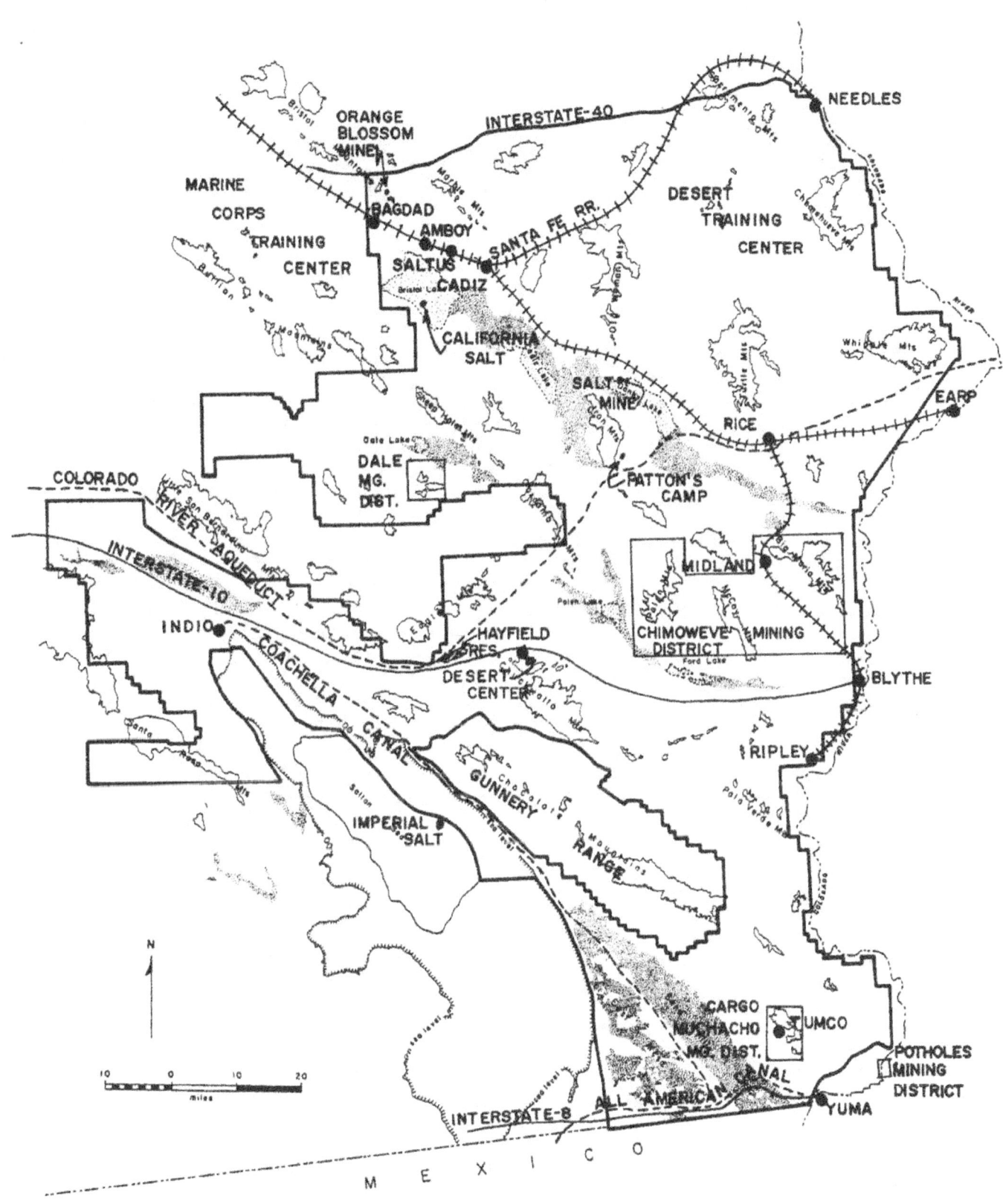

Figure 9. Historical Resources: Exploitation

-105-

Chapter VI. SUMMARY AND RECOMMENDATIONS
Elizabeth von Till Warren and Claude N. Warren

The paucity of data from prehistoric sites of the Colorado Desert has been clearly illustrated above. There are large areas from which little or no archaeological data have been recovered through excavation (e.g. in the northeastern portion of the study area). Most chronological periods for the area are poorly represented and some (e.g. Pinto Period) are speculative because of lack of data. Only the Late Period has data in quantity comparable to that of adjacent areas. Consequently, synchronic studies of settlement patterns, economic systems, and so on, are at a speculative or descriptive stage of development and most such studies have been concerned with sampling methods and techniques towards management ends rather than research problems of a largely substantive nature (Gallegos et al. 1979a, 1979b; Reed 1979 and Ritter 1978). Wilke's (1978a) ecological analysis of sites in the Coachella Valley represents the kind of study needed to further the understanding of the economic systems and settlement patterns. However, the number of localities where data are sufficient for these kinds of studies is extremely small. This lack of adequate data reflects the paucity of archaeological excavations in the Colorado Desert. The archaeology of the Colorado Desert has been, by and large, surface archaeology with the few exceptions concentrated primarily on the Colorado River. Because of the small number of sites excavated and the resultant limited understanding of the prehistory of the Colorado Desert, specific recommendations for cultural resource management are difficult to make.

The prehistoric developments of the Colorado Desert appear to have had two major centers of cultural development: the Colorado River and the Salton Basin. The Colorado River was, almost certainly, an area of relatively intense cultural activity throughout the history of man in the area. Use of the Salton Basin, however, appears to have fluctuated from intensive to marginal, as the lakes that periodically formed there receded and dried.

Other areas of relatively heavy use by aboriginal populations must have included the eastern slopes of the Peninsular Range and higher elevations in the desert ranges, especially where springs were present. Because of the extreme aridity of the Colorado Desert, water must have been one of the major determining factors in the location of habitation sites. This obviously became even more important once agriculture was introduced into the area.

The relationship of man and water in the Colorado Desert must be considered in the development of a cultural resource management plan. The largest, most productive areas of aboriginal occupation currently known are along the old beach lines of Lake Cahuilla and on the terraces of the Colorado River. These areas are of major significance in the management of cultural resources. Wherever the BLM land impinges upon these areas, careful consideration must be given to these important resources.

However, activities of prehistoric people were not limited to these areas. There was certainly seasonal movement dictated by economic and other cultural activities.

These activities took people to a variety of different environmental settings as the productivity of the various zones fluctuated with the seasons of the year. Just how and where the various environmental zones in the desert were used is not yet known. Much more data are needed before the relationship of man and his desert environment can be understood. This is probably the most critical problem for those managing cultural resources. It is a problem to which we will return shortly.

Another important factor for cultural resource management is environmental change, which has introduced variability in the distribution and function of archaeological sites. This is another variable in the cultural resources that must be considered in their management.

Cultural resource management of the California deserts includes the decision as to which sites are to be preserved in the multiple land use program of the Bureau of Land Management and which are to be subjected to greater risk or sacrificed (hopefully after proper mitigation). Such decisions would appear to require ranking sites on the basis of significance. However, "significance of an archaeological site is relative to the problem which the archaeologist is investigating, the method used, and the theoretical structure under which the program of research is developed" (Warren and McCarty 1980:90). The significance of a site is relative to the biases of the investigator and the archaeologists of the future will no doubt hold biases that we can not predict today. This means that the cultural resource manager must begin with the assumption that all sites are potentially significant while recognizing that some sites will necessarily be destroyed.

Glassow (1977) has suggested that one way of overcoming these difficulties is to determine the range of variation of sites and to preserve an adequate sample of that range of variation. Basic to a cultural resource management plan would be the preservation of the complete range of sites in the varying environmental settings. The determination of the variability of both sites and environmental settings requires considerable knowledge of the archaeological and environmental resources. The data accumulated for this overview are insufficient in themselves for making such determinations. The Bureau of Land Management Desert Planning Staff is in the best position to evaluate the data accumulated by recent surveys and overviews such as those of Gallegas et al. (1979a, 1979b), Ritter (1978), Reed (1979) and Weide et al. (1974). Consequently we do not address this problem further in this report.

Coombs (1979b) introduces four criteria for classifying sites according to the relative potential for destruction or vandalism. These are: accessibility, familiarily, value and delicacy. We are in general agreement with Coombs' evaluations of these criteria as regards possible destruction and vandalism. However, as Warren and McCarty (1980:90-91) note, when Coombs discusses the criteria of delicacy he introduces another criterion of complexity. He states (Coombs 1979b:127)

> "The criteria of delicacy brings up an important issue we think should be considered. There are, of course two basic ways of preserving a site. The first involves leaving it intact and protecting it as best as possible. The alternative is to remove the site and place it in a collection. We bring up this point here because sites which are not delicate are ones in which very little, if any, information is lost when the site is removed, provided of course that its precise provenience is recorded. Given the delicacy of isolates, in particular, we would strongly recommend that the BLM consider collecting them as they are found. We are now convinced that leaving isolates in the field is all but insuring that any further

information they may provide to archaeology will be lost forever....
Conversely, more complex sites should not be collected unless necessary,
since even most careful surface collection or excavation can destroy a
considerable amount of information."

We are in agreement with Coombs' comments, however, he has introduced another
problem. That of evaluating the method by which a site is to be preserved. In this
evaluation, delicacy and complexity must be considered as separate criteria. The
problem of the isolate is simple and straight forward because it is delicate but not
complex. Warren and McCarty (1980:91) note:

"A large fragile pattern site containing several activity areas is delicate
indeed, as is the ghost town. However, they are far more difficult to
remove than isolated finds which are equally delicate. The difference is
the number of elements involved and the interrelationships in space, the
difference is in complexity of the site."

Complexity and delicacy are two independent variables that must be considered in
management of cultural resources. The criteria of "complexity" must be considered
along with accessibility, familiarity, value and delicacy in determining procedures to
be followed in active management of the resources. When sites are endangered all
these criteria are relevant to the evaluation of means of preservation.

Finally it is essential that cultural resource management look beyond the single
site and its environmental setting. In making this point we quote from Warren and
McCarty (1980:91) the comments on the Mojave:

"Glassow (1977) and Coombs (1979) present a convincing argument for
their criteria of significance and criteria for possibility of vandalism and
destruction. However, these criteria are at the level of individual sites.
Archaeologists too often view sites as independent units. However, sites
were never independent units during the time of their occupation. It is a
fact that the prehistoric cultural systems of the Mojave Desert were not
limited to single sites, but extended networks over wide geographic areas
and through various ecological zones. Any program of site preservation in
the Mojave Desert, with a view toward future research, must include the
criteria of area network integrity. Area network integrity recognizes that
people throughout the Mojave utilized virtually all ecological zones, but
they did not utilize them in the same manner in all places. The Owens
Valley Paiute apparently had a different pattern of land use from the
Death Valley Paiute or Reese River Shoshone. To attempt to test a
hypothesis regarding settlement patterns or economic systems by utilizing
lowland sites of Owens Valley and upland sites in the Funeral Range,
regardless of the variety included, would only lead to erroneous results.
In preserving sites for future research it is not enough to protect the
variety of site types in the various ecological zones. The area in which
they are preserved must also exhibit integrity in being at least
geographically contiguous to the degree that it was usable within the
context of a single prehistoric cultural system."

In dealing with the ethnographic factors, the relationship of the local aboriginal
toward the cultural resources must be considered. The sensitivity of the Mohaves,
Quechans, Chemehuevis and Cahuillas to their culturally significant sites is well
documented. These sites represent a wide range of types, some geographically

specific and some ecologically specific.

Geographically specific sites include known sacred and mythically important places such as archaeological sites, caves, trails, trail shrines, petroglyphs, pictographs, intaglios, initiation camps and burial sites (including all camp and village sites and palm oases because of their association with the spirits of the dead). Certain mountains sacred to them as homes of the spirits (e.g. Avikwame, Newberry Mt.) are clearly included in the mythic framework of each group. Additionally, there are unspecified "power" sites with sacred significance. Any policy which would have a negative impact on these sites, or which would limit respective native American access to them, would be of interest to these groups and they should be given ample opportunity to evaluate and respond to such policies. It may be difficult to substantiate the claim of such cultural significance for a particular site, especially since the native American group may not have previously revealed the significance of a given location in an effort to keep secrets from the dominant white power structure.

Significant concern has also been expressed regarding continued access to native flora and fauna used for sacred medicine, basketry and food purposes. Thus any policy that would either endanger species traditionally utilized or limit or deny access by native American users to those species, is of great interest to them. Since these concerns focus not on specific sites but on specific plants and animals, decisions regulating the merits of protection will have to be made on an individual project basis.

As with all non-renewable resources, historical sites' management should follow a conservative approach. The history of adverse impacts on the cultural resources of the California desert is long and indiscriminate. Recent sites as well as older ones have been wholly or partially destroyed by natural and human forces. As the population pressures increase upon the resources of this still isolated region, care will have to be exercised that the historic sites and their context are protected.

Determination of which sites to preserve and which to sacrifice to contemporary needs is a constantly pressing issue. The criterion of eligibility for the National Register of Historic Places (NRHP) provides some framework for placing a given site in a ranked system of value. For this reason, nomination to the NRHP should be made for the numerous sites probably eligible but not yet listed. The problem with relying on the NRHP, however, is that systemic interrelationships are not well reflected. Historical sites did not develop in isolation: a full understanding of them requires information on their environmental setting, place in time and interrelationships with other sites. Networks of communication and supply and other systems operating within those same settings at the same time are important sources of information. Thus, preservation of a single historic site or even a historic district is not sufficient. The physical network that existed between and among them should also be available for analysis and research. Springs, trails and trail campsites are all important physical evidence of the intangible communication/supply networks of prehistoric and early historic times and, thus, also need protection and preservation.

Equally important are the physical remains of later communication/supply systems: automobile and railroad. Apart from representing the history of the development of the Colorado Desert, broader areas and other histories are also reflected in the changing pattern of relationships between and among these networks: the history of automobile and rail technology, the history of transportation; and economic history. The BLM, in its management of the area over which these networks extended, should take care that sufficient attention is paid to the physical remains reflecting these networks.

The early history of the Colorado Desert is poorly known. Documentary sources have been fragmentary and subject to varying interpretations. Since all of the histories of the Colorado Desert area have perforce been based upon these same sources, all of them are equally subject to the same inadequacies. It is therefore imperative that the BLM be cognizant that important new information relative to the Colorado Desert may become available as the historical documents recently acquired by the Arizona Historical Society from the College of Jesuits in Rome are inventoried and analyzed. Resource management policies predicated on the series of historical overviews compiled for the California Desert Conservation Area Plan should be subjected to rigorous re-examination as new data become available. While the practice of updating any plan for resource management should be followed for all areas and disciplines, the Spanish Period in the California Desert is so imperfectly known that this particular time period should receive special attention.

Management of all the cultural resources of the Colorado Desert should include interpretation of them for the general public. The BLM has a great responsibility to ensure that the complexity of life forms and their interrelationships through time and space are clearly explained to the public, which has scanty knowledge and generally little understanding of the systems which operate in the deserts of California. Good displays, popular publications and other interpretive programs can provide significant means of educating the public about the nature of desert lands and their historic uses. Programs should include information on the negative aspects of historic uses as well as on the positive ones. It would be well, for example, to include information on erosion caused by poor historic mining or agricalatural practices, so that current management policies designed to prevent similar problems will be understood better.

But perhaps the most important, fragile, historical resources of all, is the desert itself, with all the mystique the word embodies. Desert lands are fascinating; a large body of myth, legend and fantasy exists in the literature of the west that reflects this love/hate relationship between desert lands and people. This special, intangible phenomenon, should be recognized in BLM management policies. Efforts should be directed to ensure that all desert lands are not managed for consumptive uses. The eloquent plea made by John Van Dyke in 1901 in support of "empty" desert space, has even greater urgency today:

> "To speak about sparing anything because it is beautiful is to waste one's breath and incur ridicule in the bargain. The aesthetic sense--the power to enjoy through the eye, the ear, and the imagination--is just as important a factor in the scheme of human happiness as the corporeal sense of eating and drinking; but there has never been a time when the world would admit it. The "practical men", who seem forever on the throne, know very well that beauty is only meant for lovers and young persons--stuff to suckle fools withal. The main affair of life is to get the dollar, and if there is any money in cutting the throat of Beauty, why, by all means, cut her throat. That is what the "practical men" have been doing ever since the world began. It is not necessary to dig up ancient history; for have we not seen, here in California and Oregon, in our own time, the destruction of the fairest valleys the sun ever shone upon by placer and hydraulic mining? Have we not seen in Minnesota and

Wisconsin the mightiest forests that ever raised head to the sky slashed to pieces by the axe and turned into a waste of treestumps and fallen timber? Have we not seen the Upper Mississippi, by the destruction of the forests, changed from a broad, majestic river into a shallow, muddy stream; and the beautiful prairies of Dakota turned under by the plough and then allowed to run to weeds? Men must have coal though they ruin the valleys and blacken the streams of Pennsylvania, they must have oil though they disfigure half of Ohio and Indiana, they must have copper if they wreck all the mountains of Montana and Arizona, and they must have gold though they blow Alaska into the Behring Sea. It is more than possible that the "practical men" have gained much practice and many dollars by flaying the fair face of these United States. They have stripped the land of its robes of beauty, and what have they given in its place? Weeds, wire fences, oil-derricks, board shanties and board towns--things that not even a "practical man" can do less than curse at.

And at last they have turned to the desert! It remains to be seen what they will do with it. Reclaiming a waste may not be so easy as breaking a prairie or cutting down a forest. And Nature will not always be driven from her purpose. Wind, sand, and heat on Sahara have proven hard forces to fight against; they may prove no less potent on the Colorado. And sooner or later Nature will surely come to her own again. Nothing human is of long duration. Men and their deeds are obliterated, the race itself fades; but Nature goes calmly on with her projects. She works not for man's enjoyment, but for her own satisfaction and her own glory. She made the fat lands of the earth with all their fruits and flowers and foliage; and with no less care she made the desert and its sands and cacti. She intended that each should remain as she made it. When the locust swarm has passed, the flowers and grasses will return to the valley, when man is gone, the sand and the heat will come back to the desert. The desolation of the kindgom will live again, and down in the Bottom of the Bowl the opalescent mirage will waver skyward on wings of light, serene in its solitude, though no human eye sees nor human tongue speaks its loveliness."

The Desert
John C. Van Dyke, 1922.

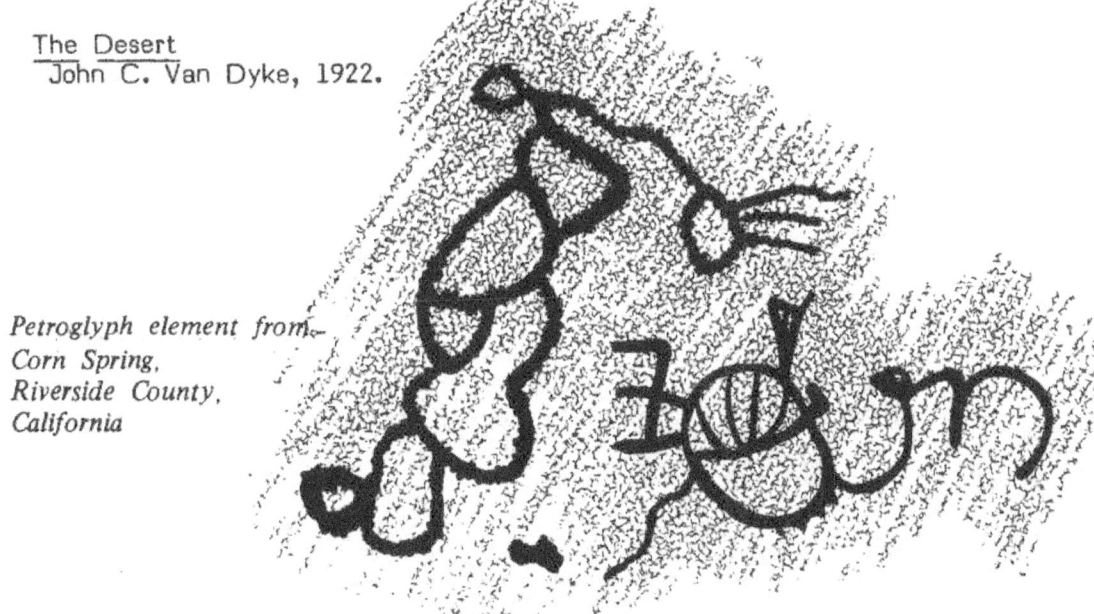

Petroglyph element from
Corn Spring,
Riverside County,
California

REFERENCES

Aikens, C. Melvin
1978 Current Research, Thomas P. Myers (ed.), American Antiquity 43(4):764.

Antevs, Ernst
1948 The Great Basin, with emphasis on glacial and post-glacial times: climatic changes and pre-white man. Bulletin of the University of Utah 38(20):168-191.

1955 Geologic-climatic dating in the west. American Antiquity 20 (4):317-335.

Aschmann, Homer
1958 Great Basin climates in relation to human occupance. Reports of the University of California Archaeological Survey 47:23-40. Berkeley.

Babcock, E. A.
1974 Geology of the northeastern margin of the Salton Trough, Salton Sea, California. Geological Society of America, Bulletin 85(3):321-332.

Bailey, H. P.
1966 The climate of southern California. University of California Press, Berkeley.

Bancroft, Hubert Howe
1890 The works of Hubert Howe Bancroft (Vol XXIV) history of California, 1860-1890. The History Company, San Francisco.

Barbour, M. G. and J. Major (Editors)
1977 Terrestrial vegetation of California. J. Wiley & Sons, New York.

Bard, Robert Charles
1973 Settlement pattern of the eastern Mojave Desert. Unpublished Ph.D. dissertation, University of California, Los Angeles.

Bartlett, John Russell
1854 Personal narrative of explorations and incidents in Texas, New Mexico, California, Sonora and Chihuahua, connected with the United States and Mexican boundary commission during the years 1850, 1851, 1852 and 1853 (2 vols). D. Appleton, New York and London. 2 vols.

Bartlett, Katherine
1938 Indian crafts of North America. Museum Notes 10(7):21-24. Museum of Northern Arizona, Flagstaff.

Baumhoff, Martin A. and R. F. Heizer
1965 Postglacial climates and archaeology in the desert west. In The Quaternary of the United States, edited by H. E. Wright and D. G. Frey, pp. 697-708. Princeton University Press.

Bean, Lowell J.
  1972 Mukat's people: the Cahuilla Indians of Southern California. University of
  California Press. Berkeley,

Bean, Lowell J. and H. W. Lawton
  1973 Some explanations for the rise of cultural complexity in native California
  with comments on proto-agriculture and agriculture. In Patterns of Indian
  burning in California: ecology and ethnohistory by Henry T. Lewis.
  Anthropological Papers1. Ballena Press, Ramona, California.

Bean, Lowell J. and William Marvin Mason
  1962 Diaries and accounts of the Romero expeditions in Arizona and California
  1823-1826. Ward Ritchie Press, Los Angeles.

Bean, Lowell J. and Katherine S. Saubel
  1963 Cahuilla ethnobotanical notes: the aboriginal use of the mesquite and
  screwbean. University of California Archaeological Survey Annual Report for
  1962-1963:55-57. Los Angeles.

Bee, Robert
  1979 Indian water and Indian economy along the lower Colorado. Paper read
  before the Southwest Anthropological Association Meetings, Santa Barbara,
  California.

  1980 Development at Fort Yuma: the Quechan Indians as Wards and Citizens, in
  press. University of Arizona Press, Tucson.

Belden, L. Burr
  1956 Pauline Weaver had Own Route to Reach River, San Bernardino
  Sun-Telegram, February 12, 1956:24.

Bell, William
  1870 New tracks in North America. Scribner, Welford, New York.

Benedict, Ruth B.
  1924 A brief sketch of Serrano culture. American Anthropologist 26:366-392.

Bergland, Lt. Eric
  1876 Report of Lieutenant Eric Bergland, in Report of the Secretary of War:
  Being Part of the Message and Documents Communicated to the Two Houses
  of Congress at the Beginning of the Second Session of the Forty-Fourth
  Congress VI (Part III) Appendix B to Appendix JJ. Government Printing
  Office, Washington, D. C.

Bettinger, Robert and R. E. Taylor
  1974 Suggested revisions in interior southern California archaeological sequences.
  Nevada Archaeological Survey Research Papers 5:1-16. Reno, Nevada.

Bischoff, J. L., W. M. Childers and R. J. Shlemon
  1978 Comments on the Pleistocene age assignment and associations of a human
  burial from the Yuha Desert, California: A rebuttal. American Antiquity
  43(4):747-749.

Bishop, Charles C. and Charles W. Jennings
1963 Reconnaissance geologic map and photogeologic interpretation of parts of the Milligan, Essex, Cadiz Lake and Danby quadrangles, California, scale 1:62,500, California Division of Mines and Geology reconnaissance mapping for the State Geologic Map.

Blackwelder, Eliot
1953 Pleistocene lakes and drainages in the Mojave Region southern California. California Division of Mines Bulletin 170:35-40.

Bolton, Herbert E. (Editor)
1908 Spanish exploration in the Southwest, 1542-1706. Barnes Noble, New York.

Bolton, Herbert E.
1916 Spanish exploration in the southwest, 1542-1706. In Original narratives of early American historical series. Scribner and Sons, New York.

1948 Kino's historical memoir of Pimeria Alta, 1683-1711 (2 vols.). University of California Press, Berkeley and Los Angeles.

1949 Coronado on the Turquoise Trail: Knight of pueblos and plains. University of New Mexico Press, Albuquerque.

1966 Anza's California expeditions (5 volumes). New York.

Bourke, John G.
1889 Notes on the cosmogony and theogony of the Mohave Indians of the Rio Colorado, Arizona. Journal of American Folklore 2:169-189. Reprinted in A collection of ethnographical articles on the California Indians, edited by Robert F. Heizer. Publications in Archaelogy, Ethnology, and History 7:77-103. Ballena Press, Ramona, California, 1976.

Brooks, Richard H.
1969 Second interim report on the archaeological survey of the lower Colorado River. Prepared for the Bureau of Reclamation, Boulder City, Nevada, by the Nevada Archaeological Survey, Desert Research Institute, University of Nevada, Las Vegas.

Brooks, Rishard H., Lawrence Alexander and Robert H. Crabtree
1970 The 1969/70 Report on the archaeological survey of the lower Colorado River. Prepared for the Bureau of Reclamation, Boulder City, Nevada, by the Nevada Archaeological Survey, Desert Research Institute, University of Nevada, Las Vegas.

Brooks, Richard H. and George Kritzman
1968 Report on archaeology in the lower Colorado River Basin. Prepared for the Bureau of Reclamation, Boulder City, Nevada. Ms. on file, Archaeological Research Center, Natural History Museum, University of Nevada, Las Vegas.

Brooks, Richard H. and Daniel O. Larson
1973 Report on archaeological resources of Tahquitz Canyon. Ms. on file, Archaeological Research Center, Natural History Museum, University of Nevada. Las Vegas.

Brooks, Richard H., Daniel O. Larson, Joseph King and Kathryn Olson
1977 Phases 1 and 2 archaeological research in Imperial Valley. Prepared for the Bureau of Reclamation, Yuma, Arizona by the Archeological Research Center, University of Nevada, Las Vegas.

Brown, John S.
1920 Routes to desert watering places in the Salton Sea region, California. U.S.Geologic Survey Water-Supply Paper 490-A. Government Printing Office, Washington, D. C.

Bryan, Alan. L.
1978 An overview of paleo-american prehistory from a circum-Pacific perspective. In Early man in America from a circum-Pacific perspective, edited by A. L. Bryan, pp.306-327. University of Alberta, Edmonton.

Bureau of Land Management
1978 Imported water report, on file with the Bureau of Land Management, Riverside, California.

1980 The California desert conservation area plan alternatives and environmental impact statement. Desert Planning Unit, Riverside, California.

Bureau of Land Management, Desert Planning Staff
1978 California desert ethnographic notes 1, 2, 5, 6, 11, 14, 17-19. Ms. on file, Bureau of Land Management, Riverside, California.

Burk, Jack H.
1977 Sonoran Desert. In Terrestrial vegetation of California edited by M. G. Barbour and J. Major, pp. 869-889. Wiley and Sons, New York.

Campbell, Elizabeth W. Crozer
1931 An archaeological survey of the Twentynine Palms region. Southwest Museum Papers 7. Los Angeles.

1936 Archaeological problems in the southern California deserts. American Antiquity 1(4):295-300.

Campbell, Elizabeth W. Crozer and William H. Campbell
1935 The Pinto Basin site. In The Pinto Basin site, Southwest Museum Papers 11. Southwest Museum, Los Angeles.

1937 The Lake Mohave site. In The archaeology of Pleistocene Lake Mohave, a symposium. Southwest Museum Papers 11. Southwest Museum, Los Angeles.

Carter, George F.
1957 Pleistocene man at San Diego, John Hopkins Press, Baltimore.

Carter, George F.
1978 The American Paleolithic. In Early man in America from a circum-Pacific perspective, edited by Alan Lyle Bryan, pp. 10-19. Occasional Paper of the Department of Anthropolgy 1. University of Alberta, Archaeological Researches International, Edmonton, Alberta, Canada.

Castetter, Edward R. and Willis H. Bell
1951 Yuman Indian agriculture: primitive subsistence on the lower Colorado and Gila Rivers. University of New Mexico Press, Albuquerque.

Chapman, Charles E.
1921 A history of California: the Spanish period. New York.

Childers, W. M
1974 Preliminary report on the Yuha burial, California. Anthropological Journal of Canada 1(1):2-9.

1977 Ridge-back tools of the Colorado desert. American Antiquity, 42(2):242-248.

Cleland, Robert G.
1918 Transportation in California before the railroads, with special reference to Los Angeles. Historical Society of Southern California, Annual Publications 11. Los Angeles.

Clements, Thomas and Lydia Clements
1953 Evidence of Pleistocene man in Death Valley. Geological Society of America, Bulletin 64(1):1189-1204.

Cline, Gloria Griffen
1963 Exploring the Great Basin. University of Oklahoma Press, Norman.

Colton, Harold S.
1939 Prehistoric culture units and their relationships in northern Arizona. Museum of Northern Arizona, Bulletin 17. Flagstaff.

1945 The Patayan problem in the Colorado River Valley. Southwest Journal of Anthropology 1(1):114-121.

1953 Potsherds. Museum of Northern Arizona, Flagstaff.

Colton, Harold S. and Lyndon L. Hargrave
1937 Handbook of Northern Arizona pottery wares. Museum of Northern Arizona, Bulletin 11. Flagstaff.

Conkling, Roscoe P. and Margaret B. Conkling
1947 The Butterfield overland mail, 1857-1869 (Vol. II). Arthur H. Clark, Glendale, California.

Cooke, R. U.
1970 Morphometric analysis of pediments and associated landforms in the western Mojave Desert, California. American Journal of Science 269:26-38.

Cooke, R. U. and A. Warren
  1973 Geomorphology in deserts. University of California Press, Berkeley.

Coombs, Gary B.
  1979a The archaeology of the northwest Mojave Desert. Bureau of Land
    Management. Cultural Resource Publications. Riverside, California.

  1979b The archaeology of the western Mojave. Bureau of Land Management.
    Cultural Resource Publication. Riverside, California.

Coues, Elliott
  1900 On the trail of a Spanish pioneer, the diary and itinerary of Francisco
    Garces (Vol. I). Frances P. Harper, New York.

Crabtree, R. H., and R. R. Ellis
  1978 East Mesa: ceramics and settlements. Ms. in possession of senior author.

Crabtree, R. H., Claude N. Warren and D. L. True
  1963 Archaeologic investigations at Batiquitos Lagoon, San Diego County,
    California. University of California Archaeological Survey, Annual Report
    319-462. Los Angeles.

Crofutt, George A.
  1883 Crofutt's New Overland Tourist and Pacific Coast Guide. The Overland,
    Omaha and Denver.

Cross, Aureal T. and Martin E. Bordner
  1977 Final report, palynological analysis Palo Verde Mesa samples. Sun Desert
    Project, Ms. on file, San Diego Gas and Electric Co., San Diego.

Cultural Systems Research, Inc.
  1978 Persistence and power: a study of native American peoples in the Sonoran
    Desert and the Devers-Palo Verde high voltage transmission line. Ms. on file,
    Cultural Systems Research, Menlo Park, California.

Curtis, Edward S.
  1907-1930 The North American Indian: being a series of volumes picturing and
    describing the Indians of the United States, and Alaska 2:15. University
    Press, Cambridge, Maryland. Reprinted by Johnson Reprint, New York, 1970.

Daggett, Stuart
  1922 Chapters on the history of the Southern Pacific. The Ronald Press, New
    York.

Dana, Samuel Trask and Myron Krueger
  1958 California lands, ownership, use, and management. The American Forestry
    Association, Washington, D. C.

Daniels, R. B., E. E. Gamble and J. G. Cady
  1971 The relation between geomorpology and soil morphology and genesis.
    Advances in Agronomy 23:51-88. Academic Press, New York.

Davenport, Lawrence C.
   1963 Mohahve. Reports from a class in local historical research. Victor Valley
      College, Victorville, California.

Davis, E. L.
   1970 Archaeology of the north basin of Panamint Valley, Inyo County, California.
      Nevada State Museum, Anthropological Papers 15:83-142. Carson City.

   1978 Associations of people and a Rancho La Brean fauna at China Lake,
      California. Great Basin Foundation and Los Angeles County Museum of
      Natural History Publication 3. Los Angeles.

Davis, E. L., D. L. True and Gene Sterud
   1965 Notes on two sites in eastern California: unusual finds. University of
      California Archaeological Survey Annual Report 1964-65:323-32. Los Angeles.

Davis, E. L. and Sylvia Winslow
   1965 Giant ground figures of the prehistoric deserts. American Philosophical
      Society Proceedings 109(1):8-21. Philadelphia.

Davis, James T.
   1961 Trade routes and economic exchange among the Indians of California.
      University of California, Archaeological Survey Report 54. Berkeley.
      Reprinted in Publications in Archaeology, Ethnology and History 3. Ballena
      Press, Ramona, California, 1974.

Dean, Leslie E.
   1977 The California desert sand dunes. Report on file with the Bureau of Land
      Management, Riverside.

Dekens, Camiel
   1962 Riverman, desertman, as told to Tom Patterson. Press-Enterprise,
      Riverside, California.

de Stanley, Mildred
   1966 The Salton Sea, yesterday and today. Triumph Press, Los Angeles

Devereux, George
   1951 Mohave chieftainship in action: a narrative of the first contacts of the
      Mohave Indians with the United States. Plateau 23:33-43.

   1957 Dream learning and individual ritual differences in Mohave shamanisn.
      American Anthropologist 59:1036-1045.

   1961 Mohave ethnopsychiatry: the psychic disturbances of an Indian Tribe.
      Bulletin of the Bureau of American Ethnology 175. United States Government
      Printing Office, Washington, D.C. Reprinted by Smithsonian Institution Press,
      Washington, D.C., 1969.

Dobyns, Henry F., Paul H. Ezell and Greta S. Ezell
   1963 Death of a society. Ethnohistory 10:105-161. Reprinted in Emergent native
      Americans: a reader in culture contact, edited by Deward Walker, pp. 192-217.
      Little, Brown and Company, Boston. 1972.

Dobyns, Henry F., Paul H. Ezell, Alden W. Jones and Greta S. Ezell
    1957 Thematic changes in Yuman warfare. In Cultural stability and cultural change, edited by Verne F. Ray. Proceedings of the American Ethnological Society for 1957:46-71. University of Washington Press, Seattle.

Douglas, John E. and John J. Wallace
    1978 Study of second home and recreation property market in the California desert. Report on file with the Bureau of Land Management, Riverside, California.

Drago, Harry Sinclair
    1967 The Steamboaters, from the early side-wheelers to the big packets. Bramhall House, New York.

Driver, Harold E.
    1937 Culture element distributions (Vol. VI) Southern Sierra Nevada. Anthropological Records 1(2):53-154. University of California, Berkeley.

    1957 Estimation of intensity of land use from ethnobiology applied to the Yuman Indians. Ethnohistory 4:174-197.

Drucker, Phillip
    1937 Culture element distributions (Vol. V) Southern California. Anthropological Records 1(1):1-52. University of California Press, Berkeley.

    1941 Culture element distributions (Vol. XVII) Yuman-Piman. Anthropological Records 6(3):91-230. University of California Press, Berkeley.

Ellis, R. R.
    1973 East Mesa: Report on the first phase of survey. Archaeological Research, Inc., Costa Mesa. Report on file with Bureau of Reclamation, Boulder City, Nevada.

Ellis, R. R. and R. H. Crabtree
    1974 Archaeological impact statement on East Mesa, areas 1 and 2 Imperial Valley, California. Archaeological Research, Inc., Costa Mesa. Report on file with Bureau of Reclamation, Boulder City, Nevada.

Euler, Robert C.
    1959 Comparative comments on California pottery, University of California, Archaeological Survey Annual Report 1958-59:41-42. Los Angeles.

Euler, Robert C., and Henry F. Dobyns
    1958 Tizon brown ware: a descriptive revision. Museum of Northern Arizona, Ceramic Series 3D, Flagstaff.

Ezell, Paul H.
    1961 Malcolm Jennings Rogers, 1890 to 1960. American Antiquity 26:532-4.

Fairchild, Mahlon Dickerson
    1933 A trip to the Colorado mines in 1862. California Historical Society Quarterly 12.

Farris, William M.
1977 Laguna Chapala, the Mexican fort. Imperial Valley College Museum Society and Imperial Valley College Museum, Publication 6. El Centro, California.

Fathauer, G.H.
1954 Structure and causation in Mohave warfare. Southwestern Journal of Anthropology 10:97-118. Albuquerque.

Fenzke, Gerhard A.
1980 History of the California highway system, expenditures and revenues. University of Michigan Press, Ann Arbor.

Ferraro, David and R. H. Crabtree
1976 Floral remains from three hearths at the Berger site, Las Vegas, Nevada. Ms. in possession of the authors.

Forbes, Jack D.
1964 The development of the Yuma route before 1846. California Historical Society Quarterly 43:99-118.

Forbis, R. G.
1974 The PaleoAmericans in North America, edited by S. Gorenstein, pp. 17-35. St. Martins Series in Prehistory, St. Martins Press.

Forde, C. Daryll
1931 Ethnography of the Yuman Indians. Publication in American Archaeology and Ethnology 28:83-278. University of California, Berkeley.

Foreman, Grant
1939 Marcy and the gold seekers, the journal of Captain R. B. Marcy, with an account of the Gold Rush over the southern route. University of Oklahoma Press, Norman.

Frickstad, Walter N.
1955 A century of California post offices, 1848 to 1954. A Philatelic Research Society Publication, Oakland.

Gallegos, Dennis, John Cook, Emma Lou Davis, Gary Lowe, Frank Norris, and Jay Theskin
1979a Cultural resources inventory of the central Mojave and Colorado desert regions, California. Westec Service, Inc., San Diego, California. Prepared for the Bureau of Land Management, Desert Planning Staff, Riverside, California.

Gallegos, Dennis, Emma Lou Davis, William Ekhardt, Cliff Gates, Gary Lowe, Frank Norris, Lorraine Pritchett, Michael R. Waters, Christopher W. White
1979b Class II Cultural resource inventory of the East Mesa and West Mesa regions, Imperial Valley, California (Vol. I), Westec Service, San Diego. Prepared for the Bureau of Land Management, Riverside, California.

Gifford, Edward W.
1931 The Kamia of the Imperial Valley. Bureau of American Ethnology Bulletin 97. Washington, D.C.

Gladwin, Winifred and Harold S.
1930 The western range of the Red-on-Buff culture. Medallion Papers V, Gila Pueblo, Globe, Arizona.

1934 A method for designation of cultures and their variations. Medallion Papers XV, Gila Pueblo, Globe, Arizona.

Glassow, Michael A.
1977 Issues in evaluating the significance of archaeological resources. American Antiquity 79:413-420.

Glennan, William S.
1976 The Manix Lake lithic industry: early lithic tradition or workshop refuse? Journal of New World Archaeology 7(1):43-61.

Grant, Campbell
1971 Rock art in California. In The California Indians, a source book, edited by R. F. Heizer and M. A. Whipple, pp. 231-243. University of California Press, Berkeley.

Grant, Campbell, James W. Baird and J. Kenneth Pringle
1968 Rock drawings of the Coso Range, Inyo County, California. Maturango Museum Publication 4. Ridgecrest, California.

Haenszel, Arda M.
1974 The Frinks and the hacienda adobe, edited version published in San Bernardino County Museum Commemorative Edition, Allen-Greendale, Redlands, California.

Hall, Mathew C. and James P. Barker
1975 Background to prehistory of the El Paso/Red Mountain desert region. Prepared for Bureau of Land Management, Desert Planning Staff, Riverside, California.

Hall, Sharlot M.
1903 The burning of a Mojave chief. Old West 18:60-65. Reprinted in Publications in Archaeology, Ethnology, and History 7, edited by Robert F. Heizer, pp. 69-74. Ballena Press, Ramona, California. 1976.

Harner, Michael J.
1951 Potsherds and the tentative dating of the San Gargonio - Big Maria Trail. University of California Archaeological Survey Reports 37:35-42. Berkeley.

1953 Gravel pictographs of the lower Colorado River region. University of California Archaeological Survey Reports 20:1-29. Berkeley.

1958 Lowland Patayan phases in the lower Colorado River Valley and Colorado Desert. University of California Archaeological Survey Reports 42:93-99. Berkeley.

Harrington, Mark R.
   1931 Gypsum Cave. Southwest Museum Papers 8. Los Angeles.

   1957 A Pinto site at Little Lake, California. Southwest Museum Papers 17. Los Angeles.

   1962 Souvenirs of the Palm Springs area. Printed by Simi for Service, Simi, California.

Hastings, J. R., R. M. Turner and D. K. Warren.
   1972 An atlas of some plant distributions in the Sonoran Desert. Arid Regions Technical Report 21, University of Arizona Institute of Atmospheric Physics, Tucson.

Haury, Emil W.
   1950 The stratigraphy and archaeology of Ventana Cave, Arizona. University of New Mexico Press, Albuquerque.

Hayden, Julian D.
   1967 A summary prehistory and history of the Sierra Pinacate, Sonora. American Antiquity 32:335-44.

   1976 Pre-Altithermal archaeology in the Sierra Pinacate, Sonora, Mexico. American Antiquity 41:274-289.

Heald, Weldon F.
   1960 With Patton on desert maneuvers, Desert Magazine, July 1960:6-7, 24.

Hedges, Kenneth
   1970 Pictographs of San Diego County. Master of Arts Thesis, San Diego, California.

Heilbron, Carl H. (editor)
   1936 History of San Diego County. The San Diego Press Club, San Diego.

Heizer, R. F. and M. A. Baumhoff
   1962 Prehistoric rock art of Nevada and eastern California. University of California Press, Berkeley.

Heizer, R. F. and C. W. Clewlow, Jr.
   1973 Prehistoric rock art of California. Ballena Press, Ramona.

Hickman, Patricia Parker
   1977 Country nodes, an anthropological evaluation of William Keys' Desert Queen Ranch, Joshua Tree National Monument, California. Western Archaeological Center, Publications in Anthropology 7. Tucson.

Hoover, Mildred Brooke, Hero Eugene Rensch and Ethel Grace Rensch
   1966 Historic spots in California (3rd edition), reviewed by William N. Abeloe. Stanford University Press, Palo Alto, California.

Hubbs, Carl L. and George S. Bien
1967 La Jolla natural radiocarbon measurements V. Radiocarbon 9:261-294.

Hubbs, Carl L., George S. Bien and Hans E. Suess
1960 La Jolla natural radiocarbon measurements. American Journal of Science, Radiocarbon Supplement 2:197-223.

1963 La Jolla natural radiocarbon measurements III. Radiocarbon 5:254-272.

1965 La Jolla natural radiocarbon measurements IV. Radiocarbon 7:66-117.

Huning, James R.
1978 A characterization of the climate of the California desert. Report on file with the Bureau of Land Management, Riverside, California.

Indian Claims Commission
1959 Findings of fact, docket 295 and 283. Reprinted in Mohave Indians:129-156. Garland Publishing, New York.

Jackson, J. Brantley
1977 Plane sense: a technological and functional analysis of a stone tool category. Master of Arts thesis, Washington State University, Pullman.

Jaeger, Edmund C.
1941 Desert wild flowers (revised edition). Stanford University Press, Stanford, California.

1957 The North American deserts. Stanford University Press, Stanford.

Jennings, Bill
1979 "Desert Steve" the town founder, Desert Magazine 42(6):20-22.

Jennings, Jesse D.
1978a Origins. In Ancient native Americans, edited by Jesse D. Jennings, pp. 1-42. W. H. Freeman, San Francisco.

1978b The prehistory of Utah and the eastern Great Basin. University of Utah Anthropological Papers 98. Salt Lake City.

Johnston, Francis J.
1972 Stagecoach travel through San Gorgonio Pass, Journal of the West XI(4) October 1972.

1976 The Bradshaw Trail, edited by John R. Brumgardt and Tom Patterson. Historical Commission Press, Riverside, California.

Johnston, Francis J. and Patricia H. Johnston
1957 An Indian trail complex of the central Colorado desert: a preliminary survey. University of California Archaeological Survey, Reports 37:22-34. Berkeley.

Kelly, Isabel T.
  1934 Southern Paiute bands. *American Anthropologist* 36:548-560.

Kelly, Marsha C.
  1972 The society that did not die. *Ethnohistory* 19:261-265.

King, Chester
  1967 The Sweetwater Mesa site (LAn-267) and its place in southern California prehistory. University of California Archaeological Survey *Annual Report* 1967:25-76. Los Angeles.

King, Chester and Dennis G. Casebier
  1976 *Background to historic and prehistoric resources of the east Mojave Desert region.* Bureau of Land Management, Desert Planning Staff, Riverside.

King, J. E. and T. R. Van Devender
  1976 Pollen analysis of fossil packrat middens from the Sonoran Desert. *Quaternary Research* 8:191-204.

King, Thomas F.
  1975 *Fifty years of archaeology in the California desert: an archaeological overview of Joshua Tree National Monument.* Western Archaeological Center, National Parks Service, Tucson.

King, T. J., Jr.
  1975 Late Pleistocene-early Holocene history of coniferous woodlands in the Lucerne Valley. In *Archaeological impact evaluation of upper Johnson and Lucerne valleys,* edited by C. Mortland, et al. Drylands Research Institute, University of California, Riverside.

  1976 Late Pleistocene-early Holocene coniferous woodlands in the Lucerne Valley region, Mojave Desert, California. *Great Basin Naturalist* 36:227-238.

Knack, Martha C.
  1978a Ethnographic interviews, Chemehuevi.

  1978b Ethnography of the Central Mojave Basin, with ethnohistorical notes. Ms. on file, Bureau of Land Management, Riverside, California.

Kowta, Makoto
  1969 The Sayles complex: a late millingstone assemblage from Cajon Pass and the ecological implications of its scraper planes. *University of California Publications in Anthropology* 6. Berkeley and Los Angeles.

Krieger, Alex D.
  1964 Early man in the new world. In *Prehistoric man in the new world,* edited by J. D. Jennings and Edward Norbeck, pp. 23-81. University of Chicago.

Kroeber, Alfred E.
  1902 Preliminary sketch of the Mohave Indians. *American Anthropologist* 4:276-285. Reprinted in *Selected Papers from the American Anthropologist, 1888-1920,* edited by Frederica de Laguna, pp. 506-515. American Anthropological Association, Washington, D.C., 1960 [1976].

Kroeber, Alfred E.
    1925 Handbook of the Indians of California. Bulletin of the Bureau of American
        Ethnology 78. United States Government Printing Office, Washington, D.C.
        Reprinted by Dover Publications, New York, 1976.

    1953 Report on aboriginal territory and occupancy of the Mohave tribe:
        testimony before the Indian Claims Commission; docker 283. Reprinted in
        Mohave Indians, Ethnohistory Series, pp. 23-108. Garland, 1974.

    1959 Desert Mohave: fact or fancy? Publication in American Archaeology and
        Ethnology 47:294-307. University of California, Berkeley.

Kroeber, Alfred E. and Michael J. Harner
    1955 Mohave Pottery. University of California Anthropological Records 16.
        Berkeley and Los Angeles.

Kroeber, C.B.
    1965 The Mohave as nationalist, 1854-1874. Proceedings: American Philosophical
        Society 109:173-180.

LaFuze, Pauliene
    1971 Saga of the San Bernardinos (Vol I). San Bernardino County Museum
        Association, San Bernardino.

Laird, Carobeth
    1976 The Chemehuevis. Malki Museum Press, Banning, California.

Lanning, Edward P.
    1963 Archaeology of the Rose Spring site Iny 372. University of California
        Publications in American Archaeology and Ethnology 49(3):237-336. Berkeley
        and Los Angeles.

Laudermilk, J. D. and P. A. Munz
    1934 Plants In the dung of Nothrotherium from Gypsum Cave, Nevada. Carnegie
        Institution of Washington Paleontological Contributions 453:29-37.

    1938 Plants in the dung of Nothrotherium from Rampart and Muav Caves,
        Arizona. Carnegie Institution of Washington Paleontological Contributions
        487:271-281.

Lavender, David
    1972 California: land of new beginnings. A Regions of America Book. Harper
        Row,New York, Evanston, San Francisco, London.

Lawton, Harry and Lowell J. Bean
    1968 A preliminary reconstruction of aboriginal agricultural technology among the
        Cahuilla. The Indian Historian 1(5):18-24, 29.

Lee, W. Storrs
    1963 The great California deserts. G. P. Putnam's Sons, New York.

Long, A. and P. S. Martin
    1974 Death of American ground sloths. Science 186:638-640.

Longwell, C. R.
    1954 History of the lower Colorado river and the Imperial depression. California
        Division of Mines, Bulletin 170:53-56.

McCown, B. E.
    1954 Archaeological survey of (Salton Sea) beach line. Archaeological Survey
        Association of Southern California, Newsletter 1(3):10-11.

    1955 The Lake LeConte beach line survey. The Masterkey 29:89-92. The
        Southwest Museum, Los Angeles.

    1957 The Lake LeConte survey. Archaeological Survey Association of Southern
        California, Newsletter 4:3-4.

McCown, B. H.
    1974 Progress report on the Lake LeConte survey material. Archaeological
        Survey Association of Southern California, Newsletter 21(2):27-28.

MacDougal, Daniel Trembly, W. P. Balke, G. Sykes, E. E. Free, W. H. Ross, G. J.
Peirce, M. A. Brannon, J. C. Jones and S. B. Parish
    1914 The Salton Sea: a study of the geography, the geology, the floristics, and
        the ecology of a desert basin. Carnegie Institution of Washington Publication
        193. Washington, D. C.

Madsen, Rex
    1977 Prehistoric ceramics of the Fremont. Museum of Northern Arizona Ceramic
        Series 6, Flagstaff.

Malouf, Carling and A. Arline Malouf
    1945 The effects of Spanish slavery on the Indians of the Intermountain West.
        Southwestern Journal of Anthropology 1:378-391. Reprinted in The emergent
        native Americans: a reader in culture contact, edited by Deward Walker, pp.
        426-435. Little/Brown, Boston, 1972.

Marks, J. B.
    1950 Vegetation and soil relations in the lower Colorado Desert. Ecology
        31:176-193.

Massey, William C.
    1966 Archaeology and ethro-history: lower California. Handbook of Middle
        American Indians,4:38-58. University of Texas Press, Austin.

Mathison, Richard R.
    1968 Three cars in every garage: the story of the automobile and the Automobile
        Club in Southern California. Doubleday and Company. Garden City, New
        York.

Matson, Fredrick R.
1960 The quantitative study of ceramic materials. Viking Fund Publications in Anthropology 28:34-59.

Matson, Fredrick R. (editor)
1965 Ceramics and man. Viking Fund Publications in Anthropology 41.

May, Ronald V.
1978 A southern California indigenous ceramic typology: a contribution to Malcolm J. Rogers' research. Archaeological Survey Association of Southern California Journal 2(2):1-54.

Mehringer, Peter J., Jr.
1967 Pollen analysis of the Tule Springs area, Nevada. In Pleistocene Studies in Southern Nevada, edited by H. M. Wormington and Dorothy Ellis. Nevada State Museum Anthropological Papers 13:129.200. Carson City.

Meighan, Clement W.
1959 Archaeological resources at Borrego State Park. University of California Archaeological Survey. Annual Report 1958-59:27-46. Los Angeles.

1976 Two views of the Manix Lake lithic industry: introductory comments. Journal of New World Archaeology 1(7):41-42.

Meller, Sydney
1946 The desert training center and the C-AMA, historical section, Army Ground Forces Study 15.

Mendenhall, Walter C.
1909 Some desert watering places in southeastern California and southwestern Nevada. United States Geological Survey, Water Supply Paper 224, Washington, D. C.

Michels, Joseph W.
1964 The Snow Creek rock shelter site (Riv-210). University of California Archaeological Survey, Annual Report 1963-64:85-128. Los Angeles.

Minshall, Herbert L.
1975 The lower Paleolithic bipolar flaking complex in the San Diego region: technological implications of recent finds. Pacific Coast Archaeological Society Quarterly 11(4):45-55. Santa Ana, California.

Morrison, Roger
1965 Quaternary Geology of the Great Basin. In The Quaternary of the United States, edited by H. E. Wright and D. G. Frey, pp. 265-285. Princeton University Press, Princeton.

Muffler, L. J. P. and D. E. White
1969 Active metophorism of upper Cenozoic sediments in the Salton Sea geothermal field and the Salton Trough, southeastern California. Geological Society of America, Bulletin 80(2):157-182.

Munz, Philip A.
 1974 A flora of southern California. University of California Press, Berkeley.

Murray, K., J. Bell and B. Crowe
 1976 Stratigraphy and structure of the Orocopia, Chocolate and Cargo Muchacho mountains, southeastern California. In Early Site Review Report, Sundesert Nuclear Power Project, Appendix 2.5-L, San Diego Gas and Electric.

Musser, Ruth A.
 1979 Notes on the Blythe petroglyphs. Pacific Coast Archaeological Society Quarterly 15(2):33-49. Costa Mesa, California.

Myrick, David F.
 1963 Railroads of Nevada and eastern California (Vol 2). Howell-North Books, Berkeley, California.

Nance, J. D.
 1970 Lithic Analysis: Implications for the prehistory of central California. University of California Archaeological Survey Annual Report:66-103. Los Angeles.

Norris, Frank and Richard L. Carrico
 1978 A history of land use in the California desert conservation area. Westec Service, San Diego, California. Report prepared for the Bureau of Land Management, Desert Planning Staff, Riverside, California.

O'Connell, James, Philip J.Wilke, Thomas F. King and Carol L. Mix (editors)
 1974 Perris Reservoir archaeology: late prehistoric demographic changes. California Department of Parks and Recreation Archeological Report 14. Sacramento.

Palmer, William Jackson
 1869 Report of surveys across the continent in 1867-1868 on the Thirty-Fifth and Thirty-Second Parallels, for a route extending the Kansas-Pacific Railway to the Pacific Ocean at San Francisco and San Diego. W. B. Selheimer, Philadelphia.

Parke, Lieutenant John G.
 1854 Report of exploration of that portion of a railroad route near the Thirty-second Parallel of North Latitude, lying between Dona Ana on the Rio Grande and Pima Village on the Gila. Quarto Edition of the Pacific Railroad Reports II.

 1855 Report of explorations for a railroad route from San Francisco Bay to Los Angeles, California west of the Coast Range and from the Pima Villages on the Gila to the Rio Grande near the Thirty-Second Parallel of North Latitude (1854-1855). Pacific Railroad Surveys VII.

Parker, R. B.
 1963 Recent volcanism at Amboy Crater, San Bernardino County, California. California Division of Mines, Special Report 76.

Payen, L. A., C. H. Rector, E. Ritter, R. E. Taylor and J. E. Ericson
1978 Comments on the Pleistocene age assignment and associations of a human burial from the Yuha Desert, California. American Antiquity 43(3):448-453.

Peck, Stuart L.
1953 Some pottery from the Sand Hills, Imperial County, California. Archaeological Survey Association of Southern California, Paper 1. Southwest Museum, Los Angeles.

Perkins, Edna Brush
1922 The white heart of Mojave. Boni and Liveright. New York.

Phinney, Robert A. (Editor)
1968 The history of the earth's crust: a symposium. Princeton University Press, Princeton, New Jersey.

Priestley, Herbert I..
1913 The Colorado River campaign 1781-82, diary of Pedro Fages, Publications of the Academy of Pacific Coast History 3(2):135-233.

Rector, Carol
1976 Rock art of the east Mojave Desert. In Background to historic and prehistoric resources of the east Mojave Desert region by Chester King and Dennis G. Casebier, Appendix 5:236-259. Prepared for the Bureau of Land Management, Riverside.

Reed, Judyth
1979 Archaeological investigations in the southeastern California Desert. Paper presented at the Society for California Archaeology meeting, San Luis Obispo. On file at the Bureau of Land Management, Riverside.

Ritter, Eric W.
1978 Archaeological/historical sampling in the Whipple Mountains, Big Maria and Picacho planning units. Reports on file with Bureau of Land Management, Riverside.

Rogers, Malcolm J.
1936 Yuman pottery making. San Diego Museum of Man, Paper 2. San Diego.

1939 Early lithic industries of the lower Basin of the Colorado River and adjacent desert areas. San Diego Museum of Man, Paper 3. San Diego.

1945 An outline of Yuman prehistory. Southwestern Journal of Anthropology 1(2):167-198.

1958 San Dieguito implements from the terraces of the Rincon-Pantano and Rillito drainage systems. The Kiva 24:1-23. Tucson.

1966 Ancient hunters of the Far West, edited by Richard Pourade. Copley Press, San Diego.

Roske, Ralph J.
   1968 Everyman's Eden, a history of California. The Macmillan Company, New
        York; Collier-Macmillan Ltd., London.

Roth, George
   1976 Incorporation and changes in ethnic structure: the Chemehuevi Indians.
        Unpublished Ph.D. dissertation, Department of Anthropology, Northwestern
        University.

   1977 The Calloway affair of 1880: Chemehuevi adaptation and
        Chemehuevi-Mohave relations. Journal of California Anthropology, Winter
        1977.

Rowlands, Peter G.
   1978 The vegetational dynamics of the Joshua Tree in Southwestern United
        States. Unpublished Ph.D. dissertation, University of California, Riverside.

Ruby, Jay W.
   1964 Excavations at One Horse Canyon rockshelter (Riv-8). University of
        California Archaeological Survey Annual Report 1963-64:129-38. Los Angeles.

Russell, I. C.
   1885 Geological history of Lake Lahonton: A Quaternary lake in Northwestern
        Nevada. Monographs of the United States Geologic Survey 11.

Russell, Susan Higley and Jean Lotridge
   1978 Survey of residents of the California desert. Report on file with the
        Bureau of Land Management, Riverside, California.

Ryan, John, Mary Ivory, Cynthia Kroll, Jean Smith, Sue Mara, Keith Duke, Marilyn
Duffey-Armstrong
   1978 Demographic and economic trends in the California desert. Report on file
        with Bureau of Land Management, Riverside, California.

Sample, L. L.
   1950 Trade and trails in aboriginal California. University of California
        Archaeological Survey, Report 8. Berkeley.

Schroeder, Albert H.
   1952 A brief survey of the lower Colorado River, from Davis Dam to the
        international border. Ms. on file, National Park Service, Santa Fe.

   1957 The Hakataya cultural tradition. American Antiquity 23(2):176-78.

   1958 Lower Colorado Buff Ware. Museum of Northern Arizona Ceramic Series
        30. Flagstaff.

   1961 The archaeological excavations at Willow Beach, Arizona, 1950. University
        of Utah Anthropological Papers 50. Salt Lake.

1975 The Hohokam, Sinagua and the Hakataya. Occasional Paper 3. Imperial Valley College Museum Society, El Centro. (Originally published in Society for American Archaeology, Archives of Archaeology 5 (1960)).

Sharp, R. P.
1964 Wind-driven sand in the Coachella Valley. California Geological Society of America, Bulletin 75:785-804.

1976 Field Guide to Southern California. K/H Geology Field Guide Series. Kendall/Hunt, Dubuque, Iowa.

Shepard, Anna O.
1968 Ceramics for the archaeologist. Carnegie Institute of Washington, Publication 609. Washington, D. C.

Sherer, Lorraine
1965 The clan system of the Fort Mohave Indians. Southern California Quarterly 47:1-72.

1967 The name Mohave. Southern California Quarterly 49:1-36, 455-458.

Shlemon, R. J.
1978 Quaternary soil-geomorphic relationships, Southeastern Mojave Desert, California and Arizona. In Quaternary soils: Geo Abstracts Ltd., edited by W. C. Mahaney, pp. 187-207. University of East Anglia, Norwich, England.

Shumway, Gary L., Larry Vredenburgh and Russell Hartill
1980 Desert fever: an overview of mining in the California desert conservation area. Report on file with the Bureau of Land Management, Riverside, California.

Shutler, Richard, Jr.
1967 Cultural chronology in southern Nevada. Nevada State Museum Anthropological Papers 13:303-308. Carson City.

Simpson, Ruth D.
1976 A commentary of William Glennan's article. Journal of New World Archaeology 7:63-66.

Singer, Clay and Robert O. Gibson
1970 The Medea Creek village site (4-LAn-243): a functional lithic analysis. University of California Archaeological Survey, Annual Report:163-183. Los Angeles.

Smith, Gerald A., W. C. Schuiling, L. Martin, R. J. Sayles and P. Jillson.
1957 Archaeology of Newberry Cave, San Bernardino County California. San Bernardino County Museum Association, Scientific Series 1. San Bernardino, California.

Smith, Gerald A. and Clifford Walker
1965 Slave trade along the Mohave Trail. San Bernardino County Museum Press, San Bernardino, California.

Smith, G. I.
  1968 Late-Quaternary geologic and climate history of Searles Lake, southeastern
    California. In Means of correlation of Quaternary successions, edited by R. B.
    Morrison and H. E. Wright, International Association for Quaternary Research,
    University of Utah Press, Salt Lake City.

Smith, Melvin T.
  1972 The Colorado River: its history in the lower canyon area. Unpublished Ph.D
    dissertation, Brigham Young University, Provo, Utah.

Spicer, Edward H.
  1962 Cycles of conquest: the impact of Spain, Mexico, and the United States on
    the Indians of the Southwest, 1533-1960. University of Arizona Press, Tucson.

Spier, Leslie
  1953 Some observations on Mohave clans. Southwestern Journal of Anthropology
    9:324-342.

Steward, Julian H.
  1929 Petroglyphs of California and adjoining states. University of California
    Publications in American Archaeology and Ethnology 24(2):47-258.   Berkeley.

  1938 Basin-plateau aboriginal sociopolitical groups. Bulletin of American
    Ethnology 120. United States Govenment Printing Office, Washington, D.C.
    Reprinted by University of Utah Press, Salt Lake City, 1970.

Stewart, Kenneth
  1947a Mohave hunting. The Masterkey 21:80-84. Southwest Museum, Los
    Angeles.

  1947b Mohave warfare. Southwestern Journal of Anthropology 3:257-278.

  1957 Mohave fishing. The Masterkey 31:198-203. Southwest Museum, Los
    Angeles.

  1965 Mohave Indian gathering of wild plants. Kiva 31:46-53.

  1966a Mohave Indian agriculture. The Masterkey 40:4-15. Southwest Museum,
    Los Angeles.

  1966b The Mohave Indians and the fur trappers. Plateau 39:73-79.

  1966c The Mohave Indians in Hispanic times. Kiva 32:25-38.

  1967 Chemehuevi culture changes. Plateau 40:14-21.

  1968 Culinary practices of the Mohave Indians. El Palacio 75:26-37.

  1969a The aboriginal territory of the Mohave Indians. Ethnohistory 16:257-276.

  1969b A brief history of the Mohave Indians since 1850. Kiva 34:219-236.

Stewart, Omer C.
    1939 The Northern Paiute bands. _Anthropological Records_ 2(3):127-149. University
        of California, Berkeley.

Strain, B. R. and V. C. Chase
    1966 Effect of past and prevailing temperatures on the carbon dioxide exchange
        capacities of some desert perennials. _Ecology_ 47:1043-1045.

Strong, William D.
    1929 Aboriginal society in Southern California. _Publications in American
        Archaeology and Ethnology_ 26:1-349. University of California, Berkeley.

Sykes, Godfrey
    1970 The Colorado Delta. American Geographical Society _Special Publication_ 19,
        edited by W. L. G. Joerg. Kennikat Press, Port Washington, New York and
        London. Originally published in 1937.

Thompson, D. G.
    1929 The Mohave Desert region, California-a geographic, geologic and hydrologic
        reconnaissance, U.S. Geologic Survey _Water Supply Paper_ 578.

Treganza, Adan E.
    1942 An archaeological reconnaissance of northeastern Baja California and
        southeastern California. _American Antiquity_ 8:152-163.

    1945 The "ancient stone fish traps" of the Coachella Valley, southern California.
        American Antiquity 10:285-294.

    1947 Possibilities of an aboriginal practice of agriculture among the Southern
        Diegueño. _American Antiquity_ 12:169-173.

True, D. L. and Jan Townsend
    1976 Archaeological reconnaissance of the Santa Rose Mountains. Report on file
        with the Bureau of Land Management, Riverside.

Turnage, W. V. and A. L. Hinckley
    1938 Freezing weather in relation to plant distribution in the Sonoran Desert.
        Ecology Monograph 8:529-550.

Tyler, Daniel
    1964 _A concise history of the Mormon battalion in the Mexican War, 1846-1847._
        The Rio Grande Press, Chicago. (Originally printed, 1881).

U.S. Government
    1857 _U.S. Government Report of the United States and Mexican boundary survey_
        (3 volumes in 2). Government Printing Office, Washington D.C.

Van Camp, Gena Ruth
    1972 A study of Diegueño pottery: extrinsic qualities and regional distribution.
        Ms. on file, San Diego Museum of Man.

Van Devender, T. R.
    1976 The biota of the hot deserts of North America during the last glaciation: the packrat midden record. American Quaternary Association, Abstracts of Fourth Biennial Meeting, pp. 62-67.

    1977a Holocene woodlands in the southwestern deserts. Science 198:189-192.

    1977b Comment on: Macrofossil analysis of woodrat (Neotoma) middens as a key to the Quaternary vegetational history of arid North America, by P. V. Wells. Quaternary Research 8:236-237.

Van Devender, T. R. and J. E. King
    1971 Late Pleistocene vegetational records in western Arizona. Journal of the Arizona Academy of Science 6:240-244.

Van Devender, T. R. and W. G. Spaulding
    1979 Development of vegetation and climate in the southwestern United States. Science 207:701-710.

Van Dyke, Dix
    1927 A modern interpretation of the Garces route. Historical Society of Southern California, Annual Publications XIII.

Von Haake, A.
    1910 Post route map of the states of California and Nevada. U.S. Postal Service, Washington, D.C.

Van Valkenburgh, Richard F.
    1934 Chemehuevi notes. Ms. on file, Museum of Northern Arizona Library, File #6315, Flagstaff. Reprinted in Paiute Indians II: American Indian Ethnohistory Series, pp. 225-253. Garland, New York, 1976.

von Werlhof, Jay C.
    1965 Rock art of Owens Valley, California. University of California Archaeological Survey, Reports 65. Berkeley.

von Werlhof, Jay C. and Sherilee von Werlhof
    1968 Archaeological examinations of west and north perimeters Sun Desert site and request for determination of eligibility for the National Register. A twin report, Imperial Valley College Museum.

    n.d. Archaeological examinations of the Sun Desert Nuclear Plan site. Imperial Valley College Museum.

Wallace, W.J.
    1953 Tobacco and its use among the Mohave Indians. The Masterkey 27:293-202. Southwest Museum, Los Angeles.

    1962 Prehistoric cultural developments in the southern California deserts. American Antiquity 28:172-180.

1964 An archaeological reconnaissance in Joshua Tree National Monument. _Journal of the West_ 3:90-101.

1977 _Death Valley National Monuments' prehistoric past: an archaeological overview._ National Park Service. Western Archaeological Center, Tucson.

Walter, H..
1971 _Ecology of tropical and subtropical vegetation._ Van Nostrand Reinhold, New York.

Warren, Claude N. (editor)
1966 The San Dieguito type site: M. J. Rogers' 1938 excavation on the San Dieguito River. San Diego Museum _Papers_ 6, San Diego.

Warren, Claude N.
1967 The San Dieguito complex: a review and hypothesis. _American Antiquity_ 32(4):168-185.

1970 Time and topography: Elizabeth W. C. Campbell's approach to the prehistory of the California deserts. _The Masterkey_ 44(1):5-14. Southwest Museum, Los Angeles.

Warren, Claude N. and J. De Costa
1964 Dating Lake Mohave artifacts and beaches. _American Antiquity_ 30:206-209.

Warren, Claude N. and Richard McCarty
1980 The archaeology and archaeological resources of the Amargosa-Mojave Basin planning units. In A cultural resource overview for the Amargosa-Mojave Basin planning units, C.N. Warren, M. Knack and E.von Till Warren. Report prepared for the Bureau of Land Management, Riverside.

Warren, Claude N. and Anthony J. Ranere
1968 Outside Danger Cave: a view of early man in the Great Basin. Eastern New Mexico University, _Contributions in Anthropology_ 1(4):6-18. Portales.

Warren, Claude N. and D. L. True
1961 The San Dieguito complex and its place in California prehistory. University of California Archaeological Survey _Annual Report_ 1960-61:246-338. Los Angeles.

Warren, Claude N., D. L. True and Ardith A. Eudey
1961 Early gathering complexes in western San Diego County. University of California Archaeological Survey _Annual Report_ 1960-61:1-105. Los Angeles.

Warren, Elizabeth von Till
1974 Armijo's trace revisited, a new interpretation of the impact of the Antonio Armijo route of 1829-1830 on the development of the old Spanish trail. M. A. thesis, University of Nevada, Las Vegas.

Warren, Elizabeth von Till and Ralph J. Roske
1978 Cultural resources of the California desert, 1776-1880: historic trails and wagon roads. Report prepared for the Bureau of Land Management, Riverside, California.

Wassaja
  1979 Quechans to receive 25,000 acres if others do not claim. Wassaja 7:1:8
  (January 1979). San Francisco.

Weide, Margaret L.
  1973 Archaeological inventory of the California desert: a proposed methodology.
  Bureau of Land Management, Riverside.

Weide, Margaret L., James P. Barker, Harry W. Lawton and David L. Weide
  1974 Background to prehistory of the Yuha Desert region. Bureau of Land
  Management, Riverside.

Weide, D. L.
  1976 Regional environmental history of the Yuha Desert. In Background to
  prehistory of the Yuha Desert, edited by P. J. Wilke. Anthropological Papers
  5. Ballena Press.

Weinman-Roberts, L.
  1979 History: narrative overview, In An overview of the cultural resources of the
  western Mojave Desert. Report prepared for Bureau of Land Management,
  Desert Planning Staff, Riverside, California.

Wells, P. V.
  1976 Macrofossil analysis of wood rat (Neotoma) middens as a key to the
  Quaternary vegetational history of arid America. Quaternary Research
  6:223-248.

Wells, P. V. and R. Berger
  1967 Late Pleistocene history of coniferous woodland in the Mohave Desert.
  Science 155:1640-1647.

Whalen, Norman M.
  1976 An archaeological survey in southeastern Imperial County, California.
  Pacific Coast Archaeological Society Quarterly 12(2):25-50.

Wheeler, George M.
  1876 Geographical surveys west of the One Hundredth Meridian, in California,
  Nevada, Utah, Colorado, Wyoming, New Mexico, Arizona and Montana, annual
  report for the fiscal year ending June 30, 1876. Report of the Secretary of
  War, 44th Congress, 2nd Session, Ex. Doc. 1, Pt. 2, Ser. 1745.

White, Christopher
  1974 Lower Colorado River area aboriginal warfare and alliance dynamics. In
  Antap: California Indian political and economic organization, edited by L. J.
  Bean and T. F. King. Anthropological Papers 2:111-135. Ballena Press,
  Romona, California.

Wilke, Philip J.
  1974 Settlement and subsistence at Perris Reservoir: a summary of archaeological
  investigations. In Perris Reservoir archaeology: late prehistoric demographic
  changes in southeastern California, edited by James O'Connell, Phillip J.
  Wilke, Thomas F. King and Carol L. Mix. California Department of Parks and
  Recreation Archeological Report 14:20-29. Sacramento.

Wilke, Philip J.
  1975 Aboriginal occupation of Tahquitz Canyon: ethnography and archaeology. *Anthropological Papers* 3:45-73. Ballena Press, Ramona, California.

  1978a Late prehistoric human ecology at Lake Cahuilla, Coachella Valley, California. *Contributions of the University of California Archaeological Research Facility* 38. Berkeley.

  1978b Cairn burials of the California deserts. *American Antiquity* 43(3):444-447.

Wilke, Philip J. and Harry W. Lawton
  1975 The Cahuilla Indians of the Colorado Desert: ethnohistory and prehistory. *Anthropological Papers* 3. Ballena Press, Romona, California.

Wilke, Philip J., Thomas W. Whitaker and Eugene Hattori
  1977 Prehistoric squash (*Cucurbita pepo* L.) from the Salton Basin. *Journal of California Anthropology* 4(1): 55-59.

Williamson, Lieutenant Robert S.
  1856 Report of expeditions in California for railroad routes to-connect with the routes over the 35th and 32nd Parallels of North Latitude. *House Document* 129, 33rd Congress, 1st Session, Government Printing Office, Washington, D. C. (Also in *Railroad Surveys* V, 1856.)

Worman, Frederick C. V.
  1969 *Archaeological investigations at the U. S. Atomic Energy Commission's Nevada Test site and Nuclear Rocket Development stations.* Los Alamos Scientific Laboratory of the University of California, Los Alamos, New Mexico.

Wyss, M. and J. N. Brune
  1968 Seismic movement, stress and source dimensions for earthquakes in the California-Nevada Region. *Journal of Geophysical Research* 73:4641-4694.

APPENDIX I. COLLECTIONS AT THE UCLA MUSEUM OF CULTURAL HISTORY

Museum Number	Site Name/Number	Date Collected	Collector	Number of Entries
	RIVERSIDE COUNTY			
320	Palen Dry Lake	1961-63	A. Koloseike	299
232	Perris	1951	E. Nickens	4
62	Salton Sea, NW Shore	Pre-1953	G.Guthrie	1
61	Riv-4	1953	Meighan/Hurst	6
513	Riv-8 One Horse	1959-61		1
319	Riv-8		J. Ruby	8
324	Riv-8	1963	J. Ruby	28
314	Riv-10	1962	J. Smith	1
314	Riv-32 Corn Springs	1962	J. Smith	1
507	Riv-58 Willow Hole	1965	J. Ruby	4
314	Riv-89 Black Mountain	1962	J. Smith	1
314	Riv-98	1962	J. Smith	2
145	Riv-117 (RV-65) Palm Springs	1955	Harrison/F. Davis	1
146	Riv-118 (RV-64)	1955	Harrison/F. Davis	3
63	Riv-129 (RV-62)	1953	Meighan	13
64	Riv-131 (RV-11)	1953	Meighan	2
513	Riv-150	1959-61		4
314	Riv-150	1962	J. Smith	5
513	Riv-151	1959-61		2
147	Riv-155 (RV-66)	1955	Harrison/F. Davis	3
148	Riv-156 (RV-67) Deep Canyon	1955	G. Redfeldt	14
513	Riv-159	1959-61	G. Redfeldt	1
513	Riv-182	1959-61	G. Redfeldt	1
513	Riv-183	1959-61	G. Redfeldt	1
513	Riv-186	1959-61	G. Redfeldt	10
272	Riv-186	1954	M. McKusick	3
513	Riv-187	1959-61		1
376	Riv-210 Snow Creek	1963	J. Michels	318
345	Riv-241	1969	J. Ruby	3
513	Riv-241 Hayfield	1959-61		2
483	Riv-258	1965	E.L. Davis	4
482	Riv-260	1965	E.L. Davis	2
484	Riv-261	1965	E.L. Davis	4
473	Riv-364	1965	J. Chartkoff	35
473	Riv-365	1965	J. Chartkoff	1
473	Riv-366	1965	J. Chartkoff	4
	SAN BERNARDINO COUNTY			
355	Harvard Hill	1972	W. Glennan	no cat.
84	Coyote Hills, 29 Palms			1
124	Old Woman Spring	1955	R. & N. Troike	4
53	Searles Lake			11
80	East Cronise Lake	1949	S. Peck	2
9	Silver Lake, Soda Lake	1949	Brainerd/Peck	167
55	SBr-28	1948	Bierman/Mohr	10

Museum Number	Site Name/Number	Date Collected	Collector	Number of Entries
59	SBr-29	1947	Mohr/Bierman	8
56	SBr-30	1948	Bierman/Mohr	6
16	SBr-32	pre-1953		20
57	SBr-34	1948	Bierman/Mohr	3
58	SBr-35	1948	Bierman/Mohr	4
66	SBr-36	1948	Bierman	3
67	SBr-37	1948	Bierman	2
68	SBr-38	1948	Bierman	5
69	SBr-40	1948	Bierman	7
314	SBr-40 Rock Spring	1962	J. Smith	1
456	SBr-102	1965	C. Singer	65
293	SBr-113	1960	J. Smith/G. Grosscup	4
293	SBr-114	1960	J. Smith/G. Grosscup	1
293	SBr-122	1960	J. Smith/G. Grosscup	1
293	SBr-126	1960	J. Smith/G. Grosscup	6
293	SBr-127	1960	J. Smith/G. Grosscup	13
293	SBr-128	1960	J. Smith/G. Grosscup	6
65	SBr-129	pre-1953	S. Peck	44
293	SBr-129	1960	J. Smith/G. Grosscup	5
293	SBr-130	1960	J. Smith/G. Grosscup	2
293	SBr-132	1960	J. Smith/G. Grosscup	7
293	SBr-133	1960	J. Smith/G. Grosscup	4
293	SBr-134	1960	J. Smith/G. Grosscup	3
293	SBr-208	1960	J. Smith/G. Grosscup	7
293	SBr-261	1960	J. Smith/G. Grosscup	11
293	SBr-267	1960	J. Smith/G. Grosscup	4
314	SBr-285	1962	J. Smith	2
314	SBr-288	1962	J. Smith	13
321	SBr-288	1962	J. Smith	111
314	SBr-332	1962	J. Smith	
314	SBr-333	1962	J. Smith	2
314	SBr-335	1962	J. Smith	3
314	SBr-336	1962	J. Smith	4
314	SBr-337 Sunflower Springs	1962	J. Smith	2
314	SBr-338	1962	J. Smith	4
314	SBr-339	1962	J. Smith	2
314	SBr-340 Paiute Springs	1962	J. Smith	1
314	Rancho Potrero #2	1962	J. Smith	1
314	Cook's Well	1962	J. Smith	4
314	Trail Site #1	1962	J. Smith	2
314	Trail Site #2	1962	J. Smith	1
365	SBr-335 near Essex	1963	C. Donnan	missing
506	SBr-350 Baker Site	1963-64	N. Nakamura	1371
517	SBr-356	1965	N. Nakamura	12
450	SBr-381 New York Mts.	1965	E.L. Davis	8
450	SBr-382 Coats Spring	1965	E.L. Davis	15
450	SBr-383 Indian & Malpais Springs	1965	E.L. Davis	8
450	SBr-384 Malpais Spring	1965	E.L. Davis	6
450	SBr-385 Carothers Canyon	1965	E.L. Davis	4
450	SBr-386 Carothers Canyon	1965	E.L. Davis	14
450	SBr-387 Carothers Canyon	1965	E.L. Davis	2
450	SBr-388 Carothers Canyon	1965	E.L. Davis	7
450	SBr-389 Carothers Canyon	1965	E.L. Davis	3
450	SBr-390 Carothers Canyon	1965	E.L. Davis	3

Museum Number	Site Name/Number	Date Collected	Collector	Number of Entries
450	SBr-391 Carothers Canyon	1965	E.L. Davis	2
450	SBr-392 Carothers Canyon	1965	E.L. Davis	35
450	SBr-393 Carothers Canyon	1965	E.L. Davis	7
450	SBr-394 Carothers Canyon	1965	E.L. Davis	6
450	SBr-396 Carothers Canyon	1965	E.L. Davis	11
450	SBr-397 Round Valley	1965	E.L. Davis	9
450	SBr-398 Round Valley	1965	E.L. Davis	6
450	SBr-399 Round Valley	1965	E.L. Davis	11
450	SBr-400 Wild Horse Canyon	1965	E.L. Davis	30
450	SBr-401 Fenner Wash	1965	E.L. Davis	161
450	SBr-404	1965	E.L. Davis	38
450	SBr-405	1965	E.L. Davis	114
450	SBr-406	1965	E.L. Davis	14
450	SBr-407 Hackberry Mt/Fenner Wash	1965	E.L. Davis	6
450	SBr-408 Hackberry Mt/Fenner Wash	1965	E.L. Davis	40
450	SBr-409	1965	E.L. Davis	8
450	SBr-410	1965	E.L. Davis	26
450	SBr-411	1965	E.L. Davis	5
450	SBr-412	1965	E.L. Davis	5
450	SBr-413	1965	E.L. Davis	6
450	SBr-416	1965	E.L. Davis	30
450	SBr-417	1965	E.L. Davis	1
450	SBr-418	1965	E.L. Davis	36
450	Devil's Playground near Kelso	1965	E.L. Davis	1
423	near Calico	1970	A. Christenson	4

IMPERIAL COUNTY

Museum Number	Site Name/Number	Date Collected	Collector	Number of Entries
369	south of Palo Verde	1962	M. Mulroy	7
274	Imp-49	1960	F. Reinman	17
362	Imp-56	1961	Pavesik/Benito	1
362	Imp-57	1961	Pavesik/Benito	1
362	Imp-59	1961	Pavesik/Benito	1
372	Imp-80	1963	K. Johnson/F. Davis	1
372	Imp-82	1963	K. Johnson/F. Davis	7
387	Imp-85 Chocolate Mountain	1963	E. Davis	19

APPENDIX II. NATURAL RESOURCE USE TABLE

A. Plants Used as Food Sources

NAME	PART USED/PREPARATION	TRIBE
Piñon (Pinus monophylla)	Nuts stored whole, ground to flour	Chemehuevi L:109; Dr:9 Cahuilla/Serrano Ben:391;B:39
Indian rice grass (Oryzopsis hymenoides)	Important grain, seeds stored, ground to flour	Chemehuevi L:109;DR:9 Cahuilla/Serrano DR:9
Joint pine or Mormon tea (Ephedra nevadensis)	Seeds eaten	Chemehuevi *pp:6-37 Cahuilla/Serrano B:46; *pp:6-13
Cottontop or Devil's pincushion (Echinocactus polycephalus)	Seeds, stores well	Cahuilla/Serrano B:40
Mesquite (Prosopis juliflora glandulosa)	Beans eaten whole, pounded to flour, meal eaten dry or as cakes	Mohave KS:1965,47; K:736 CB:180; *pp:6-55 Quechan F:115; CB:180 Chemehuevi L:106; V:16; DR:9; *pp 6-38 Cahuilla/Serrano Ben:374; K:616; B:38; *pp:6-13
Beavertail prickly pear (Opuntia basilaris, O. engelmannii)	Joints sundried, cooked in open fire or pit cooked - later boiled - stores well	Quechan CB:204 Cahuilla/Serrano B:40
Crucifers (Stanleya elata, S. pinnata, Caulanthus crassicaulis)	Shoots eaten; leaves and stems boiled, drained and reboiled to to remove bitterness	Cahuilla/Serrano B:40
California clover (Trifolium gracilentum)	Leaves and stems, eaten raw	Cahuilla/Serrano B:46

NAME	PART USED/PREPARATION	TRIBE
Desert thorn or wolf-berry (Lycium andersonii, L. fremontii)	Berry eaten fresh, sundried, later in stews	Mohave KS:1965,50; CB:204 Quechan CB:204 Chemehuevi KN Cahuilla/Serrano B:44

Agave or mescal (Agave deserti)	Hearts pit roasted and sundried	Quechan
		  DR:21
		Chemehuevi
		  K:597; Dr:9; L:108;
		  V:16
		Cahuilla/Serrano B:41

Sagebrush (Artemisia tridentata)	Seeds and inflorescences eaten	Chemehuevi L:107 Cahuilla/Serrano B:46
Creosote (Larrea tridentata)	Stems and leaves, into tea, general medicine	Chemehuevi L:107; Kn
Palmita or banana yucca (Yucca bacatta)	Seeds	Chemehuevi L:107; *pp.6-37
Wild grape (Vitis arizonica)	Fruit eaten fresh	Chemehuevi L:107 Cahuilla/Serrano K-615

Jimsonweed (Datura meteloides)	root brewed as hallucinogen	Mohave
		  KS:1965,51
		Quechan
		  K:793; Dr:41;
		  F:202, 205
		Chemehuevi
		  *pp:6-37;
		  L:108; V:11
		Cahuilla/Serrano
		  Ben:375; *pp:6-23

Indian asparagus (Anemopsis californica)	Greens eaten raw	Chemehuevi L:108
Squawberries (Rhus trilobata)	Fruit eaten raw, sundried	Chemehuevi L:109 Cahuillá/Serrano B:40

Jumping and buck-thorn cholla (Opuntia bigelovii, O. acanthocarpa)	New growth boiled and eaten	Quechan
		  CB:204
		Chemehuevi
		  L:109

NAME	PART USED/PREPARATION	TRIBE
Acorn (Quercus dumosa turbinella)	Seeds shelled, pounded and leached for flour	Chemehuevi L:104 Cahuilla/Serrano Ben:387; K:615; B:37; Dr:8
Wild tobacco (Nicotiana trigonophylla)	Smoked,, domestic and ritual occasions	Mohave W; KS:1966,8 Quechan CB:120; DR:25 F:117 Chemehuevi Dr:25 Cahuilla/Serrano Dr:25; Ben:369
Screwbeans (Prosopis pubescens)	Beans pounded to flour	Mohave KS:1965,48; CB:180 K:737 Quechan F:115; CB:179 Chemehuevi V:16; *pp. 6-38 Cahuilla/Serrano K:615; B:38; BS:62
Tule (Scirpus acutus)	Roots eaten, pollen and sprouts	Mohave KS:1965,50; CB:207 Kamia G:23 Cahuilla/Serrano K:615; B:45
Chia (Salvia columbariae)	Seeds, eaten whole and ground to flour	Mohave CB:187 Quechan F:115; CB:187 Chemehuevi Dr:9; *pp:6-37 Cahuilla/Serrano Dr:9; B:47
Blazing star (Mentzelia albicaulis, M. reflexa)	Seeds, ground to flour	Cahuilla/Serrano B:46
Barrel cactus (Ferocactus acanthodes, Sclerocactus polyancistrus)	Seeds and leaves	Chemehuevi V:17 Cahuilla/Serrano B:40; *pp:6-13
Tuna (Opuntia megacantha)	Seeds and leaves	Cahuilla/Serrano B:40; *pp:6-13
Prickly pear (Opuntia phaeacantha var. mojavensis	Seeds and leaves	Chemehuevi *pp:6-38 Cahuilla/Serrano B:40

NAME	PART USED/PREPARATION	TRIBE
Yucca (Yucca schidigera)	Flower, stalk, root and fruit	Mohave CB:204 Chemehuevi DR:9 Cahuilla/Serrano B:42; DR:9; *pp:6-23
Sandroot (Ammobroma sonorae)	Roots eaten	Quechan CB:207
Hackberry (Celtis reticulata)	Fruits eaten while traveling	Quechan CB:204
Catclaw (Acacia greggii)	Seeds eaten	Cahuilla/Serrano B:42
Locoweed (Astragalus sp.)	Seeds eaten	Cahuilla/Serrano B:43
Palo verde (Cercidium floridum, C. micro-phyllum)	Seeds eaten	Mohave CB:187 Quechan CB:196 Cahuilla/Serrano B:43
Desert willow (Chilop-sis linearis)	Seeds eaten	Cahuilla/Serrano B:43
Ironwood (Olneya tesota)	Pods eaten	Mohave CB:187 Quechan F:116; CB:187 Chemehuevi pp:3-38 Cahuilla/Serrano B:43
Desert lily (Hespero-callis undulata)	Roots eaten raw or pit baked	Quechan CB:207 Cahuilla/Serrano B:45
Cattail (Typha lati-folia)	Roots and seeds eaten	Quechan DR:9; F:127; CB:207 Cahuilla/Serrano B:45
Mariposa lily (Calochortus kennedyi)	Root eaten	Cahuilla/Serrano B:45
Sow thistle (intro-duced, Sonchus asper)	Leaves eaten	Mohave CB:201 Kamia G:24
Yerba mansa(Eriodict-yon trichocalyx)	Seeds eaten	Kamia G:24
Saltbrush (Atriplex torreyi)	Seeds eaten	Kamia G:24
Maize (Zea amylacea)	Grain cultivated; blue, white, yellow, red and mottled varieties	Mohave KS:1966,8 Quechan F:111 Kamia G:26

NAME	PART USED/PREPARATION	TRIBE
Tepary beans (Phaseolus acutifolius)	Bean cultivated; white and yellow varieties	Mohave KS:1966,8 Quechan F:111 Kamia G:26
Pumpkin (Cucurbita moschata, C. pepo, C. vulgaris)	Cultivated, strips sundried; white yellow and black skinned	Mohave KS:1966,8 Quechan F:111 Kamia G:26
Sunflowers (Helianthus annus)	Cultivated for seeds	Mohave KS:1966,9; CB:130
Crowfoot grass (Dactyloctenium aegypticum)	Semi-cultivated for seeds	Mohave KS:1966,9; CB:167 Quechan CB:167
Panic grass (Panicum hirticaule)	Semi-cultivated for seeds	Mohave CB:167 Quechan CB:167
Curleydock (Rumex crispus)	Semi-cultivated for greens	Mohave KS:1965,50; CB:167 Quechan CB:167
Quailbrush or lenscale (Atriplex lentiformis)	Seeds winnowed, leached, ground to flour	Mohave KS:1965,49; CB:187 Quechan CB:186
Pigweed or careless weed (Amaranthus palmeri)	Seeds eaten, greens boiled to remove bitterness	Mohave KS:1965,50; CB:186 Quechan CB:187 Chemehuevi *pp:6-38
Hog potato (Hoffmanseggia densiflora)	Roots eaten	Quechan CB:207
Barnyard grass (Echinochloa crusgalli)	Seeds	Mohave CB:186 Quechan CN:187
Greasewood (Sarcobatus vermiculatus)	Leaves brewed to tea for colds	Mohave *pp:6-53 Quechan F:152 Chemehuevi *pp:6-38
Tansey mustard (Descurainia pinnata)	Seeds eaten, leaves as greens	Mohave CB:191 Quechan CB:187
Sisymbrium (Sisymbrium irio)	Greens eaten	Mohave CB:201; KS:1965,50

NAME	PART USED/PREPARATION	TRIBE
Goosefoot (Chenopodium fremontii)	Greens and seeds eaten	Mohave CB:207; KS:1965,50 Chemehuevi *pp:6-38
Seepwillow (Baccharis glutinosa)	Greens eaten	Mohave CB:201 Quechan CB:201
Cattle spinach or all-scale (Atriplex poly-carpa)	Seeds eaten	Mohave CB:187 Quechan CB:187
Sprangle top (Leptochloa viscida)	Seeds eaten	Mohave CB:187
Iodine bush (Allenrolfea occidentalis)	Seeds eaten	Mohave CB:187 Quechan CB:187
Yellow nut grass (Cyperus ferax)	Seeds eaten	Mohave CB:187
Ammannia (Ammannia coccinea)	Seeds eaten	Mohave CB:187 Quechan CB:187
Evening primrose, Yellow cups (Oenothera brevipes)	Seeds eaten	Mohave CB:187
Spring aster (Aster spinosus)	Leaves eaten	Mohave CB:201
Ground cherry (Physalis sp.)	Berries eaten raw	Mohave CB:204
Mistletoe (Phoradendron californicum)	Berries boiled	Cahuilla/Serrano BS:63
Mushroom		Mohave CB:203 Quechan F:115
Crucifixion thorn (Holocanthus emoryi)	Fruits eaten	Quechan CB:204
Deer nut (Simmondsia chinensis)	Nuts eaten raw when travelling	Quechan CB:188

B. Plants Used for Non-Food Uses

NAME	PART USED/PREPARATION	TRIBE
Deer grass, bunch grass (Muhlenbergia rigens)	Above joint only, core for coiled willow-core basketry, especially caps	Chemehuevi DR:20 Cahuilla/Serrano DR:20

NAME	PART USED/PREPARATION	TRIBE
Willow (<u>Salix lasiandra</u>)	Roofing, bow, inner bark for cordage, fiber coiled basketry, arrow (simple), twining	Mohave K:738,751; *pp:6-55 KS:1957,200 Quechan F:92,124 Kamia G:19,28,32 Chemehuevi L:106; BR:23;/ DR:20 *pp:6-37 Cahuilla/Serrano *pp:6-13
Devil's claw (<u>Proboscidae altheifolia</u>)	Pods peeled; black for basket patterns	Mohave *pp:6-55 Chemehuevi V:16; *pp:6-37
Tule (<u>Scirpus acutus</u>)	Roofing layer, raft, roots peeled, black for coiled basketry patterns	Mohave CB:207 Quechan F:127 Kamia G:23 Chemehuevi L:108 Cahuilla/Serrano Ben:385; K:618
Joshua tree (<u>Yucca brevifolia</u>)	Inner root, red pattern for basketry; cordage, especially for rabbit skin robe weaving	Chemehuevi B:23; L:108, V:16 Cahuilla/Serrano DR:21
Squawbush (<u>Rhus trilobata</u>)	Shoots for basketry	Cahuilla/Serrano Ben:387
Arrowweed (<u>Pluchea sericea</u>)	A layer under the mud to cover sweatlodge; unpointed arrows; weave granaries	Mohave KS:1947,263; K:751; KS:1966,13 Quechan CB:183-5; F:111,121,171 Kamia G:18,20,40 Chemehuevi DR:16 Cahuilla/Serrano BS:62; DR:16; *pp:6-23
Wild hemp (<u>Apocynum cannabinum</u>)	Cordage, bowstrings	Chemehuevi V:12 Cahuilla/Serrano Ben:388; K:615
Reed or cane (<u>Phragmites vulgaris</u>)	Arrowshafts for compound arrows	Quechan F:124; DR:15 Chemehuevi L:107 Cahuilla/Serrano BS:61
Sagebrush (<u>Artemisia tridentata</u>)	Brush for house construction	Chemehuevi L:107

NAME	PART USED/PREPARATION	TRIBE
Rush (Juncus sp.)	Basal stem for light brown basket pattern	Mohave *pp:6-55 Cahuilla/Serrano Ben:387; DR:21
Mulberry (Morus sp.)	Light color for basketry pattern	Chemehuevi Bt:23
Cottonwood (Populus fremontii)	Poles for house construction, mortar	Mohave B:85 Quechan F:116 Kamia G:19,23 Chemehuevi L:106
Carrizo	Arrow shafts	Chemehuevi L:107
Wild grape (Vitis arizonica)	Vine for tying	Chemehuevi L:107
Agave (Agave deserti)	Fiber for cordage, sandals	Cahuilla/Serrano Ben:389
Mesquite (Prosopis Juliflora glandulosa)	Inner bark for cordage, roots for weaving cradles, gum for dye for fiber and hair; wood for digging sticks, bows, war clubs, mortars	Mohave KS:1957,199; K:751; KS:1947,262;1966,9 Quechan F:112,171; CB:180 Kamia G:32,36,39,42 Cahuilla/Serrano *pp:6-23
Gourd, domestic (Cucumis sp.)	Canteen, storage contained, rattle	Quechan F:111 Kamia G:16
Screwbean (Prosopis pubescens)	Wood for bow, clubs, digging stick	Mohave KS:1966,11; K:751 Kamia G:28,30
Pumpkin (Cucurbita moschata)	Seeds for fishbait	Mohave KS:1957,200
Greasewood (Sarcobatus vermiculatus)	Used in construction of home and ceremonial house for mystic protection; resin for sealing containers; arthritis cure	Mohave KS:1970,23 Chemehuevi *pp:6-37 Cahuilla/Serrano *pp:6-23
Ironwood (Olneya tesota)	Wood for tools, especially hoes; some sacred connotations	Mohave KS:1966,12 Cahuilla/Serrano *pp:6-23

NAME	PART USED/PREPARATION	TRIBE
Palm (<u>Washingtonia</u> <u>filifera</u>)	Fronds for roof, especially of ceremonial house	Cahuilla/Serrano *pp:6-23; BS:62
Mistletoe (<u>Phoradendron</u> <u>californicum</u>)	Leaves for black basketry dye	Cahuilla/Serrano BS:62
Yucca (<u>Yucca</u> sp.)	Cordage	Quechan DR:21

C. Animals Used

NAME	PART USED/PREPARATION	TRIBE
Eagle (<u>Aquila</u> <u>chrysaetos</u>)	Feathers, cermonially	Mohave KS:1947,84 Quechan F:226; DR:29 Kamia G:42,48 Chemehuevi L:1151 Cahuilla/Serrano Ben:377
Cottontail (<u>Sylvilagus</u> <u>audubonii</u>, <u>S</u>. <u>nuttalii</u>)	Meat, skin for robes	Mohave KS:1947,82 Quechan F:92,118; CB:216 Kamia G:26 Chemehuevi K:597; DR:7; L:112 Cahuilla/Serrano B:58; Ben:375; K:615 DR:7
Jackrabbit (<u>Lepus</u> <u>californicus</u>)	Meat	Mohave KS:1947,82; C:50; Kr:277 Quechan F:92; CB:216 Kamia G:6,20,26 Chemehuevi K:597; L:112 Cahuilla/Serrano B:58; BS:63
Wood rat (<u>Neotoma</u> sp.)	Meat	Mohave KS:1947,83; CB:217 BLM:5 Quechan CB:212; DR:7 Chemehuevi K:597; DR:7 Cahuilla/Serrano BS:63; B:58; DR:7
Lizards (<u>Cnemidophorus</u> sp., <u>Gerrhonotus</u> sp., <u>Sceloporus</u> sp.)	Meat	Chemehuevi K:597; L:116; DR:8

NAME	PART USED/PREPARATION	TRIBE
Mountain sheep (<u>Ovis</u> <u>canadensis</u>)	Meat, hide, horns boiled for glue	Mohave 　KS:1947,81; CB:215 Quechan 　CB:215; F:118 Kamia　G:27 Chemehuevi　L:112 Cahuilla/Serrano 　B:157; BS:63
Common Flicker (<u>Colaptes</u> <u>auratus</u>) "Red-shafted"	Feathers used for basketry patterns	Cahuilla/Serrano 　Ben:391
Cambel's Quail (<u>Lophortyx</u> <u>gambelii</u>)	Meat, eggs	Mohave 　KS:1947,84; C:50 Quechan 　CB:215; DR:7 Kamia　G:26 Chemehuevi 　DR:7; V:17 Cahuilla/Serrano 　B:60; BS:63
White-footed mice (<u>Peromyscus</u> sp.)	Meat	Quechan　CB:153 Cahuilla/Serrano　B:58
Chuckwalla (<u>Sauromalus</u> <u>obesus</u>)	Meat	Mohave 　CB:213; SK:1968,36 Quechan 　CB:213; DR:9 Chemehuevi　L:116 Cahuilla/Serrano　B:61
Black tailed or mule deer (<u>Odocoileus</u> <u>hemionus</u>)	Hoofs for rattles, meat, sinew for bow backing and string	Mohave 　CB:215; DS:1947,80 Quechan　CB:215; 　F:91,118,131 Kamia　G:27 Chemehuevi 　L:112; DR:7 Cahuilla/Serrano 　Ben:379; Dr:7; B:57 　BS:63
Coyote (<u>Canis</u> <u>latrans</u>)	Eaten in extreme famine, hide	Mohave 　KS:1947,83; CB:213 Chemehuevi　L:111
Antelope (<u>Antilocapra</u> <u>americana</u>)	Meat and hide	Quechan 　F:91; CB:211 Chemehuevi　L:112 Cahuilla/Serrano 　B:57; BS:63

NAME	PART USED/PREPARATION	TRIBE
Desert tortoise (Gopherus agassizi)	Meat	Quechan CB:212 Chemehuevi L:116; DR:8 Cahuilla/Serrano B:61
Squirrels (Spermophilus sp., Sciurus sp., Ammospermophilus sp.)	Meat	Mohave CB:213;KS:1947,83 Kamia G:26 Cahuilla/Serrano B:58; BS:63
Black spider (Arachnidae)	Bite used as counter-irritation and in shamanistic cures	Cahuilla/Serrano Ben:385
Chipmunks (Eutamias sp.)	Meat	Mohave KS:1947,83 Quechan CB:212 Chemehuevi DR:8 Cahuilla/Serrano B:58
Ducks and Mudhens (various)	Meat and eggs	Mohave KS:1947,84; C:50 Quechan CB:212 Kamia G:26 Cahuilla/Serrano B:60
Rattlesnake (Crotalus sp.)	Meat	Cahuilla/Serrano B:61
Ants (Formicidae)	Meat	Cahuilla/Serrano B:61
Grasshopper (Acrididae)	Meat, fish bait	Mohave KS:1957,198 Kamia G:14 Cahuilla/Serrano B:61
Cicada (Cicadidae)	Meat	Cahuilla/Serrano B:61; BS:63
Cricket pupae (Gryllidae)	Meat	Cahuilla/Serrano B:61
Sphinx moth larvae (Hyles lineata)	Meat	Quechan CB:214 Cahuilla/Serrano B:61
Crow (Corvus brachyrhynchos)	Feathers	Mohave KS:1947,84 Quechan F:171 Chemehuevi DR:8 Cahuilla/Serrano DR:8

NAME	PART USED/PREPARATION	TRIBE
Gopher (Thomomys sp.)	Meat	Mohave KS:1947,83 Quechan CB:212 Kamia G:26 Chemehuevi DR:8
Mourning dove (Zenaida macroura)	Meat	Quechan CB:70 Kamia G:26 Chemehuevi DR:8
Bobcat (Lynx rufus)	Skins for quiver, occasionally eaten	Mohave KS:1947,83 Quechan CB:172 Kamia G:14,29
White salmon, minnow (Ptychocheilus lucius)	Meat	Mohave KS:1957,198 Quechan CB:219 Kamia G:26
Humpback sucker (Xyrauchen cypho)	Meat	Mohave KS:1957,198; K:737 Quechan CB:219 Kamia G:26
Whitefish, boneytail (Gila eligans)	Meat	Mohave KS1957,198 Quechan CB:219 Kamia G:26
Beavers (Castor canadensis)	Meat	Mohave Kr:277;KS:1947,83 Quechan F:91 Kamia G:27
Mountain lion (Felis concolor)	Hides only, not eaten	Mohave KS:1947,83
Raccoon (Procyon lotor)	Meat	Mohave KS:1947,83
Badger (Taxidae taxus)	Meat	Mohave KS:1947,83
Muskrat (Ondatra zibethicus)	Meat	Mohave KS:1947,83 Quechan F:91
Fox (Vulpes sp., Urocyon cinereoargenteus)	Hides, only old may eat	Mohave KS:1947,83; CB:213

CULTURAL RESOURCE MANAGEMENT SUMMARY

Elizabeth von Till Warren and Claude N. Warren

The Colorado Desert Cultural Resources Overview clearly illustrates the paucity of data from prehistoric sites within that region. There are large areas from which little or no archaeological data have been recovered through excavation (e.g. in the northeastern portion of the study area). Most chronological periods for the area are poorly represented and some (e.g. Pinto Period) are speculative because of lack of data. Only the Late Period has data in quantity comparable to that of adjacent areas. Consequently, synchronic studies of settlement patterns, economic systems, and so on, are at a speculative or descriptive stage of development and most such studies have been concerned with sampling methods and techniques towards management ends rather than research problems of a largely substantive nature (Gallegos et al. 1979a, 1979b; Reed 1979 and Ritter 1978). Wilke's (1978a) ecological analysis of sites in the Coachella Valley represents the kind of study needed to further the understanding of the economic systems and settlement patterns. However, the number of localities where data are sufficient for these kinds of studies is extremely small. This lack of adequate data reflects the paucity of archaeological excavations in the Colorado Desert. The archaeology of the Colorado Desert has been, by and large, surface archaeology with the few exceptions concentrated primarily on the Colorado River. Because of the small number of sites excavated and the resultant limited understanding of the prehistory of the Colorado Desert, specific recommendations for cultural resource management are difficult to make.

The prehistoric developments of the Colorado Desert appear to have had two major centers of cultural development: the Colorado River and the Salton Basin. The Colorado River was, almost certainly, an area of relatively intense cultural activity throughout the history of man in the area. Use of the Salton Basin, however, appears to have fluctuated from intensive to marginal, as the lakes that periodically formed there receded and dried.

Other areas of relatively heavy use by aboriginal populations must have included the eastern slopes of the Peninsular Range and higher elevations in the desert ranges, especially where springs were present. Because of the extreme aridity of the Colorado Desert, water must have been one of the major determining factors in the location of habitation sites. This obviously became even more important once agriculture was introduced into the area.

The relationship of man and water in the Colorado Desert must be considered in the development of a cultural resource management plan. The largest, most productive areas of aboriginal occupation currently known are along the old beach lines of Lake Cahuilla and on the terraces of the Colorado River. These areas are of major significance in the management of cultural resources. Wherever the BLM land impinges upon these areas, careful consideration must be given to these important resources.

However, activities of prehistoric people were not limited to these areas. There was certainly seasonal movement dictated by economic and other cultural activities. These activities took people to a variety of different environmental settings as the productivity of the various zones fluctuated with the seasons of the year. Just how and where the various environmental zones in the desert were used is not yet known. Much more data are needed before the relationship of man and his desert environment can be understood. This is probably the most critical problem for those managing cultural resources. It is a problem to which we will return shortly.

Another important factor for cultural resource management is environmental change, which has introduced variability in the distribution and function of archaeological sites. This is another variable in the cultural resources that must be considered in their management.

Cultural resource management of the California deserts includes the decision as to which sites are to be preserved in the multiple land use program of the Bureau of Land Management and which are to be subjected to greater risk or sacrificed (hopefully after proper mitigation). Such decisions would appear to require ranking sites on the basis of significance. However, "significance of an archaeological site is relative to the problem which the archaeologist is investigating, the method used, and the theoretical structure under which the program of research is developed" (Warren and McCarty 1980:90). The significance of a site is relative to the biases of the investigator and the archaeologists of the future will no doubt hold biases that we can not predict today. This means that the cultural resource manager must begin with the assumption that all sites are potentially significant while recognizing that some sites will necessarily be destroyed.

Glassow (1977) has suggested that one way of overcoming these difficulties is to determine the range of variation of sites and to preserve an adequate sample of that range of variation. Basic to a cultural resource management plan would be the preservation of the complete range of sites in the varying environmental settings. The determination of the variability of both sites and environmental settings requires considerable knowledge of the archaeological and environmental resources. The data accumulated for this overview are insufficient in themselves for making such determinations. The Bureau of Land Management Desert Planning Staff is in the best position to evaluate the data accumulated by recent surveys and overviews such as those of Gallegos et al. (1979a, 1979b), Ritter (1978), Reed (1979) and Weide et al. (1974). Consequently we do not address this problem further in this report.

Coombs (1979b) introduces four criteria for classifying sites according to the relative potential for destruction or vandalism. These are: accessibility, familiarily, value and delicacy. We are in general agreement with Coombs' evaluations of these criteria as regards possible destruction and vandalism. However, as Warren and McCarty (1980:90-91) note, when Coombs discusses the criteria of delicacy he introduces another criterion of complexity. He states (Coombs 1979b:127)

> "The criteria of delicacy brings up an important issue we think should be considered. There are, of course two basic ways of preserving a site. The first involves leaving it intact and protecting it as best as possible. The alternative is to remove the site and place it in a collection. We bring up this point here because sites which are not delicate are ones in which very little, if any, information is lost when the site is removed, provided of course that its precise provenience is recorded. Given the delicacy of isolates, in particular, we would strongly recommend that the

BLM consider collecting them as they are found. We are now convinced that leaving isolates in the field is all but insuring that any further information they may provide to archaeology will be lost forever.... Conversely, more complex sites should not be collected unless necessary, since even most careful surface collection or excavation can destroy a considerable amount of information."

We are in agreement with Coombs' comments, however, he has introduced another problem. That of evaluating the method by which a site is to be preserved. In this evaluation, delicacy and complexity must be considered as separate criteria. The problem of the isolate is simple and straight forward because it is delicate but not complex. Warren and McCarty (1980:91) note:

"A large fragile pattern site containing several activity areas is delicate indeed, as is the ghost town. However, they are far more difficult to remove than isolated finds which are equally delicate. The difference is the number of elements involved and the interrelationships in space, the difference is in complexity of the site."

Complexity and delicacy are two independent variables that must be considered in management of .cultural resources. The criteria of "complexity" must be considered along with accessibility, familiarity, value and delicacy in determining procedures to be followed in active management of the resources. When sites are endangered all these criteria are relevant to the evaluation of means of preservation.

Finally it is essential that cultural resource management look beyond the single site and its environmental setting. In making this point we quote from Warren and McCarty (1980:91) the comments on the Mojave:

"Glassow (1977) and Coombs (1979) present a convincing argument for their criteria of significance and criteria for possibility of vandalism and destruction. However, these criteria are at the level of individual sites. Archaeologists too often view sites as independent units. However, sites were never independent units during the time of their occupation. It is a fact that the prehistoric cultural systems of the Mojave Desert were not limited to single sites, but extended networks over wide geographic areas and through various ecological zones. Any program of site preservation in the Mojave Desert, with a view toward future research, must include the criteria of area network integrity. Area network integrity recognizes that people throughout the Mojave utilized virtually all ecological zones, but they did not utilize them in the same manner in all places. The Owens Valley Paiute apparently had a different pattern of land use from the Death Valley Paiute or Reese River Shoshone. To attempt to test a hypothesis regarding settlement patterns or economic systems by utilizing lowland sites of Owens Valley and upland sites in the Funeral Range, regardless of the variety included, would only lead to erroneous results. In preserving sites for future research it is not enough to protect the variety of site types in the various ecological zones. The area in which they are preserved must also exhibit integrity in being at least geographically contiguous to the degree that it was usable within the context of a single prehistoric cultural system."

In dealing with the ethnographic factors, the relationship of the local aboriginal toward the cultural resources must be considered. The sensitivity of the Mohaves,

Quechans, Chemehuevis and Cahuillas to their culturally significant sites is well documented. These sites represent a wide range of types, some geographically specific and some ecologically specific.

Geographically specific sites include known sacred and mythically important places such as archaeological sites, caves, trails, trail shrines, petroglyphs, pictographs, intaglios, initiation camps and burial sites (including all camp and village sites and palm oases because of their association with the spirits of the dead). Certain mountains sacred to them as homes of the spirits (e.g. Avikwame, Newberry Mt.) are clearly included in the mythic framework of each group. Additionally, there are unspecified "power" sites with sacred significance. Any policy which would have a negative impact on these sites, or which would limit respective native American access to them, would be of interest to these groups and they should be given ample opportunity to evaluate and respond to such policies. It may be difficult to substantiate the claim of such cultural significance for a particular site, especially since the native American group may not have previously revealed the significance of a given location in an effort to keep secrets from the dominant white power structure.

Significant concern has also been expressed regarding continued access to native flora and fauna used for sacred medicine, basketry and food purposes. Thus any policy that would either endanger species traditionally utilized or limit or deny access by native American users to those species, is of great interest to them. Since these concerns focus not on specific sites but on specific plants and animals, decisions regulating the merits of protection will have to be made on an individual project basis.

As with all non-renewable resources, historical sites management should follow a conservative approach. The history of adverse impacts on the cultural resources of the California desert is long and indiscriminate. Recent sites as well as older ones have been wholly or partially destroyed by natural and human forces. As the population pressures increase upon the resources of this still isolated region, care will have to be exercised that the historic sites and their context are protected.

Determination of which sites to preserve and which to sacrifice to contemporary needs is a constantly pressing issue. The criterion of eligibility for the National Register of Historic Places (NRHP) provides some framework for placing a given site in a ranked system of value. For this reason, nomination to the NRHP should be made for the numerous sites probably eligible but not yet listed. The problem with relying on the NRHP, however, is that systemic interrelationships are not well reflected. Historical sites did not develop in isolation: a full understanding of them requires information on their environmental setting, place in time and interrelationships with other sites. Networks of communication and supply and other systems operating within those same settings at the same time are important sources of information. Thus, preservation of a single historic site or even a historic district is not sufficient. The physical network that existed between and among them should also be available for analysis and research. Springs, trails and trail campsites are all important physical evidence of the intangible communication/supply networks of prehistoric and early historic times and, thus, also need protection and preservation.

Equally important are the physical remains of later communication/supply systems: automobile and railroad. Apart from representing the history of the development of the Colorado Desert, broader areas and other histories are also reflected in the changing pattern of relationships between and among these networks: the history of automobile and rail technology, the history of transportation; and economic history. The BLM, in its management of the area over which these networks extended, should take care that sufficient attention is paid to the physical remains reflecting these networks.

The early history of the Colorado Desert is poorly known. Documentary sources have been fragmentary and subject to varying interpretations. Since all of the histories of the Colorado Desert area have perforce been based upon these same sources, all of them are equally subject to the same inadequacies. It is therefore imperative that the BLM be cognizant that important new information relative to the Colorado Desert may become available as the historical documents recently acquired by the Arizona Historical Society from the College of Jesuits in Rome are inventoried and analyzed. Resource management policies predicated on the series of historical overviews compiled for the California Desert Conservation Area Plan should be subjected to rigorous re-examination as new data become available. While the practice of updating any plan for resource management should be followed for all areas and disciplines, the Spanish Period in the California Desert is so imperfectly known that this particular time period should receive special attention.

Management of all the cultural resources of the Colorado Desert should include interpretation of them for the general public. The BLM has a great responsibility to ensure that the complexity of life forms and their interrelationships through time and space are clearly explained to the public, which has scanty knowledge and generally little understanding of the systems which operate in the deserts of California. Good displays, popular publications and other interpretive programs can provide significant means of educating the public about the nature of desert lands and their historic uses. Programs should include information on the negative aspects of historic uses as well as on the positive ones. It would be well, for example, to include information on erosion caused by poor historic mining or agricultural practices, so that current management policies designed to prevent similar problems will be understood better.

But perhaps the most important, fragile, historical resources of all, is the desert itself, with all the mystique the word embodies. Desert lands are fascinating; a large body of myth, legend and fantasy exists in the literature of the west that reflects this love/hate relationship between desert lands and people. This special, intangible phenomenon, should be recognized in BLM management policies. Efforts should be directed to ensure that all desert lands are not managed for consumptive uses. The eloquent plea made by John Van Dyke in 1901 in support of "empty" desert space, has even greater urgency today:

> "To speak about sparing anything because it is beautiful is to waste one's breath and incur ridicule in the bargain. The aesthetic sense--the power to enjoy through the eye, the ear, and the imagination--is just as important a factor in the scheme of human happiness as the corporeal sense of eating and drinking; but there has never been a time when the world would admit it. The "practical men", who seem forever on the throne, know very well that beauty is only meant for lovers and young persons--stuff to suckle fools withal. The main affair of life is to get the dollar, and if there is any money in cutting the throat of Beauty, why, by all means, cut her throat. That is what the "practical men" have been doing ever since the world began. It is not necessary to dig up ancient history; for have we not seen, here in California and Oregon,

in our own time, the destruction of the fairest valleys the sun ever shone upon by placer and hydraulic mining? Have we not seen in Minnesota and Wisconsin the mightiest forests that ever raised head to the sky slashed to pieces by the axe and turned into a waste of treestumps and fallen timber? Have we not seen the Upper Mississippi, by the destruction of the forests, changed from a broad, majestic river into a shallow, muddy stream; and the beautiful prairies of Dakota turned under by the plough and then allowed to run to weeds? Men must have coal though they ruin the valleys and blacken the streams of Pennsylvania, they must have oil though they disfigure half of Ohio and Indiana, they must have copper if they wreck all the mountains of Montana and Arizona, and they must have gold though they blow Alaska into the Behring Sea. It is more than possible that the "practical men" have gained much practice and many dollars by flaying the fair face of these United States. They have stripped the land of its robes of beauty, and what have they given in its place? Weeds, wire fences, oil-derricks, board shanties and board towns--things that not even a "practical man" can do less than curse at.

And at last they have turned to the desert! It remains to be seen what they will do with it. Reclaiming a waste may not be so easy as breaking a prairie or cutting down a forest. And Nature will not always be driven from her purpose. Wind, sand, and heat on Sahara have proven hard forces to fight against; they may prove no less potent on the Colorado. And sooner or later Nature will surely come to her own again. Nothing human is of long duration. Men and their deeds are obliterated, the race itself fades; but Nature goes calmly on with her projects. She works not for man's enjoyment, but for her own satisfaction and her own glory. She made the fat lands of the earth with all their fruits and flowers and foliage; and with no less care she made the desert and its sands and cacti. She intended that each should remain as she made it. When the locust swarm has passed, the flowers and grasses will return to the valley, when man is gone, the sand and the heat will come back to the desert. The desolation of the kindgom will live again, and down in the Bottom of the Bowl the opalescent mirage will waver skyward on wings of light, serene in its solitude, though no human eye sees nor human tongue speaks its loveliness."

The Desert
John C. Van Dyke, 1922.

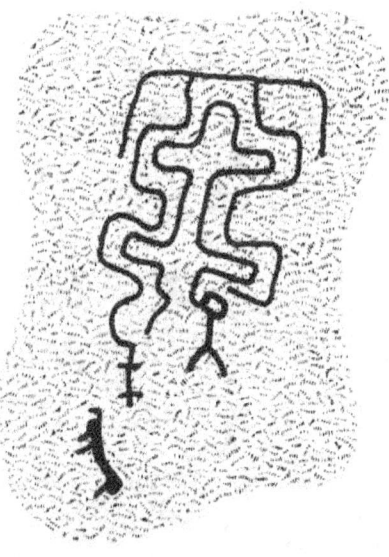

*Petroglyph element from
Corn Spring,
Riverside County,
California*

✿ U.S. GOVERNMENT PRINTING OFFICE: 1981-784-758/2673